Two *MAGIC* Rupees and a *SPACE* Chillum

Copyright © 2024 Neil Rock

Coolgrove Press, an imprint of
Cool Grove Publishing, Inc. New York.
512 Argyle Road, Brooklyn, NY 11218
All rights reserved under the International and
Pan-American Copyright Conventions.
www. coolgrove. com
For permissions and other inquiries write to info@coolgrove.com

ISBN 13: 978-1-887276-25-2
Library of Congress Control Number: 2023942347

This book is distributed to the trade by IngramSpark

Acknowledgements:

Ardha

Front cover photo by Claudia Hinterseer
Neil Rock's full name is James Neil Rock

From the publisher, thanks to Brice Bowman and Susan Kovacs
for preserving, compiling and editing Neil Rock's essays.

Media alchemy by Kiku

Cool Grove Press

Easy roads

Two *MAGIC* Rupees and a *SPACE* Chillum

NEIL ROCK

Cool Grove Press

Table of Contents

Foreword by Susan Kovacs viii
Foreword by Brice Bowman.. ix

1. First Travels 1
2. Hobbit Country 5
3. Strutting the Music Stuff 19
4. Skiffling, Scuffling and Busking.. 23
5. At the Royal Court of Soho 33
6. Up and Down Penny Lane 40
7. Meeting Christine 46
8. Ketama 1962 47
9. Moses and the Tooth 52
10. Eddie's Leg 57
11. Algerian Adventures 60
12. Cops and Cobbers 64
13. The Great Pyramid 68
14. Bombed in Beirut 73
15. Kundalini 76
16. Riding as the Raj 79
17. Jasper and Mataji at Varanasi 83
18. Two Magic Rupees and a Space Chillum........................... 85
19. View from the Howdah.. 94
20. Dead Elephant 98
21 Rollin' with the Rabbi.. 102
22. Girls in Goa.. 104
23. Even More Elephant 107
24. Tihar Prison 108
25. The Bamiyan Buddhas, Ali's Dragon, Kohr-i-Baba Pass .. 121
26. Tribal Cues... 130
27. Room in the Bin... 134
28. The Northwest Frontier 139
29. Naked at Night... 147
30. Buzkashi 149
31. Afghan Road Cuisine... 152
32. A Drive from the Steppe 153
33. A Short Real Glasnost... 158

34. Donkey Doings... 159
35. Communist Constrictions 164
36. The Latvian Law.. 172
37. La Maison Perdue 177
38. Rockin' through Poland 187
39. Skirt, Skis, and Skates 193
40. The Green March 196
41. Ethernet 210
42. Hi-Ho for No Silver 214
43. Christmas in Balafia.. 216
44. A Formentera Visit.. 219
45. A Tangier Day.. 227

APPENDIX
United Nations Presentation on Environment & Tourism 234

PHOTOS
First set 86
Second set 200

Foreword by Susan Kovacs

I was seven years old when Neil left home to join the RAF at 15. Don't know how he managed that. The silver tongue approach, I imagine! My memories of him before that time are fond but vague since he was rarely at home, anyway.

Mam and Dad were extremely forward thinking and liberal in their approach to our upbringing. Regular attendance at school was never Neil's interest or intention. Even as a young boy he would disappear for days at a time to explore the wilderness of the North Yorkshire Moors and Dales. Our Mam just knew that he could take care of himself, even at such a young age, and that it would be a futile task to try and put a halt to his wanderings. She realized she had brought an extraordinary child into the world and it quickly became clear that he would only live life on his own terms.
As a teenager, I would hear about Neil's adventures through his letters home.

Our parents and myself were in awe of his travels and he truly did inspire us all to leave our lives in Leeds behind and see the world for ourselves. I flew the coop myself at 18, to France and Germany before moving to the USA at 21. Mam and Dad also traveled Europe and then emigrated to the USA when they retired: a huge decision to make at that age. It was Neil who opened the door to the world for us all.

After he left home, I only saw him once before I went to the USA, and then only twice more before our parents passed away. My husband Paul and myself caught up with Neil again in Ibiza shortly after he married Barbara, but it wasn't until 2013—when I began visiting him annually—that a stronger brother-sister bond began to gel. Neil's thirst for adventure, his generous spirit, his love for his friends, and his pure joy of living have inspired me since childhood.

James Neil Rock, 1936-2018. Easy Roads, brother.

Foreword by Brice Bowman

Neil Rock taught me what it meant to be part of a scene. He helped me understand how to be a true friend. He certainly qualifies to be included in a sequel to Meetings with Remarkable Men.

His passing is not an ending but a continuation, because he gave his friend and late-life carer Ardha a handwritten note for me: "Brice, Time to move on. You are the best friend I ever had. I hope that we meet again somewhere along the way. With all my love, I wish you Easy Roads."

Two Magic Rupees and a Space Chillum

1.

First Travels

One late evening in early summer of 1944, I was lifted-up from the ground by a hefty warehouseman and hoisted by the driver from above into the cab passenger seat of a huge Perkins diesel engine truck. It smelled of oil and grease and there were rags and cans in a box on the floor. The engine had a diamond-patterned black leather engine heater cover; above it, dials quivered on the dashboard. The driver sat in the right-hand seat with the huge steering wheel in front of him and the giant motor absolutely throbbed. Once it was sure that I was properly seated the engine made a roaring sound and we were offon a two-hundred mile nighttime journey from Leeds to London. My father was staying with a brother for a few days, waiting to be shipped back to Africa after being in a London hospital while having treatment for a serious scorpion bite got while fighting against the German Afrika Korps in the Libyan Desert. My birthday being two days from now, my dad had taken advantage of having mates owning a Leeds clothing company to deliver me overnight to the capitol so he could see me reach 8 years old. Driving at night to avoid being daytime targets for German fighter planes, Britain's long-distance commercial traffic snail-paced along its arterial roads in the dark at 25 miles-per-hour, with hooded headlights giving dull light no more than twenty feet ahead. There were not many enemy fighter aircraft attacks on roads at night, or even anywhere at all by this stage of the war, although some damage was done still in cities being bombed between nightfall and dawn. This I had frequently experienced and cowered under, my mother and I both wearing anti-gas masks, amongst piles of coal in the cellar of our house, sometimes for several nights a week as planes droned and bombs fell. Occasionally, when a bomber was shot down nearby, any dead or wounded were removed, the police would guard it and the locals would troop off in the morning to visit it. There were often unexploded bombs deep in street concrete and buried in house gardens. One night in my hometown, German bombers attacked Quarry Hill Flats, the largest block of apartment houses in Europe. Amazingly, they completely missed. An entire adjoining housing estate more than a mile long and a quarter mile wide was completely flattened except for two buildings still left standing unscathed. A church and a pub. Wags had it that Satan went to pray, and God went for a pint. Because of all the bombing, I was moved round homes of family and family friends six times during WWII. So, in the summer of '44, at night and in the care of a friendly driver, I am on the road in a motor vehicle (other than a bus or tramcar) for the first time in my life. The view from high in the cab was wide open to the moon and I knew immediately that viewing the world rolling by from a motor vehicle was to be a lifetime exciting encounter. Within two minutes traveling I was forever hooked. It always seems to me that by driving you Go Somewhere, whereas by airplane or ship you are merely taken.

I slept for a while on the diamond-patterned leather engine cover and was shaken awake about one o'clock in the morning by the truck-driver, as we pulled into a black-out curtained but still open all night trucker's diner. The driver and I joined other truckers he knew. I was greeted and hair ruffled all round. I tell you truly that right there and then I surrendered to motorway grease of scrambled eggs, a pile of bacon on the side and giant slabs of toast and a huge mug of coffee. If only I could live on the road forever, then I knew I would survive anywhere on any kind of food forever. So far, I have eaten from hedgerows, car back seats, five-star hotels, roadside curry shacks, Micks Café to La Tour D'Argent from gutter to gourmet. After that midnight dinner my truck rolled on through the night and we reached the company depot in London at dawn. My dad, in army uniform was there to meet me. I was impressed by the stripes he wore on his uniform sleeves and the campaign ribbons on his chest. I had a memory of having seen him only one time previously when I was 5, and once when he was on leave in February of this same year. It took all that day at my uncle's house to get used to him. My uncle I did not know at all. The next day my dad said he would take me to a cinema that night as an early birthday treat. For my birthday itself, the following day, we were to visit family friends living in the countryside south of London. The visit to the cinema being my birthday treat, I wanted to go to the late show, starting at 8.30 pm. No, said my dad, it was the 6 o'clock show or nothing. The first German V-1 rocket bombs had fallen on London for three nights previously and my dad wanted us home early in case of more. We went to see a film called "Madonna of The Seven Moons." The film show started at 6:15 and finished at 8 pm. My dad and I were already back at my uncle's house when the first heavy concentrations of German V-1 rockets of the war rained down on London. That night, 16th June 1944, over one hundred V-1 rockets hit London and then fifty every day and night for the next two months. During the first days of attacks the rockets targeted the Ford Motor Works in Dagenham near where my uncle lived. The cinema my dad and I had been in was hit 45 minutes after we had left it and 82 people were killed. A Woolworth department store across the street was completely obliterated. That night I dozed and was shaken in bed in a room outside of which flashes and explosions rocked the house all night long. In the morning I looked through the curtains to outside and in front of me for a quarter of a mile was a pile of smoking rubble with nothing intact more than a garden wall two feet high. The only thing standing high amongst the shattered ruined former streets was a forked tree completely stripped of its leaves, the bark, and small branches. My birthday was over before the day started as my father was called back to his army base. I did not see him again until the end of the war. The V-1 rocket had no guidance system. It was just a rocket bomb. Its fuel load was calculated to reach London and it was simply pointed at the city and launched. It burbled along at 350 miles per hour. If you heard one overhead you hoped that the motor kept on running until the rocket had passed, otherwise at termination of fuel the rocket dropped, wiggled out of control and its 1 ton payload exploded on impact, destroying anything where it fell. The Londoners called them Buzz Bombs and Doodlebugs.

Amazingly, British fighter pilots shot thousands of these flying bomb Doodlebug rockets so that they exploded in midair. The pilots also learned to fly alongside the rockets, get their aircraft wingtips under the rocket stabilizer fins and flip them away from London so that they fell and exploded in countryside. Despite this bravery, thousands of people were killed in those air raids. It seems that my first venture onto The Road being in a time of war was a sign of things to come, as I have since been in Algeria and Afghanistan, each while a coup d'etat was taking place, and in Morocco, Lebanon, and Pakistan at times of the opening of war hostilities. No matter, all adventures have been wonderful. From the first sight of the neighborhood rubble and the stripped tree in Dagenham that morning—which has never left my memory—all recollection of the continuance of that trip faded away. I have never been able to remember leaving London or how I traveled home to my mother in Leeds, but I never lost all memories of any trip, and I never lost the love of road travel.

© Neil Rock

2

Hobbit Country

Yorkshire is England's largest county, an area of industrial cities and large open countryside with quiet valleys dotted with small agricultural villages. Most settlements are old and full of tradition. On the northern edge of the city of Leeds is a district called Harehills where I grew up from childhood to teenager. My playgrounds were places that have names of early English historic provenance: Oakwood, Roundhay, Temple Newsham, Seacroft, Harewood and Cross Gates. In the county there are towns and villages with names such as Streoneshlh-(Whitby), Ulaskelf, Thriebergh, Jervaux and Rievaulx, which reveal Yorkshires' Saxon, Viking, and Norman French history. When a boy and youth I wasn't often in towns. I spent most of my free time hill walking in the countryside of the Yorkshire Dales and Cumberland Lake District. There are many counties in England with the word Shire appending to their names, which are those of the principal cities. The Shire of York is Hobbit country, the *real* Hobbit Country, which having been born in I came to love by exploring it since I was a child of eight years old.

While he was Senior Reader at Leeds University, JRR Tolkien lived not five miles from the home of my parents. There, he collaborated with EV Gordon on writing the famous edition of "Sir Gawain and The Green Knight." He also invented and wrote his "Elvish" languages while living in Leeds, and worked on The Hobbits too, after adapting the names of the Yorkshire fable little people to Hobbits from Hobs. Many original Yorkshire folktales are of the Hobs, and they are there in the written tales in the Yorkshire Folktale Storybooks; the Shire is their home, although some Hobs were known to live further north on the Yorkshire borders with Northumberland and County Durham close to the Lake District. The word Hob comes from Holbitian, a Northern dialect word from 5th century Saxon Old English and meaning Hole Builder, or Hole Dweller.

Some Hobs were famous across Yorkshire. There was one named Hob in The Hole, a respected herbalist living in his cave at Runswick Bay and who made medicinal remedies that were used for centuries. People trekked from all over the county to consult him. A Hob who lived at Farndale turned almost Gollum-like after working for a farmer many years for a jug of cream a day. Then, after the farmer's wife died a second wife refused to feed him. He followed this woman everywhere even to the bedroom and when the farmer tried to escape him by moving his family to another part of the Shire this Hob moved with them. He would not go away until he got his cream wages. You cannot afford to cheat a Hob.

There was also a highly-regarded Hob who bred ponies; canny he was and traded with gypsies. He lived on the North Yorkshire Moors in a village named Castletown.

People familiar with Hobs say that they have never seen one more than four feet tall, and that a significant difference between Hobs and Hobbits in olden days is that Hobs used to go about without any clothes on. People are mistaken and are thinking of The Celts, who went into battle naked. If Hobs of olden days did not wear clothes, then either they did not socialize a lot or—well, like many Yorkshiremen—they are thick skinned.

Of course, all little folks are founded on the characteristics of rural people. Any Hob or Hobbit will tell you that elves, pixies and their cousins, sea sprites, fairies, leprechauns, gnomes, and trolls, can be seen in parts of the British Isles, Ireland, Eastern Europe, and Scandinavia respectively any day of the week if you have the gumption and appreciative eye to recognize them. But then, on the other hand, we know that Tolkien's Orcs and many of the dark creations of malignant priests and sour governesses—such as ogres, goblins, and various more vicious creatures of devilry—are fictions of imagination that cannot exist if disbelieved in.

Hobbit Country

Traveling into Hobbit Country is a journey into a magical landscape of eight rivers running through rolling dales and valleys. You can find faerie rings of toadstools under chestnut trees and walk in forests of hazelnut trees and beech trees; these forests are filled with bluebells, bracken, and brilliant green ferns. Oak trees are still there too. There are waterfalls, and deep dark ponds reputed to be bottomless and home to wily old Pike, swift running streams with Bream and Perch, sometimes having Trout. In some places Wishing Wells can be found and there is one in a cave on a river path close to the town of Knaresborough. Visitors for many centuries have made wishes and left gifts of hundreds of personal objects on the walls and hanging from the roof, all these now turned to stone by Mother Shipton's magic. Mother Shipton was a white witch who lived in this cave and predicted that the end of the world will come when an old stone bridge falls from its place crossing a local river.

Hobbit Country has rural family seats (of human families to be sure), stately halls and mansions of great Lords and Ladies, of Aristocrats and Nobles with bloody histories and hidden pasts, priest holes and secret passages, ancestor ghosts and pixie helpers. Before my teens I had explored some long ago abandoned ancient abbeys, priories, and monasteries, crumbling fortifications and watchtowers. There are echoing empty castles fallen into ruin, in which I played as a child and from where crusaders really did ride out to join King Richard the Lionheart. From the tower of Roundhay Castle I saluted brave men who rode to Jerusalem to fight Saladin for The Holy Land. In many battles for this castle my childhood friends and I launched our spears and arrows at the ghosts of England's enemies.

One of the mediaeval places favored in my memory, certainly one of the most peaceful and to which I was first introduced as a boy eleven years old by my most enlightened schoolteacher, is a tiny 11th century granite chapel set in the center of a walled cypress grove close to a many century-old cairn atop a hill named Beamsley Beacon. The chapel sits alone with its swaying cypress trees on a windswept endless moor and many miles from the nearest village. There in the dusty mote interior, a carved stone life size effigy of a fully armored mediaeval warrior lays on a sarcophagus and guards a thousand-years-old sleeping Norman Knight buried inside it. Some people say that elves visit the cypress grove and sweep the chapel clean. Who would ever say nay?

Norman crosses with weather-blasted names are seen on graves in churchyards; some lichen-covered Saxon graves at country crossroads date from 460 AD. Romans were here from 100BC, Celts and their Druids were already here from France and Austria 400 years before that—and there are rune stones and religious sites from other ancient cultures. On the horizon of a line of hills to the northeast of Ilkley town is a cleft named Wingate Nick. Climb the hills and scramble up through the cleft and on a high plain you will find huge mushroom shaped stones ten feet high. Channels cut into the mushroom caps are stained rusty red. These stones are mysteries thought to be from some unknown ancient sacrificial religion.

The land also holds its natural mysteries. Near Bolton Abbey in Wharfedale the river Wharfe is forced into a deep chasm under rocks and compressed between a gap a misleading two yards wide. From the chasm the water rushes into a fierce roaring whirlpool called The Strid. Throughout known history many foolish people have tried to jump the gap. Failure has always been fatal as the falling people are sucked down into The Strid. It is thought that the bodies have been drawn down into deep underground caves and caverns. Stories are that The Strid is the gate to Hell. It has never given up a single body of its many unfortunate victims.

Much of the natural beauty of the Yorkshire is unsurpassed. Away from the cities and highways you can walk for days through purple heather on rolling high hills, the home of hawks, skylarks, grouse and curlews, meeting nobody except maybe a few stray sheep in summer pasture. In the valleys there are small quiet villages, lush deep grass fields full of fat cows, wheel-rutted lanes lined with chestnut trees, elderberry bushes loaded blackberry brambles, rosehip, and wild apple trees. Where else but The Yorkshire Dales would Hobbits live?

Everybody knows that Yorkshire has a rich lore of communication between humans and other inhabitants of the Shire. It is well known that some of the country folk in Yorkshire had special relationships with the Hobs and animals. Of course, pixies, elves, and fairies all had friends amongst the creatures of the fields and woodlands. Well, birds had a human friend. Whitby Abbey, built by The Saxons in 653ce had a first Abbess named Hilda, later sainted. Saint Hilda cleared the adjoining land of poisonous snakes and fed the birds of the seas and moors. Such was her piousness and kindness that even today, although the abbey was demolished by Henry VIII in 1536, migrating geese flying to summer and winter habitats are observed never to fly over the ruins, but to swerve left or right to fly around Whitby Abbey in salute and respect for Saint Hilda In York, the Shire capitol, the Shire's oldest market town, 12th century streets named Whipma Whopma Gate, The Shambles, Shield Makers Street, Monkgate, and Beggersgate still exist and are national heritage treasures. The Shambles is a narrow passage and the plaster and wooden beam faced top floors of houses on each side jut out so close to one another across the streets that the many centuries of inhabitants have been able to reach out and shake hands with each other from their bedroom windows. York Minster, built in the 12th century, is arguably the oldest Cathedral in Europe and is replete with guardian gargoyles to drive away evil spirits. The Minster is still a place of worship every day. York is a walled city, its bastion museum filled with mediaeval arms, armor and siege weapons. York, battling with Lancaster, was the winner of The Wars of The Roses, which decided the future succession of English Kings. Wallis, The Brave Heart of Scotland, seeking freedom from England for his country, invaded York. He was later captured, sent to London, where he was hanged, intestines drawn out while still alive, then quartered. His parts, stuck on spikes, were carried on horseback around England and exhibited at various cities. No wonder that The Hobbits and other little people fought against cruel kings.

The little people had their own villains of course. Dick Turpin, the most famous of all highwaymen robbed his way across the York Shire and held up countless coaches using a pistol with a carved brass gargoyle on its grip. His command of "Stand and Deliver" became the standard order of every English-speaking highway robber in the world. He escaped the sheriffs many times. Once to escape capture while in southern England, Turpin was said to have ridden his horse "Black Bess" from London to York, 225 miles in 24 hours. This feat is not true as it was originally accorded a feat of, yet another Yorkshire highwayman named Will Nevison who was hanged in York in 1684 while Dick Turpin was still a boy. Said to rob the rich to give to the poor, Dick Turpin was captured and his hanging at York in 1739 for the theft of a chicken was bemoaned by the little people across the county.

Another famous fighting robber and a champion of the little people was Robin Hood, and as everybody knows he lived and hid in Nottingham Shire's Sherwood Forest. But he did travel outside and there are quite a few folk tales about the York Shire activities of Robin Hood. One tale relates how Robin recruited Friar Tuck from his work as hunting dog expert at Fountains Abbey on the river Ure near the town of Ripon by challenging Tuck to an archery contest. Robin, losing, begged the friar to join his band. There is even a Yorkshire town on the North Sea coast named Robin Hood's Bay, though I never heard of him as a pirate or coastal smuggler. He is buried in Hobbit Country. In old age he left Sherwood Forest and traveled with Little John to Kirklees Priory near Brighouse in South Yorkshire. He died there while staying in a gatehouse, which still stands. He is buried nearby in his named grave.

Until the mid-20th century, (and possibly still) on May Day in Hobbit Country, the farming folk in some villages really did dance around colored beribboned Maypoles. There were raffles for cakes and pies, potato sack races, hand wrestling games, and strapping young farm lads lifting wooden logs. There were May Queen competitions to choose the loveliest lass, then, kisses at a small coin each for a new church window. Paganism and plant seeds stir thickly at May Day celebrations in the Yorkshire, the spring wind is blustery, young men are boisterous and some easily flustered homemakers and sprightly young girls really must take extra care. The parson keeps his eyes peeled. Cricket is played, bowls also, and your dad will tip you a wink and sneak a hint of beer into your glass of lemonade while you sit at a wooden trestle table near the sundial outside the Jug and Firkin pub on the village green.

In my hometown of Leeds, every autumn, except during WWII, for a week at Harvest Festival time there was held the biggest feast in England. It has taken place for centuries in the district of Hunslet on the Holbeck Moor (The Holy Stream). My mother was born there. Hunslet Feast was the biggest annual gathering event on Yorkshire's calendar. In the evenings and nights of Harvest Festival week the working people from the wool mills, factories, tanneries, coal mines, and iron and steel foundries came to Hunslet Feast from all over Leeds and other nearby

Hobbit Country

cities in their thousands. There were whole families, stray kids, courting couples, and a lot of lads and lasses looking for each other.

At Hunslet Feast, every carnival in England, Wales and Scotland was there. Every animal circus, human and flea circus came. Every steam calliope and hand cranked music organ, every mummer, performing clown and dwarf, roving musician and every gipsy and hawker family on the road would gather in Hunslet for the week. There were so many tents of Giants, Tom Thumbs, Skeleton Men, Fat Women, Tumbling Fools, Jugglers, Fire Eaters, Hoop Jumpers, Escape Artists, Sword Swallowers, Gipsy Fortune Tellers, Turkish Knife Throwers, and Bearded Ladies from Egypt that you couldn't decide what to see and pay for, or even put a number on them all.

This fairground was over a mile in length, a quarter mile across. You could see it and hear it from miles away. Thousands and thousands of colored light bulbs powered by throbbing generators flickered, popped, and dazzled. The music and noise from dozens of steam engines driving whirling fairground rides was roaring tremendously. There was so much of meat pies with mushy peas and pickled onions, toffee apples, fizzy soda pop, jacket potatoes stuffed with cheese, rock candies, smoked kippers, brandy snaps, sausage rolls, licorice sticks, nougats, and fish and chips that you could never eat it all.

A huge blazing bonfire a hundred feet high was kept snapping and raging at a safe distance of half-a-mile away on a stretch of bare earth wasteland out on the moor. People left wood for the fire at this spot for weeks before the feast. Dozens of multicolored gipsy horse-drawn caravans and motor homes were parked in this area. There was dancing by the bonfire to whistles and accordion, singing and tippling.

Red bandana throated men wearing peaked flat caps, their trouser legs tied close to the knees with string, gambled and matched tossed-up silver coins for prized horses, piglets, rabbits, money, and chickens. Owners of racing dogs and hunting dogs compared animal talents and scores with hawk fanciers, pigeon racers and ferret handlers. Hunslet Feast was all great excitement and Thousands of firework skyrockets, whizzing pin wheels, jumping crackers and bang sticks were fired off round the bonfire. By Gum! Hunslet Feast was grand! Them Yorkshire Hobbits know what's what!

For a while, as a child, and taken out of danger from WWII German bombing raids on the city, I lived with my Nanny, my father's mother, in her lead window paned and low wood beamed stone cottage in the village of Pudsey outside Leeds, on the very edge of the moors. Every Sunday, she, in her black cape, best watered taffeta dress, button shoes, glaze flowered straw hat, and me in wool sweater, best short pants, thick socks and nailed boots, would ride a country bus, and walk the last two miles up the wild heather hills to a fieldstone farmhouse high in Bronte Sister Country where Nanny would buy jars of hand-churned butter, home-bottled fruit preserves, and fresh farmyard eggs. Rain or shine, we never failed. Nanny could cook and bake like you would not believe. With and without Nanny I walked a lot. After WWII and my father came home from soldiering in Africa my parents thought nothing of a local 12 miles Sunday walk, even with my mam wheeling my new sister in a pushchair. We would walk 10 miles to a hamlet named Collingham, do some canoeing or punting on the river, have tea on the riverbank, then walk another couple of miles to the town of Weatherby and catch a bus home. With school friends I walked miles to search for frogs, newts and salamanders in old quarries and reed-filled marshes. My favorite places were marshes near Ulaskelf, a village where Tolkien's Orcs once ruled in the shape of Norseman Viking marauders. The Vikings crossed the North Sea to raid the East Yorkshire coast at Scarborough Town and at Whitby, where Bram Stoker later lived and wrote *Dracula*. They plundered their way up a river in the Shire and built their wattle and daub village and earthen barrows of Ulaskelf near a Saxon settlement called Church Fenton (Church in The Fens). We kids fought a lot of Eric the Reds and Black Barons during those childhood forays round Ulaskelf and Church Fenton.

Church Fenton has a Royal Air Force airfield, and like some other English east coast military bases it has its own folklore. During WWII, The Allied fighter pilots were flying at night on the North Sea coastal run out of Church Fenton and other air force bases, along with bombers raiding Germany out of RAF/USAF airfields on Yorkshire's east coast. Pilots frequently reported to command authorities that they were saved from being shot down in combat with enemy German aircraft by friendly small creatures riding on the wings of Spitfires, Hurricanes and Flying

Fortresses. On black winter nights the fighter pilots also reported being escorted home after battles. British and American bomber pilots too, with their wounded crews and planes shot full of holes and in severe weather swore that they were met by strange unidentifiable aircraft which flew alongside and guided them home. The fighter pilots and bomber crews identified the wing riders as Gremlins. They had a name for the strange aircraft too: they called them Foo Fighters. So, you see, the Gremlins and the flyers of some UFOs are human allies just like the Hobbits are, joke Hollywood movies and bad press notwithstanding. People who do not know the truth of a story most times mess it up.

On one Sunday each summer my mam and dad would take my little sister and me for a special day treat out to a wonderful place called Shipley Glen. Our bus would pass through a wool mill town named Bingley. My Granddad was born and worked in Bingley. My dad worked with him. They were coach painters to the carriage gentry. It was all hand-trimmed paintbrushes of squirrel hair and camel hair, mix your own colors, fingertip judge the consistency, hand paint, and varnish the coaches in those days. My dad became known to be the expert color mixer and best coach painter of all; there was nobody to better him, the world over. Granddad did the finest highlighting and gold leaf work you ever saw.

Well, anyway, Shipley Glen is a natural tree-filled gorge gashed into the side of a very steep hill with a flat plateau and plain above. Lots of Yorkshire families go there on summer weekends. You pay to pass through a revolving gate if you want to go in. There is a scenic miniature railway with climbing steel rails carrying small open carriages and powered by a pulley attached to a chugging engine at the end of the track above the glen. People would climb into the train coach, the whistle would toot, and you could ride all the way up through the trees to the top like a Toff. When you got there at the Glen Tearooms, you would find waiting for you fresh tea, watercress and ham sandwiches, and hot buttered scones with clotted cream and strawberry jam. A pub waited for men wanting something stronger.

After tea, adults and babies would sleep the afternoon away on the grass in the breeze, by the shade trees and in the sun. Kids would bowl hoops, play football, fly kites; throw sticks for dogs. Back on the cable car at dusk you could lick an ice cream, real slow-like, while riding all the way down the glen to the bottom from the top. Hobbits and humans have a lot of fun on Sunday afternoons at Shipley Glen.

Saltaire, built by a Victorian businessperson named Titus Salt, is a town of wool mills near Shipley Glen. Bales of raw wool from Australia, New Zealand, South America and anywhere else in the world that sheep were raised and shorn came by sea to Liverpool and were sent up the Leeds and Liverpool Canal by horse drawn barges to Saltaire Mills. One mill is huge, four stories high and many streets distance in size from end to end. My Uncle George was a weaving room foreman in this mill. For more than thirty years, in his derby hat, three-piece brown wool suit, lace-up brown boots, with his Masons medals and his fob watch on a chain across his flat stomach and thumbs in waistcoat pockets, all five foot two handsome inches of my Uncle George rocked from heel and toe and ruled over what was then the biggest room in the whole wide world. This room is half-a-mile long, fifty yards wide and from the early nineteenth century until sixty years ago it was filled with two thousand women and young girls—all weaving woolen cloth. How my Uncle George kept his hands on his waistcoat and went home to my Aunt Edna every night is anybody's guess. My Uncle George must have had a will of iron and nerves of steel.

Summer holidays my family—like millions of other Britons—went to the seaside. Sometimes we went to a caravan on Bempton Cliffs at Flamborough Head, where I could fish, wade in the rock pools, gather whelks and mussels and catch large crabs. Mostly we went to stay with my aunt May who lived in a seashore town called Redcar. Each year in Redcar from me being eight years old to fourteen, early morning before breakfast I would swim half-a-mile out and round the wreck of a torpedoed merchant ship laying there since the war. All day I could swim and sun around the beach. At night I would fish in the sea with my uncle John in his boat.

And if you have ever strolled along a Yorkshire or Lancashire promenade, seen a Punch and Judy show on the pier, laughed your head off at a cheeky variety show, gawped in wonder at El Magnifico The Magician, peeped through a lens at what the butler saw, whistled at paddling ladies in skirted one piece bathing suits, and along with dozing grandmothers you've listened to an open air concert of the town brass band while laying with a pin and a bag of winkles in a deck chair on the beach—then you know, you really know—where The Beatles got their fabulous Sergeant Pepper thing.

If you travel to the northeastern border of Hobbit Country, you are in County Durham, where some Hobs are known to have lived and there are famous stories of the region's own historic fables. People tell a story and sing songs about the giant Lambton Worm, a vicious water dragon caught from a river by Lord John Lambton near his home, Lambton Hall, during the twelfth century. It wriggled free of Lord Lambton's net, dove into a deep hole, and lived there many years. This worm was a very strange creature, it grew to six feet long with a curling body that twisted like a moving corkscrew to slither across the ground. It had the face of a dragon, dagger-like horns, rows of sharp teeth, and nine holes down each side of its head from where it breathed malodorous vapors. At night it roamed the countryside, killing and eating cattle and terrorizing the district until the Lord Lambton slew it. Men of nine generations of the Lambton family were cursed to die outside of their beds. The last surviving member of the ninth generation fell off a bridge over the River Wear, one hundred and sixty years ago. The Lambton family records reveal what happened to others.

Northwest Yorkshire borders on Cumberland (Cumbria) a land of lakes, hills and sharp crags that is known as the Lake District. It is an area of much beauty and a favorite for lake sailing, hill walking and rock climbing. Some Hobs and humans enjoy rock climbing; it's good in North Hobbit Land where there is a lot of hard granite. In my teens and early twenties, I climbed an area south of the Cumbrian Mountains called the Langdale Pikes.

Children stories author Beatrice Potter lived close to Langdale Valley, on her farm near the country market town of Ambleside. An honorary Hobbit she was—and you know very well that *she* knew *all* about talking rabbits. She even walked around with a pet rabbit hopping on a leash. Eccentric? Well, she was English.

Well now, with all this talk of Hobs, pixies, gremlins and talking rabbits—I tell you plain that for those who seek it there is a right good bag full of bright magic in Hobbit country. Even "Found, Lost and Found"

15

the last written book of J B Priestley, Yorkshire's own prolific author, famous pacifist and super imagination icon is a fairy tale love story.

Rock climbing is a hot business, dangerous, but bracing too. After a day on the face, a well-earned ale is sweet.

The watering hole for rock climbers in Langdale is The Climbers Bar in a solitary placed pub called The Dungeon Ghyll. Alone in the mists and climbing crags, The Dungeon Ghyll is five and a half miles from the nearest village. The only clients here are climbers, cave explorers and hill walkers. The nearest neighbor is a farmer with a barn in which the climbers sleep. Every type of ground hole male Hob, mining Gnome and mountain cave Troll that exists drinks, talks shop round the fireplace and feels right at home in that pub.

The interior of The Dungeon Ghyll Climbers Bar is hacked out of solid rock and is the only pub I know with rock climbs up the interior walls and across the ceiling. Climbers hang like spiders amongst the tobacco smoke and pints of drinkers, above tables littered with crampons, coiled ropes and climbing irons. The floor is reasonably close if you fall, but the climbs are tough nuts to crack, some are rated super severe. Wall climbing competitions, boozing and fights roll on all night. To keep things reasonably safe from carousing members of rival clans of Scots and English climbing clubs and any foreign visitors doing serious damage to each other and to his property, the pub landlord has taken every precaution, including that every bench, table, and chair in the room are securely bolted to the flagstone floor. Some of the rock climbs in this area are very dangerous, accidents are frequent, people do die on the crags and The Dungeon Ghyll has its own mortuary where the bodies of dead climbers are stored until collected by ambulances from the nearest town. Walking and climbing in the hills of North Hobbit Land you can meet some of the rare eccentric folk who step straight out of storybooks. I met some new and long-time future friends amongst the adventurous characters there. I enjoyed the hiking company of an elderly, red-faced, gnome-like hill-walking gentleman named Corey who reveled in open spaces. Corey received many penalty fines from country magistrates for rampant destruction of newly erected and blot on the landscape Chi-Chi townies weekend country cottage fences. He was angry wherever he saw a cottage where an old wall had been removed and replaced

Hobbit Country

by wooden railings. Corey relieved much of his frustration and temper with enraged kicks and fierce whacks with walking stick. One morning, after receiving a fine from a country town magistrate, Corey walked outside and peed all over the court garden metalwork fence, was back in the same court five minutes later and fined for public indecency. He threatened to come back with a bulldozer and was fined for contempt of court. Jailed for two hours—and even then, still raving—Corey was only released when he agreed to leave town before the pubs opened. I liked Corey.

Another of my favorite moorland ramblers was an eccentric Welshman, a short-careered London policeman named Bryn, who soon got the boot from his job. When in the hills he wore a plaid deerstalker hat, tweed jacket with matching Knickerbockers and climbing boots. He also wore the shiny metal rim of an anchovy paste jar lid for a monocle, carried a blackthorn walking stick and a teakettle. When we first met, he was smoking the most unusual stuff for a copper and singing his way along a lakeside path. He should have been given a policeman job in Hobbit Land. He belonged there.

Yorkshire is a magic palace for children. The countryside was a sparkling educational experience and gave me a lot of fun as a boy –and for many years after that. If you have not been there, I hope that one day you can visit, and I hope that like me you meet a lot of Hobs and Hobbits. I finally lost touch with the Yorkshire Hobbit Country and the Lake District when I moved away from home and then England.

I think of The Shire a lot. My spirit still resonates to ancient monasteries, walking on the Yorkshire Moors, climbing sharp crags of silver rock, of exploring the North Sea Coast. I am contentedly mindful of fast-moving skies over the hills in Bronte Country, villages of slate-roofed cottages, swans on country house lakes, brown bullrush tips in marshes, and duck-filled, willow-edged farmhouse ponds. My mind still holds some childhood adventures of sword fighting sneaky beasts in the deserted Harewood Abbey, staring in terror at the whirlpool of The Strid, of letting fly my arrows from the towers of Roundhay Castle at invaders of the realm and of jousting there with villains. I frequently think of the sleeping Norman knight at Beamsley Beacon in his cypress grove and granite chapel.

For over fifty years now I have not been back to the Yorkshire Hills and Dales. But I do know that they are amongst the most magical places on Earth. And that *is* where The Hobbits live.

© Neil Rock, 2007.

3.

Strutting the Music Stuff

In 1947 I was 11 years old and sitting watching reels of cartoons and short movies in a railway terminal News Theatre in my hometown of Leeds, UK. On the screen came The Count Basie Band with an eleven-year-old guest boogie pianist named Sugar Chile Robinson. To say I was electrified is a total understatement. Boogie pulled and I was hooked. This kid's two featured songs have stuck in my head to this day. (Almost 40 years after the event, having heard me mention these songs—a friend bought me as a gift the original 78 rpm single.) Somehow, around this time in another local cinema, I also got to see the film "Hellzapoppin'" and completely flipped. My mission in life was to get up and dance, but I'm looking, and I'm talking and can't find any kids who know this jivin, swing, boogie stuff.
Just before my 14th birthday I hit the Bop, Boogie, Swing jackpot.
Standing in line for the summer opening of my local outdoor swimming pool, a gum popping 13 year or so teeny-bopper (the first I had ever seen) swung her ponytail at me, removed her windbreaker, and revealed a slightly distorted tee-shirt front that had emblazoned on it "Ooh, bop, shi bam, be doo be dop." On the back was the statement "Be Bop Spoken Here."
Well, live and learn, gotta ask, so I did. "Wha's that?" Her boyfriend, fifteen, import hip in shades, chinos and Hawaiian shirt and standing in front of her turned to me and said "that, daddy-o, is Dizzy Gillespie." "Who's he when he's at home?" I ask. Ray gives me the up-down glim— "That's right, he is at home, I'm Ray, she's Annie, and later we can make it and you can find out." In the afternoon we left the pool and walked to Ray's house. I found out about Dizzy, I also found out about Billie,

Ella, Charlie Parker, Stan Kenton, Albert Ammons, and more. I shadowboxed, war-danced homeward in a beginner groover finger poppin' haze.

The next Saturday morning, I'm down to the town record shop.

The guy said "Who? You mean Charlie Chan? Who, Albert Einstein? Never heard of 'em. American bop? Boogie? Oh, you can't get THEM records over here, kid." Back to Ray's house, he's out. His mother, as cooool as he is, invites me in, hands me a cup of hot Instant Postum, gears up the Victrola, and slides on "Big Noise from Winnetka." In came Artie Shaw and away went my mind's marbles. This soon-to-be middle-aged boppin' English housewife grabs me, teaches the steps, and tells me that her brother was a merchant seaman who brought in the music. She had been hipped to Swing during WWII while typing on an RAF/USAF airbase in Lincolnshire. This woman learned jitterbuggin' in the wild days and wild style when ladies were thrown airborne and flight insurance should have been obligatory for any woman on the dance floor. So, she is giving me the cooled down version and soon, I'm boppin,' I'm jivin', oh, am I ever jivin'! Rockin' Rock is born! Ray arrived home and made it clear he wasn't lending out no "cuts," but that I could "slide in" to his place anytime I wanted. I told him he was welcome at my house also. So, I'd go to his place and sometimes, he and his girlfriend and pals would come to mine.

I bought a second-hand 1930s wind-up HMV record player from a pawnshop; it had a needle as big as a Masai spear and a giant size built-in speaker. It lived pride of place on my bedroom floor. When friends came by to bop, we would carry this machine into my house basement and let it blast. A couple more-young aces I met in the neighborhood stopped by after school sometimes and helped me polish up my dance act. Soon, I'm slipping and sliding with the best, I'm doin' the splits without missing a beat. I thought I was the bee's knees for a while. Later I met great dancers, kids made of rubber, bounced like golf balls. I saw the film Down Rio Way with The Flash Dance Act as performed by the *real* dance masters, the Nicholas Brothers—in white tie and tails, just pure class and more class. James Brown developed his inimitable thing from here, an' if you ever saw Sammy Davis Jr. dance while *he* was still a child, well... And *you* can eat your beginner's heart out Mr. Jackson.

Skiffling, Scuffling and Busking

My dad wasn't so keen on this dance school in the cellar, but as a kid himself, having been a banjo player in a 1920s Trad Jazz Band, he didn't kick too much. My mother grooved and shimmied around the house thinking it was all great fun.

After a couple of weeks in The Cellar Club some more local bopper pals of Ray and Annie emerged, wanted to join in and things got a bit too crowded at my home. We tapped into a source of records of British Swing Bands at the local library. With the library records and Ray's stuff, we could GO for a couple of hours. The library had a garden and a long wide roofed verandah with benches against the walls, an ideal venue for reading and bopping. In the name of educational entertainment, one of our crowd had talked the library authorities into loaning us the use of this garden for out-of-hours dance classes. A local juke joint/coffee bar, The White Rose, opened just down the road. A lot of kids got off the street to these places and I met a lot of good fun dancers.

Just before my 15th birthday Rhythm n' Blues records arrived on the underground music scene in the UK in the spring of 1951. R'n'B landed on me at an edge-of-town roadside diner named "Smokey Joe's." I was completely blown away by a jukebox full of great tunes like Louis Jordan's "Saturday Night Fish Fry," Amos Milburn's "Chicken Shack," and Nellie Lucher's "Fine Brown Frame." On the café wall was a photo of TBone Walker on stage playing guitar behind his head while doing the splits. (Yo! Hendrix in heaven—with the splits, Jimi boy, with the splits.) First stop, Hairdresser, Quiff and Brilliantine. I mean, hey kids! On the boards I wore a Barathea river-boat gambler suit in Midnight Blue, cream lawn shirts, tie—and red suede shoes—Brothel Creepers with soles an inch thick! And yes, my folks were reasonably cool about all this.

So, by now there was live band boppin' and DJs flipping discs all around. My hometown was jumping! Now we could buy great records in Leeds: Lewis's Department Store record counter was the hottest Saturday afternoon venue in town. This store was hip to business: there were guys doing slides, splits, crabs, and twirls all over the polished marble floor and girls with ponytails and wraparound skirts flying. The store bought every jumping R'n'B record as soon as it came out. They put in soundproof booths so you could take records in there and listen before you bought it. I terrified my school music teacher (a snob Frenchman) by taking this stuff in for the class to listen to. Louis Jordan got him in a seething rage. In a Cashmere wool, cream-colored, flower-embroidered jacket—I struck him speechless. He practically had to nail himself to his blackboard so as not to murder me; he would have killed me too if there hadn't been a law against it. Once, for a change of beat from Tartini and Beethoven I even tried him out on Al Jolson, Fats Waller, and some Spike Jones City Slickers. He puffed up blue in the face and quivered in agony. The guy was dandruff.

Soon after I passed 15, I had a hot bopping and butterfly-stockinged ponytail girlfriend named Pat; we were out dancing seven nights a week, knew every step, and knew every dancehall for miles around. Our favorite was a place called The Starlight Roof. On quiet nights (Thursdays and Sundays) we knew two Catholic Church Halls with a couple of steaming DJ priests who could turn out discs that would burn the spots off your soul and the soles off your shoes. Their dance sessions were conservative in taste rather than raunchy, but without even creasing their cassocks these guys would recite the 23rd Psalm, pray for no train wrecks, then wind up the kids for a night on full-tilt boogie. They just loved Duke Ellington n' Ruth Brown, Glenn Miller, Basie, n' Joe Williams, The Ted Heath Band, Pete Johnson n' Albert Ammons. Whadda' ya mean, I was supposed to be a Methodist? These guys could SEND YOU where you were REALLY supposed to GO. One of these priests was the first DJ that I ever heard play Tennessee Ernie Ford's "Shot Gun Boogie". And I still play it now.

OK, so all this was a few years before Rock n' Roll came along and fitted right on in so we could go right on boppin'. But hey, were good fun and Community Family Services ever better?

© Neil Rock

4.

Skiffling, Scuffling and Busking

I love dance music; have worked as a DJ on and off over decades. But dance music is not my only music love, I also have a longtime interest in British, Irish and American folk music and have collected records and books on the subject for many years. As a radio DJ in the Air Force, I had a budget for records and spent money on blues and folk, so learned a lot during my military service. I played a lot of records too while at home and my mother and sister became folk music fans for life. My sister is still playing live gigs in America today. After I left the Air Force, I did DJ work in a dance hall, and I was in a touring band. A friend played good electric guitar, I could sing and play drums, so, with another guitarist, a tea chest base player and a banjo player, we had a 1950s Skiffle Group– The Heaven and Hell Skiffle Group, named after a club in Soho, London. For two years we toured the Northern England club circuit. Did OK too; worked hard and there was a time when on Friday nights we had two gigs in cities 20 miles apart: one finished in a pub at 10pm and the other started in a night club at 1am. We would wrap up the first gig, catch some motorway grease and coffee on the way to the nightclub and arrive right on time to set up.

The group broke up when the lead guitar and girlfriend migrated to Australia. I continued the rock 'n' roller DJ job but found that my interest in Skiffle moved to roots folk music and this was pulling me to new fields as an entertainer.

While in the DJ job I requisitioned books from the British Library and studied folk music from the early nineteenth century and early twentieth century industrial areas of Britain. There is a poignancy in the workers' folk songs of any industrial nation: the music really reflects hard times on railroads, in iron works, shipyards, farms and coal mines; there is an exuded melancholy, stories with conditions of grinding poverty and industrial tragedies. The music reflected the reality of the working class, life at the bottom and not far beneath the level I had been in most of my childhood. I decided that I should inquire more about it. I needed roots level exposure to live folk music entertainers. Leaving the DJ job, I set out to get it. Finding grass roots singers and raconteurs by traveling round the country proved difficult. It meant going to wherever I heard of locally known old or young performers still active in small towns or country areas. Having still to earn a living, I worked short jobs: driving a bread delivery van, swinging a hammer to break up flaming slag in an iron foundry, and stacking crates of produce in a wholesale fruit and vegetable market. So, after hitch hiking round England for a few months meeting, singing and exchanging information with other people with like interest, gaining odd club gigs and after spending some further time in book research, I decided that all roads led to London.

I arrived in London, knew nobody, was flat broke and got a job simply by being still asleep at 8 am under a box hedge in Soho Square when a guy wearing a bowler hat, rubber apron, rolled up pants and no shoes—whose business it was to clean cars—threw a bucket of used soapy water into the hedge and hit both hedge and me. Cockney Jock—the bowler hat—had nowhere permanent to live either, he paid his way in shelters, and he had this business cleaning a few cars on the Square and this kept him in food as well as shelter rent. He ate most of his meals in a local café; the owner gave him water for car washing and a place to store his gear. By chance this car washer also loved folk music, played banjo and washboard and knew some American industrial songs and hollers that I had never heard. Jock offered me some of his work whenever I needed it; we would wash cars while singing work ballads, blues songs and swapping songs the other didn't know. By this means I had meals in local cafes and time to visit musicians' haunts and clubs in Soho so as to live and learn. Hanging out in Hanway Street at Chiquita's Coffee Bar I got a slot performing folk songs for an hour a couple of nights a week and worked the Soho cinemas and subway stations one step in front of the cops. The only buskers that the cops "allowed "on the Soho scene were three guys known as The Happy Wanderers who played and danced nightly in Leicester Square. Anyway, the guys were busted so many times for illegal street performances that the leader held the record of being the man with more police arrests than anybody else in Britain. World famous through the 1940s to the 1960s they worked everywhere including NY Broadway, Tokyo and Moscow. There exist photographs of American and British film stars playing and singing with them.

Buskers had their own hangouts. The Gyre and Gimble coffee bar on John Adam Street at Charing Cross Road served as the real London meeting place for folk musicians and singers. None of us got paid but we sang and played there with a tin can out front to catch small change. Some later big names worked The Gyre and Gimble; Elton John took his name from two of them (Ben Elton and Long John Baldry). One customer there, Tony Ziamitis, has spent his life to hand make the finest twelve string guitars in the world; Mark Knopfler and Long John Baldry each owned several.

I never made enough money to rent somewhere to live, but that held no importance in my mind. Some nights, under the stars on a bench on The Thames Embankment or bedded down in the Waterloo Shot Tower I could reflect on the good fortune of my freedom. I learned also to sleep while traveling round the London Underground subway system on the trains of the never-ending Circle Line. Living rough didn't hurt, I learned a lot. Often after a street performance, a pub or club gig I would be on an apartment floor or maybe in a lady's bed.

At Midnight, on New Year's Eve of 1959, in Trafalgar Square after a paid club gig, I threw a bottle of champagne into the air and as it burst on the sidewalk, I swore to myself a New Year's resolution that I would never ever work at anything I did not want to do. Stuck to it from then on. As the Buddha said, "Everything is chaos, work out your own salvation diligently." Luck came my way again that winter while singing and passing the tin can when the night manager of the Gyre and Gimble offered me a job washing down the floor after working hours in exchange for coffees, money for food and me making my home in the cleaning cupboard. I slept in that broom closet for about three months. Snug. Later, after another spell of dossing down in the Shot Tower, train station waiting rooms and trains parked in overnight sidings I got a bed and a part time job running a bookstall in exchange for teaching Irish folk songs to the wife of a friend.

Soho at this time had a lot going in the way of roots music and there were several underground clubs and coffee houses from where TV folk music personalities and other recording artists came. On the Blues scene, Alexis Korner got blues men and early Rock-n-Rollers into a Friday night jam session in a Soho pub. A lot of major talent emerged in the sixties from people that Alexis put in his groups from 1958 to 1962. Some of the people he introduced to each other are now legends. Most of the biggest names in British rock today got their start with Alexis Korner. It is hard to think of anybody but The Beatles, The Animals and John Mayall who didn't get started by working with Alexis and Cyril Davis, his harmonica-playing sidekick. Alexis gave first gigs to—and introduced to each other—Mick Jagger, Charlie Watts, Brian Jones, Jack Bruce, Ginger Baker, Graham Bond, Rod Stewart, Pete Townsend… All these names and more got started by Alexis at the Soho pub gigs and were amongst the star alumni of Alexis Korner bands. I believe it was Pete Townsend who once said that Alexis should have been carried round London in a sedan chair for life for what he did for the British music industry.

Also, a little-remembered fact is that Alexis had his own BBC radio blues program and TV blues series. Alexis also was the act who opened The Cavern in Liverpool and was the act that closed it years later.

My own scene had chugged along washing cars in Soho Square and doing street busking and odd solo club gigs until 1959 when I met guitar virtuoso Davey Graham. We teamed up together and started seriously polishing up a club act, which got us a few gigs around England. And my thanks to Anji at The Farm Café in Monmouth Street, who fed us and gave us a place to practice through weeks of rehearsal. (Davey later wrote and recorded "Anji" for her.) Davey and I hitchhiked around England for a year or so while playing club and street gigs in various cities, we also spent time at my favorite outdoor activities of rock climbing, hiking and camping.

By spring of 1960 Davey and I were feeling the pull of warmer climes and decided to spend the summer working the streets and clubs in France. I left London, hitched to Dover, sang on the street and in a park, picked up 2 Pounds in coins ($5) for a boat ticket. I had nothing when I arrived in Calais after a coffee on board the ferry. Hitch hiking through a day I spent my first night in France on potato sacks in a farm shed. Next day, after a breakfast of tomatoes from a field and milk from a roadside milk churn at 5 am, I hitched a ride to Paris. Davey had caught a train from Calais to Paris the day before I left the UK; I walked into Paris from Clignancourt March Aux Puce to Boulevard Saint Germain and met up again with Davey at the Café Monaco in Le Carrefour De L'odeon. We were working within the hour, performing on the Rue Saint Michel. After an hour singing at café terraces on the street, we bought dinner, had a few beers, got a hotel room and still had $8 each and a paid late-night gig for a month singing in the bar of L'Hotel, Monsieur Le Prince. We sang on café terraces every night and by the following week we had a second nightly gig at the nightclub Café Contrescarpe, the top international folk music venue in Paris. After six weeks of performing in front of cafés on the Champs Elysees and Boulevard Saint Germain, I had a completely new wardrobe and a reasonable stash of cash. I am still told by musician friends who knew the busking scene that year that Davey and I were the best street music act in Paris. We certainly tried to be. When not working the streets and clubs we hung out with other street and club performers. Alex Campbell was the main act at the Café Contrescarpe; Les Dudiem, a great Israeli man and wife singing act worked there nightly, as did a great Andaluz classic guitarist named Pepe Vargas.

Rambling Jack Elliott turned up in town so did Peter Golding, AND-Pete Watson, my favorite 12 string guitar player (smooth as a sewing machine.) The hottest banjo player ever, Joe Locker, from NY, arrived in Paris; Joe is simply the best, he laid a lick and just blew us all away. Joe, Davey and I formed a part time trio and strutted some great street music together.

The Bennett Brothers were around, a guy named Sammy Prosser, Geno Foreman too, and a Canadian named Robin Page who I later introduced to Peter Golding. Peter and Robin formed a street double act with Pete playing great blues harmonica and guitar. Pete, a true blues man is still playing great club gigs with his own band over fifty years later. Joe Locker and Davey each amplified their careers into clubs, concert tours and recordings; Davey worked until his death and Joe is still working.

Robin Page had an original street act such as I have never seen anywhere else. He had an iron belt fastened round his waist with colored pencils stuck round it in leather slots. The belt had an iron arm welded to it with a bicycle chain, a cog and a pedal attached sticking out front of his stomach. A series of springs and a rotating wheel supported a clipboard with a clip for suspending pencils in front of it. Robin would turn the pedal, the chain and cog would turn, and the arm holding pencils in front of the clipboard would jiggle up and down, drawing squiggles on paper attached to the clipboard. Changing the colored pencils while cavorting around the sidewalk or nightclub Robin produced a drawing. Robin would sell the finished squiggle products to his audience as Action Art. Great Intuition. Which reminds me of another old friend, William Morris: Bill, a real action painter also living in Paris that year, made a canvas titled Grass and tried to ship it to the USA. As it was an art export the authorities inspected it and as the material on the canvas was half-pound of real muggles—Bill got busted. It gave us all a laugh for a while, including it seems the cops because after some hassling Bill walked free. Unfortunately, that year, Woody Guthrie was sick with Huntington's Chorea in an upstate New York hospital.

Jack Elliott got it together for some of us working at The Contrescarpe Cafe to make a live farewell music tape at the club for Woody. We recorded lots of Woody's own songs and finished the tape with Woody's biggest all-time hit "So Long It's Been Good to Know You." This being a song that everybody knows the audience joined right in. Jack sent Woody's family the tape and it was played at in the hospital. Woody died in 1967 and I cried when he passed on.

One night in the 1980s, Jack played a concert in Washington DC and in his performance dedicated a song to me. Unknown to Jack, my mother and sister Susan were in the audience. When told this, Jack honored my folks with back-stage invitations. In the 1990s, Jack received the American Arts Medal from President Bill Clinton at the White House and was himself named a national treasure for his knowledge of American cowboy music. A well-deserved award.

One of my favorite memories of Paris in 1960 is of being befriended by Frederick Rothschild, and through him I later met another raving

Skiffling, Scuffling and Busking

Rothschild living in Andalusia, but that is another story. Fred was a talented painter and liked to hang out on the Left Bank. He and I became beer-drinking friends at the Monaco Bar. Near the Monaco Bar was a cookery school for society hosts, the wives of diplomats and other dignitaries. Known to few, the school, La Cuisine, on a back street behind Boulevard Saint Germain, had six wood-fired stoves on which six lady students were each required to cook two, four-course meals every morning. All twelve meals were different. There was a wooden panel to separate the kitchen from a space with three tables and chairs for twelve diners. As the school was not a licensed restaurant it was not allowed to sell the food, instead, each diner contributed to the cost of stove wood. Bring your own wine. Fred had his own table each Wednesday lunchtime, where I became a regular. We would sit and eat a four-course gourmet lunch of whatever was served. Cost—four francs (US $0.80 cents) each. The Beat Hotel on the Rue Git La Coeur was enjoying a popularity at that time and which in legend has lasted up to now. William Burroughs, Brion Gyson, Lawrence Ferlinghetti, Sacha Jung, Peter Golding, Gregory Corso, and other Beat luminaries were all living there at one time or another. Davey Graham, Geno Foreman and I lived nearby on Rue Gregoire Du Tours. John Cassavetes was also there, and I remember him inviting a bunch of us to his apartment to watch the final cut and first presentation of his film—*Shadows*. Apart from Peter and Sacha, the people at The Beat Hotel inhabited a more intense cerebral world than I did and were people that I would see around Paris but never got to know. Peter was accessible to his friends all the time he was in Paris. Sacha, grandson of Carl Jung, just a bit more reserved than Peter, lived in the attic garret of The Beat and lived mostly indoors on a musical diet of Gregorian Chants.

During the spring of 1960, the Algerian war of independence took a vicious turn with Algerian separatists adopting a policy of killing a French police officer every day in France. Naturally, Le Flic in Paris became somewhat jumpy. Riot gun toting cops raiding bars and cafés at night and asking for ID were par for the course. In the Carrefour De l'Odeon, the window of the Patisserie next to the police station and opposite the street performers hangout, the Cafe Monaco, suddenly late one night got bullet holes in it. Davey and I met a shaky Paris police officer on the Isle de Notre Dame one day whose nerve was so shot he could not face continuing his job. It was frequent in Paris during the Algerian independence conflict that when large crowds formed round street entertainers, the mobile police patrols (regarding this correctly as being potentially dangerous to street security) would move the performers away by either driving us in their grab van to some other police district and dropping us off again or locking us up in the local cop shop until the following morning. One summer night after being pulled in while performing on the terrace of the Café La Fouquet on the Champs Elysees, Davey and I were in a cell next to a dozen or so of Les Poules and sharing a bottle or two of wine with them. A cop came to the cells and told us that Davey and I would be on French and Belgian TV in five minutes time. It was a thirty-minute music show that we had recorded for TV Francaise, Paris some weeks before. The girls insisted we were all allowed to see the show and were escorted to the guardroom for half an hour. The girls loved it. Even the cops were really impressed when Davey told them that he also had a solo show on the BBC TV in London the same night, which was a showcase special on him titled "From Bach to Hound Dog and Back."

"OOH, LA LA!" Cracked the girls "Just imagine, SREE times in one night!"

In La Bastille, I had Algerian friends who I could visit and enjoy good times with. One friend was the owner of Chez Ali, a great café for North African music and where I learned to appreciate Oud and Tambour players and the records of Egyptian Diva, Oum Kalsoom. When Ali's daughter got married, I was invited to the wedding and reception at the café. I took an American girlfriend with me and there was great dancing and singing. While my girlfriend was cutting up the floor alongside the bride and sisters I was seated amongst the audience lining the walls. The person sitting beside me poked me in the ribs and offered me a hash joint. I turned to take it and found myself face to face with a uniformed French/Algerian Pied Noir cop with a machine gun in one hand and the joint in the other. I broke out in a cold sweat and turned my face toward Ali in confusion, and only cooled it because Ali dug a neighbor in the ribs and laughingly pointed in my direction. The cop, like myself was a friend of the family. We shook hands and carried on partying.

Skiffling, Scuffling and Busking

July 14th, Bastille Day: Tout Paris flips out and parties for 24 hours then leaves the capitol the next day for summer vacation. On the 14th, in Paris, any street entertainer worth his salt could make a normal week's take in a couple of hours. Joe Locker, Davey, and I did heart-warming business. Joe still reckons that we set the record for money made for a single day of street busking. We had all earned well that summer. Joe said later that he made so much money working with Davey and I that he traveled through Europe without touching the money he had brought from America. He recently remembered an occasion of us being hauled into a cop shop for the night and no less than three different working shifts counted the money we had made on the street that night. It was more money than a police officer earned in two weeks, and we were lucky the police chief was not vindictive. He returned our cash in the morning and said we should not work at his Arrondissement again. In July 15th, each with a pocket full of cash, Joe went to work in Copenhagen and Davey, and I took off to work on the Cote D'Azur for the rest of the summer and leisurely hitch hiked down through Vichy, Clairmont-Ferrand and Frejus. We decided to busk Saint Tropez for a couple of weeks and did that. Working was cool with the laws, and we did nightly street gigs in front of waterfront restaurants, played parties at bars and on one or two boats. One boat was a large ocean-going power yacht belonging to an international land law judge. He settled boundary disputes of property owners in many different countries. Being quite wealthy he traveled the world constantly in his yacht with his wife by his side. I asked him if he enjoyed his work, and he assured me that he loved it and said "I haf stolen more money wiz a briefcase zan I ever could have done wiz a gun"

While in Saint Trop' I met up with an English guy named Des who worked in a Creperie and for a week or so he served Davey and I giant size luxury specials on the house. Twenty years later visiting Peter Golding at "Ace", his Kings Road boutique, Peter took me into the office to introduce his business partner who turned out to be Des; big laughs and amazement all round.

An English guitar player I only knew as Mike joined up with Davey and I in San Tropez to work along the Cote D'Azur. Mike's girl was a fantastic "bottler" (cash collector): she could smile sweetly, flirt, pass the hat, and rake in the cash. The trip was fun. We did the coast.

Davey played a week of solo gigs in a bar in an alley in Menton, but it had no place to sleep, and the hotels were all full. However, the bar owner had the keys to an historic museum apartment on the opposite side of the alley, so Davey got to spend a few nights sleeping in Emperor Napoleon Bonaparte's bed.

Davey returned to Paris, and I worked Venice for a couple of weeks before returning to Paris to meet a commitment to do a part as a street singer in a film with Catherine Deneuve. During shooting on this film, Pete Watson and I worked one scene on the Pont Neuf Bridge to an enormous nighttime crowd. We made good money on this film. I bought a scooter to ride to San Sebastian in Spain where Davey and I planned to do a couple of weeks. Somehow, we missed each other, but working there anyway was a no-go. The Guardia made it impossible to work the bay cafes. I sold the scooter in Bordeaux and got the train back to Paris. Things got tough as autumn came and the café terraces glassed themselves in. Davey returned to London, and I tried Amsterdam, where the weather was approaching winter, it proved impossible to earn a living. Back in London I could not settle back into the scene even though pub work was available. I lectured for a while on folk music, sold songs and taught songs to a couple of well-known American and Australian ladies preparing tours and record albums, but I was totally restless and looking for further foreign adventure. Well, I told myself, life is an open road. Busking for a living was wonderful, BUT, after almost 4 years it was time for another change. Morocco called.

© Neil Rock 2007

5.

At the Royal Court of Soho

Busking London streets and the Underground subway tunnels for a living, cleaning the odd car in Soho Square while wandering homeless around Soho, I met Johnny Pilgrim of the Vipers Skiffle Group. He had a mobile bookstall which he operated at night on Charing Cross Road in the doorway of Foyles Bookshop with permission from Mary Foyle, the store owner. Johnny and his wife, Tina, gave me a paid job running the bookstall in the midweek nights and a roof over my head at their house in Waterloo in exchange for me teaching folk songs to Tina. I had to fight with a Heinz Mix male bulldog to sleep on a sofa in front of the fire. This no-name ugly mutt picked up Johnny late at night on a train station platform in Birmingham over a shared sandwich and rode to London on the train, following Johnny home. The dog had a mouthful of rotting teeth, absolutely terrifying breath and two bad habits. One was if anybody sat on the sofa then the dog would walk around it in continual circles clicking its claws on the linoleum floor, at the same time breathing heavily like a sewer until it got the person on the sofa crazed enough to get off, whereby the dog would take possession with all teeth bared. I learned to sit tight until it gave up. The second bad habit of this dog was masturbation in front of all and anybody. The dog would jam itself into a ball between a leg and corner of the front panel of an upright piano, wrap its front paws around its weenie, wind itself up and go like the proverbial cat riding a sewing machine.

Running the bookstall was enlightening, in that I could indulge my passion for reading and get to meet a lot more with the Soho night people than I already knew. Soho at that time still had characters walking around who could only be labeled as Bohemian. Eccentric kings and queens were certainly in residence.

King David was a Soho night roamer who stood almost two meters tall. He wore a black ankle-length overcoat, newspapers for a shirt, pants held up with string, and hobnailed boots. Hair hung three feet long down his back and his full beard was almost as long.

A café called The Little Londoner stood on the corner of Charing Cross Road and Oxford Street; this café was the nighttime sandwich stop for all the night people of the Soho streets. David would come by the bookstall on most nights I worked and mind the stall for thirty minutes while I went to the Little Londoner for coffee and a chew..On coming back, I would give David enough money to go get himself a bite to eat. David never spoke. He would just arrive and stand with me. You had to trust David to know him, he looked like he could at any minute turn into Goliath. He had a very peculiar habit in that from the breast pocket of his overcoat he would take a pencil, a piece of cardboard and a metal bottle cap. Placing the bottle cap on the cardboard he would flick the pencil against the underside of the cardboard to flip the bottle cap over and over. He would do this for hours. One night after several months of him being at the bookstall I asked him his purpose, he replied, "Fun, while watching the world go by, and congratulations, you are the first person to ask in seventeen years." He was in his late 60s or early 70s and sometime not much later, he no longer turned up at night and I was told that he had died.

Author Colin Wilson once wrote a book titled *Adrift in Soho* in which he focused on one or two street characters he briefly met, people who I knew and who were part of a larger group of Soho Bohemians and Beats. These people were functioning in a world apart from much resemblance to normal existence, but it would have been of interest to any social anthropologist studying urban tribal living. King David had introduced me to their common cave hang out in Soho, a pub known as The French.

Inside, The French looked like a bistro: the décor was French 1930s and French language newspapers on reading sticks hung in a wall rack by a circular marble-topped table in the doorway. The French had a clientele, some of whom made the inhabitants of The Beat Hotel in Paris seem like weekend wonders in comparison. Foxy, the two hundred pounds weight, five-foot-two-inch undisputed Queen of Soho and The French Clan, was the scourge of the Soho police force and a terror to anybody who crossed her. Her Friday night parties at her home in Highgate were the underground event of every week all year round. Guests were a worldwide crowd of drinkers, dopers, musicians, theatre and film people, writers and gamblers, of which for the night each type was allotted various parts of floors of the house to set up their fancy. Some nights, close to a hundred people would attend these soirees and Foxy's only rule was "Don't hustle anybody on the premises."

Once, standing at the bar of The French, Foxy's bloomers fell after someone behind her had done a neat dip job and quietly cut the elastic, everybody laughed. Foxy also laughed, said it was her birthday and invited everybody in the place to an oyster and champagne lunch at Wheelers Restaurant. Foxy disappeared to the bathroom before dessert, but never returned. The management held everybody else hostage for the king-sized bill. The police told them to forget it because they would never see a penny. The diners were released and returned to The French to find Foxy at the bar saying, "Caught you with your pants down."

Foxy was a cantankerous, iron carapace and ugly wild-eyed hostage to daily fortune who also had a heart of gold. She would have stripped the glue off the back of a postage stamp (anybody's postage stamp) had it been possible to sell it, BUT, if she discovered that anybody in the crew had a money problem then it was for sure that Foxy would put the screws on every single person she was in contact with until the problem was solved. I once saw Foxy on a crusade for new arrivals on the scene, a young couple that she didn't even know, had never met nor heard of before that morning and then—on the same day—find them a house, hustle them up the first month's rent and all the furniture. And I mean *all* the furniture, right down to kitchen utensils. She was out on the street cajoling for money, beds, pots, pans from total strangers—and allotting people she knew (and didn't know) with vehicles—to collect and deliver. When Foxy was on philanthropic quests for whatever grail she was seeking it was a case of coughing up or getting boiled in vitriol for ten years or so. You had to go along with Foxy or be in danger of segregation from the rest of humanity. Her tongue could kill an alligator.

One Christmas Eve, after a party at a house on Ibiza, when Foxy was well into her sixties, Sam of The Stones, as a fellow house guest, found her forcing her way into his bed and asking "Well, are you going to give me one?" Sam didn't. When seeing her from then he on lived in mortal fear of biblical proportion retribution.

Foxy's two classic coups were:
Successfully suing British Airways for money after claiming to having been bit in the ass by a flea on one of their aircraft. Never allowed on a BA flight ever again.
Appearing at the British Embassy in Paris and selling the Consul a box of kippers (Smoked herrings) after telling him she was broke and the box was all she had, and it was either that or he would have to pay to send her back to London.

Foxy is buried on Ibiza where she lived for the last years of her life. Her headstone carries no name, no date of birth or death. A beautifully inscribed and flower-etched, sculptured piece of white marble on her grave in the new cemetery on a hill outside Santa Eulalia simply reads "For Foxy, from all her friends." A half-page obituary was published in *The Telegraph* in the UK. As far as I know, from the 1950s to her death, I am the only person who she allowed to call her by her real first name. She once told me so. I think I will keep it that way.
Iris Murdoch, Dylan Thomas, Quentin Crisp, the Irish terrorist and poet Brendan Behan and his brother Dominic all frequented The French and were members of the floating cast. A writer friend recently reminded me that other French customers included Irish poet Paddy Kavanagh, Lucian Freud, and Francis Bacon. I am also told that when Dylan Thomas died, a wake was thrown in the pub that topped any party since the end of WWII.
One of the mainstays at The French was Iron Foot Jack, a long-haired, six-foot-tall club-footed tramp and gambler who wore a stovepipe beaver hat and claw-hammer coat and was closely loved by all, certainly by Gaston and his wife. Jack's photograph, looking like Captain Ahab, hung large and in pride of place above the bar. Jack lived in the cellar of a house in Notting Hill near Portobello Road and loaned a space on the floor to Colin Wilson now and again. For a while in the early 50s, Jack

had slept in the bath at Foxy's house; Foxy considered herself honored. Jack looked like a tramp, but he was a regular at The French and sat drinking in a corner and reading the horse racing papers. Local wisdom had it that Jack's claw-hammer coat was lined against winter cold by lots of racetrack won banknotes. Ray Cortenz, a brooding and electrically vibrating eccentric, who also wore long hair and beard, was a client of The French since it opened during WWII. He roamed coatless and barefoot around Soho for twenty years and more while claiming to be Jesus Christ and could recite The New Testament forwards and backwards to any who doubted him. I was told by a French regular that one night in the mid-50s in a Soho pub, when challenged by an American airman to show his dick "because Jesus Christ was Jewish," Ray circumcised himself with a pocketknife right there and then at the table.

During the opening night performance at a west end theater of a play written by his brother Dominic, I saw Brendan Behan leap on stage and scream to the audience, "The first time Oi come to England Oi come here wid a bag of gelignite to blow yez all te fuck. Oi did years in prison fer tryin' and now Oi've decided that youse English rat bastards ain't too fuckin' bad after all." After this, he sat down again in peace, and it must be said that one of the theater management nor any member of the audience had the chops to call for his removal by the police.

Many more wild characters were denizens of The French, one of my favorites was the tramping court astrologer and wanderer, Ernest Page, who hummed classical music constantly and went everywhere carrying two suitcases full of Ephemeris books on Astrology. Ernest worked as an astrologer through WWI, WWII and until he died in the 1960s. From the early 1950s on he made his living and his home traveling back and forth on the England/Denmark sea ferry doing horoscopes for fellow passengers in the cafeteria and for strollers he would meet while sitting on park benches at either end of the ferry ride.

Another of my favorite characters, Benny the Busker, had a great street entertainment act. Dressed in a suit of alternating blue and red panels, matching trilby and tap-dance shoes, this character rode the London underground subway trains. He carried a mechanical wind-up Victrola and a swing music record. He would wind up the Victrola, put it on the ground, stick the record on and tap dance on the train or in the train stations. On the stations Benny would do a single minute dance act, pass the hat, collect the cash and be back on the first outgoing train to any next stop before the station guards could even move to bust him. He had a certain influence on 60s freaked out fashion, for I once met my American friend photographer Bill Wassman while he was walking along Knightsbridge wearing an identical suit.

I was also friendly with someone in The French crowd who shall remain nameless. He was a direct descendant of a former and historically famous British Prime Minister and by inheritance controlled a large family fortune. My friend was an investigative street sociologist and spent years of his life tramping in London and talking with unemployed people in front of a particular London district labor exchange. Once in some argument over his right or not to sleep on the sidewalk outside the labor exchange, he struck a policeman. No criminal charges were brought against him, but his family took advantage, and had him committed to a mental hospital purely out of the dubious reasoning that he was now of violent nature and might dissipate the fortune. I would take him the odd bag of grass while he was at the hospital, and we would sit comfortably in the garden for hours. One day a doctor protested at this unlawful activity and my friend threatened to call the press and cause a scandal for the hospital and his own entire family on charges of mistreatment. The hospital authorities decided he would be less of a problem back on the street. He did get released after half a year or so. In later years his father gained control of his money and totally ripped him off.

Nothing new under the sun: Old Henry the lyrics writer was eighty-one years old in 1958 and spent his days mostly in a quiet state of daze at a table in The French and in other various Soho pubs while reading newspapers and quietly smoking Player's brand cigarettes that were syringe-loaded with liquid cocaine. His cigarettes, freshly prepared and dried at home before starting the day, allowed Henry to get totally stoned without anybody knowing what was happening. I do not recall Henry getting crazed and mugging people; still, it must be said that he didn't have to: England was civilized in those days. Henry picked up his requirement legally and free of charge from his doctor twice a week; though it did cost one shilling (US $0.14 cents) for the chemist to fill the prescriptions. Even then Henry would get his full money's worth at the pharmacy by sliding a licked finger of cocaine dust off the pan while the chemist filled paper packets with Henry's weighed daily ration.

Although almost all the members of the 1950s French crowd are dead now, a few of us latecomers survive. One still sits in the pub across Old Compton Street and tells rebel stories and another guy is a host on a NY radio talk show. Barry, of Camden Town Market, regarded as the world master ocarina craftsman, only recently died. A few years ago, while walking through Soho, I went to see The French and found it too crowded to enter. Recently, travel writer and friend Robin Brown told me that he did not believe such people as the 50s French cast exist anymore. I agreed, regretfully. But then there is an elderly bearded character on Ibiza riding around on a bicycle while wearing a tutu. There is a spark of hope for the future.

© Neil Rock 2006

6.

Up and Down Penny Lane

Trading to travel and traveling to trade have been a way of life for me and many of my friends for many years. It has led me into some roller-coaster adventures. 1963 to 1965 for me was red carpet craziness. Occasionally opportunity knocks, or you see it in front of your nose when it is there for the taking. Sometimes you re-invent yourself to turn in a new direction. All the free-wheeling travelers carry memories of missed schooners heading East or West, or the ride we caught which helped get us where we are today.

While wandering around Marrakech in the autumn of 1961, I had the good fortune to discover pawnbrokers and metal traders in the souk who were selling antique silver jewelry by weight. Looking further around the markets revealed embroidered tent hangings, carpets, old brass furnishings, and other articles which should be saleable in Europe. I hitchhiked north, checking out markets in Meknes, Fez, Tetuan and Tangier, and found goods in those markets also.

In the UK some years previously a friend had made me a gift of a few valuable drawings by the painter Augustus John. The drawings were in London. I now wrote and asked that they be sold, then the money forwarded to me in Gibraltar. It arrived and I was in business. I bought a used car and set off to the markets, paying some of my way by carrying tourists who booked me and my car for guided tours around the country. Basing myself in Tangier for the next 2 years I traveled, carried paying passengers, and bought goods around Morocco, selling in Paris, London, and Brit enclaves in southern Spain. After a couple of trips south to Agadir, then Tantan and Goulimine in the Sahara, I determined that most of the goods worth having were already further north in the established market cities and from then on, I concentrated my efforts north of the Atlas Mountains around Marrakech and in Fez, Tetouan and Tangier.

In the spring of 1963 while in Marrakech for a few days buying jewelry and embroideries, I learned of a Moroccan who supposedly had the wardrobe from the film Lawrence of Arabia. It transpired that this clothing had supposedly fallen off the back of a truck somewhere in the Sahara Desert. The film having been shot in Morocco and Jordan—this story had a ring of possible truth. Anyway, it made a great sales line. Indeed, in a back street off the Djemaa el Fna Market, I met up with the Moroccan, a container of Arab male garb and a few WWI British Army uniforms. He also had some ladies' used caftans, also left over from some kind of a theatrical event or other.

Buying some of this clothing projected me into a couple of years of a not always enjoyable but continually exciting experience.

I traveled to London. Through a friend, Danny Buckley, who had a boutique in D'Arblay Street, Soho, I sold the "Lawrence" costumes and the ladies' caftans. For a few weeks, Sheikhs, Tribal Chiefs, WWI British Army Officers, Mata Haris, and Salomes were gliding, parading, or slinking around King's Road and Portobello Road pubs.

While I was selling the film clothing and caftans, Danny, in the boutique, was working on a beautiful range of designs for soft cloth toys and was busy making samples in his workshop. Created by a brilliant animated cartoonist friend of Danny's, these toys, named "Gonks," were a variety of multi-colored, hilariously comical character figures about a foot high, each with a body and head in a single globular shape, stuffed with synthetic cotton and with floppy hands and feet attached. The toys were designed to target kids and teens to girls in their twenties. The sales posters and ads planned for girls' magazines were of a young girl sleeping in bed with a Gonk beside her on the pillow and a slogan reading "Go Get a Gonk." A winner. Added to the retail line was an edition of smaller models, designed as promotional brand leaders for various commercial products. These models targeted Advertising Agencies. Danny found an interested financial backer for both lines, and somebody was needed to research manufacturing costs and production supply from toy manufacturers.

I was there. I got the job. With a car full of various Gonks and paper patterns, I visited Britain's toy factories.

The Beatles had a couple of British top ten records out at this time and in 1963 gave a Royal Command Performance for Queen Elizabeth, the Royal Family, and guests at The London Palladium. This was the show where John Lennon told the Queen that she should not bother to clap, but instead, just rattle her jewelry. The show was an enormous success and launched The Beatles into international orbit.

Danny and I both realized the potential of having a Beatle Gonk in the toy line, so we decided that Danny should apply to Brian Epstein, owner of NEMS Enterprises, The Beatles management company for the manufacturing and sales rights of such a soft toy. Epstein and his lawyers liked the design: It was a rotund composite one-piece head and body with Beatle haircut. It looked like Paul McCartney and carried a guitar (It really brought out a teenage crush). Amazingly, we got the rights to make and sell the soft toy and when telling me this on the telephone from Epstein's office, Danny pointedly asked me if we wanted any other merchandising rights on The Beatles. Nobody else had asked Epstein before. I dazedly reeled off the top of my head a list of about 30 items. Danny read the list to Epstein's lawyer. We not only got the exclusive rights to sell contracts for the manufacture and sale of all these items, later we amplified the list to over a hundred. The addition of The Beatle Gonk to the toy line enabled me to sell the manufacturing and distribution rights of Gonk Toys to Chad Valley Toys, Britain's largest toy company.

Danny and I buckled down to selling manufacturing licenses on a wide variety of Beatles products. Within weeks we were flooded with requests from manufacturers in many countries and our efforts expanded into becoming international business operations run by London money people and in which Danny became a major shareholder and director and I was also hired as a working director.

Beatlemania was born right then. Yes, sorry, kids, I am one of the people who signed up all those companies making and selling Beatles wigs, fan club badges, Beatles imaged tee-shirts, funny hats, plastic guitars, handbags, make-up cases, wind-up toys, plastic dolls, your kid sister's bedsheets, her bedroom curtains, schoolbook covers, balloons, sneakers and chewing gum wrappers, etc., *ad nauseum*, and organizing screaming hordes of hysterical teenage girls at airports and concerts.

Business success guaranteed: It was easy. It has been most famously said: When the Beatles played a live show, there wasn't a dry seat in the house. And, *no*, I did not know The Beatles and they would not have known me from a hole in the wall. Any contact was conducted between our respective management and lawyers. The only time The Beatles and I met was at a press call in the Georges Cinq Hotel when they played the Paris Olympia. However, I did keep close track of their business progress around the world to link it with Beatles product manufacture and did a lot of Beatles promotional drum beating. Amongst other things, filling French department store windows with mechanical models wearing Beatle gear and personally, arranging with the US Military and Capitol Records for The Beatles' records to be played on American Armed Forces Network Radio in Europe. I kept no souvenirs of all the junk sold in their names (now, collector memorabilia), but I do still own copies of some of their business papers, including their signed personal management contracts with Brian Epstein. Along with the salary for my job came expense accounts, a leased flat in Chelsea, a leased car, airplane tickets and five-star hotel accommodation anywhere anytime I wished to travel on business. Fast Track? During, 18 months I don't remember ever spending more than two weeks at a stretch in the UK.

In the Spring of 1964, The Beatles made the cover and three pages of *Newsweek*, and the magazine predicted fifty million dollars of retail sales in the USA for Beatlemania products that year. It was somewhat beyond reality, but business was so successful that by autumn that year the company lawyers were busy in litigation fights over product piracy by crooked companies everywhere; ninety-six of them in the USA alone. By showing just cause in American courts we had US judges nailing up American pirate factories in 48 hours flat. There were lawyers chasing each other around the world and looking for multi-million dollars' worth of debts in unpaid royalties.

Once, after the death of Brian Epstein, John Lennon was asked if he thought Brian Epstein knew what he was doing. Lennon replied, "He certainly did, he robbed us blind." There is room for recognition of this in the Beatles/Epstein management contracts. In other papers that

Epstein and his lawyers signed (including The Beatles music recording contracts and merchandising contracts), it can be recognized that he was also incredibly naïve. His incompetence cost The Beatles millions of dollars in lost income. In the fights over payment of royalties to The Beatles, Brian Epstein and his lawyers were the definitive idiots of the piece. Although I was only a sales director in the merchandise licensing company and not involved in royalty collection matters or having the concerns of shareholders on my shoulders, all this mismanaged financial nonsense threatened my job and my newly adopted lifestyle. Coupled with domestic strain, I received my share of nerve frazzling fallout. I had a marriage and a divorce in less than two years and was using drugs at a serious turn of speed. By December of 1964, I was just another Rock 'n' roller casualty. And how another good friend in the Rock 'n' roller business kept his nerve through "Altamont" and two stomach ulcers I really do know how to appreciate. I take my hat off to you, Sam. Recognizing my lifestyle as being untenable, I resigned from my job in 1965 after almost two years of having imagined I was enjoying this trip, then dumbly blew my entire saved stash of cash on one more single year of frantic living and a Mark 7 Jaguar saloon to do it in. I totally wrecked the car while flying it off a winter snowbound Hamburg autobahn. Waking to consciousness as a guest in the barracks of a military base of the British Army on The Rhine, I decided that enough was enough. I gave away my apartment lease and everything else I had in London and fled back to the much less stressful life of being a Traveling Trader. After a friend and I made a buying trip around Morocco and Algeria, I settled down to living on Ibiza and Formentera, where my friend Brice helped me pull myself back together. Mind you, I could at least still grin when remembering that I had gone through a wild wow of a ride with some high-flying travel and some very crazy laughs. Being on the road and finding a way to pay for it is a challenge that many of our friends have successfully met, and it has enabled us to see large slices of the planet and to have adventures that would have otherwise been inaccessible. Some of us have been fortunate enough to keep going. I have bought, sold, and traded everywhere I have traveled: To and from the USA, Africa, Western and Eastern Europe and Asia. I have sold everything from Beatlemania contracts to the world, battery-driven handheld air-cooling

fans in India, American clothing in Morocco, English shirts in Istanbul, and hand-tooled cowboy boots in Kabul and bought tribal jewelry and clothing in Africa and Asia and sold it in Europe and the USA. In recent years with small effort, I have paid my summer vacation costs by trading in amber, buying in Poland and from the Russian mines at Kaliningrad, and selling in Scandinavia and Western Europe. My friends around the world deal in antiques, jewelry, gemstones, model airplane engines, clothing and leather goods, army surplus vehicles, and garbage-skip findings. The owner of a restaurant named Nostalgia, near to Slupsk in Poland trades in—and decorates his property with—nineteenth century sewing machines, ancient cars and motorcycles, church wall hangings, church pews, old farm implements, and industrial machinery. A Frenchman I first met in London at the close of the 1950s drove around Europe by Rolls Royce for some 50 years and made a comfortable living out of buying and selling the granite balls topping country house gateposts. In Sweden a few years ago I met a German camper-van wanderer dealing in old coal mining lamps. Most of the people that we all know on the road are traders grown of an incurable urge to travel and an insatiable curiosity to see what lies around the next bend. Each year I sort through and sell some odd, cherished treasures from my travels and I always look forward to the next adventure. And, frequently, driving up the road, I still sing my cracked-voice, laughing-ass off.
Yeah, Yeah, Yeah, Yeah, Yeeaaahh!

© Neil Rock 2006

7.

Meeting Christine

The same mid-day in 1963 that the News Media announced a 20-year-old English call girl Christine Keeler had brought down British Defense Minister, John Profumo and scandalized the Government, Parliament and the British people by sleeping with both Minister Profumo and the Russian naval attache in London, Yuriev Ivanov. Mr Profumo also told the press that he had been unable to resist seeing her for the first time as she stepped naked out of a swimming pool, he thought she was the most beautiful woman he had ever seen. I had to agree—for, at that moment of the news release, I was meeting Christine for the first time while she was sitting in her bath.

© Neil Rock

8.

Ketama—1962

Smoking marijuana and smoking hashish are peaceful tastes and it may be that one of these in particular catches your fancy. With me it was hash. During the many decades that I smoked it, unlike grass it got me high without ever a headache or being hit with the monster munchies. Ever since those heady 1950s London days of scoring that finest Charras of Harry The Hat, or later the best Red Leb of The Hot Dog Man and since musing long on Algerian backcountry finest and in Asia on the best they have to offer I have striven for the best, and the conditioning of my head has been a most interesting reward.

In the Autumn of 1962, a couple of like-minded souls were living in Tangier at the same time as I. One had run wet apron-clad and joyfully through the fields of the Bekkaa Valley and had also scraped the whitewashed walls of a few Lebanese farmhouse barns. The other was a seasoned grass smoker and recent convert to hash, stunned into enlightenment by the hospitality of His Blessedness, The Oran Hadj.

Daily we did our best to keep up gourmet appetites and standards by scoring the best grass possible, such as was delivered to us at Ab' Kaddas' café. But unfortunately smoking light Moroccan grass on its own gives a nervous high that just doesn't cut the mustard and smoking it long-term a´ la Moroccain -mixed as kif with raw uncured tobacco - cuts one's throat. Spoiled we were, and even with fresh daily arrival of Ketama's best product, we felt still committed to grumble by the kif cough.

To gain top quality hash from grass, the extraction of resin-rich pollen must be no more than one percent. Reducing the quality of a hundred grams of grass at even relatively low Tangier prices just to winnow out and savor solely one gram of pure hash, was above and beyond the call of reason. As hashish did not exist in Moroccan culture and no Moroccan had ever known about it, we three decided that ignorance must rise to bliss, so we planned a visit to the Rif Mountains. The marijuana harvest was just in. Between us The Maestro had his experience in Lebanon, I had my car, a tank full of juice and money for food and supplies. The third friend had boundless enthusiasm and one hundred dollars for grass. We decided to equitably divide whatever would be our take. After purchasing a large sheet of clear plastic and some small cotton bags, we set off early one morning on our mission.

Ketama is a Rif Mountain district well known now as having the perfect climate and a soil rich in phosphates for the successful growing of cannabis plants, which are the yearly cash crop for the local farmers. The Maestro and I, both having been in the region on plantation tours and sampling the fresh flower buds on previous occasions, had an idea of which village to try for business.

Ketama was a remote area to foreigners back then and many of the locals had not much idea of the world outside. On our arrival at the village we had chosen, somebody asked where we were from and The Maestro replied "America". Some villager remarked, "Oh, there was an American on a donkey who passed through Ketama last year. Do you know him?" The crazy thing is that The Maestro and I did know him, as we had met this guy the previous year while he was traveling in The Rif by donkey and at which time, he was living in a tree on the riverbank outside the mountain town of Chef Chouen and had told us he was heading through Ketama on his way to the city of Fez.

So, in French, an elderly villager introduced himself as the headman and asked what he could do for us. We explained that we wanted an amount of marijuana equal to one hundred US dollars and a place to live for a day or two where we could chop kif and smoke in peace. My car was stashed and hidden in the middle of a stand of cane, and we were shown into a wide and long wooden hut (a mountain Gite) and were served mint tea along with hard boiled eggs. A fire was lit in a central stone fireplace and a line of villagers stacked along the walls one hundred kilos of still-on-the-stalk fresh grass for our appreciation. Yes, I'll say we blinked. We had hit the proverbial jackpot. At one dollar a kilo for the grass we would get a 1-kilo yield of hash. We paid for the grass, then, naturally, the twenty people from the village hung around to see just how fast these foreign madmen could smoke it.

We had known when planning this gig that we intended to build a two meter long by one meter width and one meter height shaker box from the sheet plastic and local cane stalks but had figured on getting thirty kilos of grass or thereabout for our money and doing our work alone in a hut for a day or so. Now that we had one hundred kilos of grass to shake, and to scrape the separated pollen from the plastic sheet, we realized that there was no way of doing this in less than a few days, or of doing it in privacy.
Quietly, The Maestro told the village headman that we had a secret to show him and asked him to keep everyone out of the hut except himself and whoever would be bringing in our food and firewood until we left. When there were only a handful of men left in the hut and The Maestro explained what we were to do, there were shrugs and "Hmms", and "OKs", but no understanding or excitement.

At first light the next day we cut the box frame from a stand of cane in the village and erected the box in the Gite, cutting two circular hand size holes in a long side of the plastic sheet and hinging the top cane along the rear edge of the box as a lid. Lifting the first bundle of grass into the box, our Maestro put his hands through the holes in the side, picked up the bundle in two halves, and gently beat them together so that pollen drifted off and stuck to the walls and underside of the box lid. The headman and one other guy who had entered the Gite watched this and thought us crazy when seeing us throwing the used kilo of grass into a corner. After beating a couple of more kilos of grass we stopped to scrape some pollen off the box walls, sampled the product, found it most agreeable and gave a couple of pipes full each to the headman and his sidekick. Result: two instantly and thoroughly stoned first-timers. As soon as he felt that he was able to speak, the headman asked two questions: Did many foreigners smoke this? Where did they get it? At our statement that it usually came from Lebanon and Central Asia and on Allah's name it was becoming very popular in parts of Europe and stood every chance of spreading to a worldwide rage, there was profound understanding of everything from the headman and sidekick – work for the whole village, a whole new market in Morocco and abroad, transport costs cut, and a product they could wail on without the raw tobacco. In the next few hours as we worked, at least four different guys were delivering tea and boiled eggs and sampling the product about every five minutes. Whenever we reached a hundred grams of the pollen, we pressed it in a cotton bag using the heated bricks we kept by the fire.

The three of us sharing the jobs, it still took us three days and most of the nighttimes to get through the work.

The entire village kept its cool during the whole visit and when we three had completed our work we all shared a giant chicken couscous. The headman and his council shook hands with us, each touched his breast and wished us well. Two men escorted us safely out of the area when we left.

The Ketama villages were, until that year, so far off the beaten track that in later years when business was being done by smugglers with suitcases full of money and with a combined product of several villages amounting to boats full of hash, it was not uncommon for baksheesh to be asked for in the form of Cadillac cars and four-wheel- drive pick-up trucks. Yet, as we left in October of 1962, a villager showed me a dog-eared male clothing magazine and asked me that when I came back I should bring him a pair of Y Fronts underpants

Back in Tangier our financier took off and made a successful home-run to money. The Maestro and I cut our stashes into monthly smoke pieces and stayed high for about a year.

Why did the Moroccan culture not know hashish when they had a custom of the growing and daily smoking of Marijuana? Right next door in Algeria the Bedouin had been enjoying smoking hashish for centuries. Egypt, Lebanon, Syria and Turkey all know hashish. Why don't other marijuana-growing African countries know it, or the mountain tribes of Thailand?
Why don't the Mexicans know it? Uh, Oh, there goes somebody again!

Before writing of this adventure today I have only told this tale to two other people during the past fifty years. After living long enough to see our product reach half the world, both The Maestro and The Financier have departed to their peace in scented clouds of cool appreciation. (RIP MM and PG). An old man with a contented smile, maybe now I can be allowed to tell it to you for us all.

The Maestro and I never made hashish in Morocco again.

We rested on historic achievement.

© Neil Rock, 2011.

9.

Moses and the Tooth

The Jemaa el-Fna market (Place of The Dead) in Marrakech is the oldest market and trading post in North Africa. Caravans from Arabia to the Kalahari have met and done business there for millennia. Products have varied over the centuries, but it is recorded that some 200,000 English slaves were sold on this market, and the one up the coast at Safi, from the beginning of the 16th century to the end of the 17th century. Barbary pirates raiding the English coastline were the cause of this. At times there was a glut on the market and one Englishman is reported as being sold for an onion. Up to the 20th century criminals were executed in the Jemaa el-Fna as a public entertainment, hence the name Place of The Dead. It still was, in 1961, a far more wild place than the sanitized tourist attraction that it is today. Nobody working on the market had even dreamed of plastic tablecloths on numbered food stalls under rows of electric lights. Hippydom hadn't yet been invented (I think we were being called Beatniks then) and Crosby Stills and Nash were probably still in junior high school. Sure, there were a few guys cooking on fire buckets and oil cans, selling chickpeas and kebabs, and bread. Occasionally maybe even a boiled sheep head, steamed goat eyes and fried goat balls were on offer; a few green olives and a sardine on the side if you were lucky. No Europeanized cous-cous, tajine and lamb chops then. Up to the 1950s and early '60s, storytellers, magicians, musicians, sword swallowers, wrestlers, bead stringers, mat weavers, metal workers, machine mechanics, thieves, other assorted villains, flea bitten donkeys, and farting camels were still much more in abundance.

Moses and the Tooth

Now, my friend Moses was in great pain, he had a badly swollen face through a serious toothache. Between us we had NO money, were tired and hungry—and wafting around us was a certain interesting aroma of "je ne sais quoi" from several unwashed days of meandering hitch-hiking and sleeping in the forests and occasional tea houses of the Rif Mountains along the road through Chef Chouen and Fez from Tangier. Having only one eye (The other missing and the space being just a wet empty glaring red socket), Moses, with a Zapata moustache, face unshaven and a head of wild hair round his shoulders, combined with dusty floral waistcoat, blue-jeans and bright yellow Moroccan floppy slippers, might be said to have been—in those pre-hippy days—somewhat of a tourist attraction. And it was this appearance that saved the toothy day. Dental Treatment for Moses was urgently needed. Deciding as usual that being laid back was the better part of valor, Moses and I squatted in a dusty alley and sucked up a few of our remaining sebsis of Ketama kif, then, suitably grooved, we wandered off into the heat and clamor of noon on the Jemaa el-Fnaa in search of a dentist.

After having gone through half a kilometer of hundreds of everybody and his entire family trying to sell us everything from plastic teaspoons to tethered ostriches, recycled razor blades, battery acid wart remover, evil eye protection pouches to wear over our crotches, old doorknobs, bat toenails and rubber bath frogs, we were overly boggled. Then we got to German Afrika Korps WWII army webbing and a selection of machine parts, pencil sharpeners, dyed cloth, spices, herbs, rush mats, baskets of molting chickens and dried lizard skins until we finally came across a middle-aged gentleman wrapped in a ragged Djellaba and asleep on the ground beside a box and a stool. There was no mistaking his trade. Leaning against the stool were two evil looking large colored drawings of rotting teeth. One drawing was of a tortured eye-tooth, black and beige, pulsing with striated lines of pain and leaking a stream of venomous orange colored pus. The other drawing was of a greenish black molar, split down the middle and with a jagged red lighting flash spiked right through it. This publicity was to let you know what would excruciatingly happen to you if you did not submit to Jemaa el-Fna dental treatment immediately if not sooner.

Moses stuck out a foot and poked The Mister Doctor awake. At the

sight of Moses and fluorescent swollen jaw, (this fantastic gift of a money-spinning one-eyed Djin delivered straight into his hands by the munificence of Allah), the dentist sprang to his feet and went into a whirling series of swoops, salaams, scraping and bowing. Moses explained in sign language that we had no money. The minor triviality of not being able to pay for treatment was extravagantly pooh-poohed aside. It was understood immediately by all parties concerned that the absence of mere cash was no hindrance at all to the Hollywood Production that was about to begin. The Doc shoved a grimy finger under my nose and offered to do us both for free, I pointed at Moses and politely declined.
First, Moses was sitting on the stool and the drawings laid out on the ground in front; Moses was handed a chunk of majoun to suck on and chill him into moldable material. Our new-found medic then reached out, grabbed a passing eight-year-old snotnose by the neck, snarled throatily at this kid and threatened much of dire dearth, drought, cholera, shriveled intestines, worms, and baldness on his entire family and all descendants forever if the kid should run away. Then, by oily finger rubbing there was promise of much cash reward. The urchin was handed the dentist's embroidered skull cap and sent striding off into the throng to collect financial contribution for the pending operation, while at the same time screaming the Arabic curtain opener, a sort of—"Miracle cure in motion! Straight from a stupendous sell out season at Lourdes! Doctor Ali Mashhad! One- time only performance in Marrakech! Dentist to the world!"
The dentist in the meantime went into his own arm waving, gyrating spiel.
"Allah be my witness, I am known! Blessed with medical genius! Far and wide is my fame! Wealthy Firangi travel from the ends of the earth to celebrate my internationally blessed style! Thanks be to God for my education at the University of Timbuctoo! I swear by Holy Fatima that the King himself and your Sainted Grandmothers never saw such talent," etc. So on and so on.
A crowd of about a curious hundred joined us to gather in a circle round Moses and the dentist. Moses not yet quite mellowed out by the majoun, glowers in pain at everybody. Everybody is pleased. The Doc powers up a sebsi and slips it to Moses, Moses woofs it down and asks for more. Doc

obliges. The Doc calls snotnose over, examines the take in the skullcap, shakes his head, smacks snotnose round the ear and sends him off into the crowd again. Some further haranguing of the viewers and collection-taking by the kid; some crossed-finger waving and swiftly muttered incantations of desert ju-ju spells from suspicious and wary observers fascinated by Moses. Another hundred or so mesmerized onlookers appear. The Doc staggers round in a coughing fit, hacks a glob of phlegm, the crowd is worried. The Doc recovers, the crowd relaxes.

To keep the audience enthralled by Moses until they sic up enough funds to buy a large supply of halvah for his girlfriend, the dentist lights up a couple more well-stuffed pipes of kif in quick order, samples the taste and hands them to Moses. Moses accepts, is getting nicely wasted on kif and majoun and sways for a while to Oud music coming from a radio in a nearby spice shop.

The Doc chews on a bag of peanuts while offering ear cleaning and nose-hair clipping service to anybody interested. After determining that there really are no takers, the Maestro performs a couple of three card tricks and Moses is fed another chunk of majoun.

Now, having judged to a tee the fine psychological tuning of Moses—and the tension necessary to keep the attention level of the inward leaning watchers—the Doc opened the main act.

First, another blast of a pipe to doze Moses. Then, slurping up a pipe for himself in one enormous sucking drag, the Maestro picks up his box from the ground and blows a massive dose of smoke into a small hole in its side. Big question-mark all round, audience mystified. After pirouetting for the crowd while pointing at the box and waving it in their faces the Doc then produced La Piece de NO Resistance. He reaches into the dope smoke-filled box and pulls out a rather whacked but still writhing seven-feet-long cobra. The snake hisses, Moses flinches, the crowd quivers. Without a moment's hesitation, Doc flails the snake around in the air to facilitate rapid cannabis circulation in the brain and wraps the cobra around Moses' head. It sits there, dazed. Moses is frozen. Instant Anesthetic. None better.

Guaranteed state of total cooperation from Moses—come hell or high water—any agony—if the French are invading again—Martians in the Sahara—no matter what, Moses isn't moving, even if shit really hap-

pens. BIG sucked-in breaths and gasps of appreciation from the audience. They know a master hustler when they see one.
Doc bows to the crowd.
Signaling the kid with the money collection cap to exert one last further effort at extortion from the admirers, and urging me to move the crowd back, the Doc circles 'round Moses, chin in fist to make a final external examination of the patient. Moses and the snake continue stoning together. Having secured Moses and the audience, our Maestro again reaches into the box and takes out a pair of long-nose pliers. He grabs Moses' nose, forces his mouth open and, after peering around inside he waves cheerily to the crowd, takes one last look at the kid with the cash. Receiving a nod of an assured week's takings, the Doc sticks in the pliers and jerks out the offending molar. Moses doesn't even have time to moan, he spits a gout of blood onto the ground while Doc waves the tooth around for all to see. Oohs, aahs, much shuffling of feet, applause, complete satisfaction from the crowd. Moses is handed the tooth, an expert extraction. The dentist unwrapped the snake from Moses, put it, the photos, and the pliers back in the box and paid off the kid as the crowd dispersed in search of other entertainment. Picking up the box and stool our doctor smilingly shook hands with me, then Moses.
Having slipped into my palm enough small change for a couple of mint teas with flatbread and a pack of kif, the Doc wandered happily away, leaving Moses with a smile and both of us with a warm feeling of business having been well done.

© Neil Rock 2006.

10.

Eddie's Leg

Having broken his leg while falling down the flight of steps leading from the Medina to the port in Tangier—Eddie wasn't feeling too good. The hospital had done a good job of resetting the break and fitting a plaster cast, and had done it free of charge, so that at least was a boon. The biggest problem was it happened just as Eddie ran out of money; the day he was leaving his Pension and needing somewhere to stay.

While collecting Eddie's belongings from the Pension before getting him from the hospital, I was stopped as I left by one of the ladies who lived in the sporting house across the alley; she told me she had heard of Eddie's accident and asked how he was doing. Zorah, who was 20 years age, of curved chocolate, beautiful on five foot nine of carved sculpted muscle and carried a haughty aura that promised to eat you with nails at bedtime and leave you sweet as a peach in the morning, went immediately into mothering high gear when I told her that Eddie had no money and that I was trying to get him into my Pension. Zorah commented that the female spider who ran my Pension would keep Eddie there until she had sucked him, me, and any other friends, dry of any money coming through for food and care.

NO, and Wakha, Shuf Hada Sidi! Eddie was to live with the girls until he got well.

Being the chief whip for her Madame, Zorah had the clout in the house to organize Eddie's care and this was arranged on the spot.

The girls were expressly motivated and prepared a spare room; hot

Harira soup, kebabs and fruit were ordered from the souk and were to be in the house by the time I got back with Eddie.

Anybody wondering at all this enthusiasm should know that if James Dean and Elvis had walked down the street with Eddie then only Eddie and Elvis would have drawn a second glance. Eddie was 25 years old and ladies' blonde candy from six feet head to foot. There was not a girl on window duty in the house across the alley who had not leaned a little further out when Eddie went in and out his Pension. Cricked necks were par for the course amongst the girls in any town where Eddie lived. So, getting Eddie settled in with Zorah, Iyelda, Ayesha and a few more helpers, all had been accomplished with ease and Eddie began the luxury care road to recovery. The Kedive of Cairo never had it so good. Eddie was coddled like the Caliph of Baghdad.

Within a week, the cast on Eddie's leg was signed by everybody except the Madame. There were times in the next three weeks when Eddie looked sometimes flushed and decidedly sleepy, but the leg was healing well and as the girls and Eddie reported, nothing more than everything was OK—I didn't ask. Came the day that Eddie left the house to take a stick-assisted walk for a glass of mint tea in the Zocco Chico. I fetched him from the house with girls looking on like baby is leaving home. In truth, apart from the cast and limp Eddie looked smilingly fit. The waiters at the café commented on Eddie's health, congratulated him on his progress, prayed each for a broken leg. During further morning forays, speculation on his treatment and improving condition became daily banter. Sex, being understood as the best exercise there is—nobody bet on anything less than a full recovery. After a month and when Eddie finally left the care of the ladies, they couldn't let go without straight faces smiling fondly while hiding some twitching blubbers. Eddie could only mumble. To complete his recuperation and before the cast was removed, I took him on a car trip around Morocco. After his full recovery, we left Tangier to live for a while in the Atlas Mountains.

Sixteen years later I again met Zorah, striking as ever, on the Boulevard Mohammed V in uptown Tangier. Dressed chic, like she was on the Paris Champs Elysees, her career was successful. She remembered

Eddie's Leg

Eddie, and although not clearly being able to place me as having been on sheet or on street, when I said Eddie had fully recovered, she replied that she was sure of it as she personally had taken responsibility for the rotation of Eddie's physical recuperation therapy. She smiled, nodded and walked on.

The noticeable thing is that if Eddie had had money, he would have been nothing more than a John. Well, maybe a one-night cuddled trophy John.

As it was, the story of the heart of gold was proven true.

© Neil Rock

11.

Algerian Adventures

Nik and I drove by car through Morocco, meandering leisurely over much of the country. Blithe we were, first cruising down south, then drifting northeast up to the Spanish Moroccan enclaves of Melilla and Nador and over the border into Algeria. A large ball of majoum purchased in Tangier had lifted us some few hundred feet above sea level and put us on course for conversations on the purpose and function of the Great Pyramid of Giza, the Egyptian gods, and the tomb of Tutankhamen. Nik expounded on the genetic engineering of man by the Annuaki (and this is decades before Zecharia Sitchen wrote of the decoded tablets of Ur, the 12th Planet space invaders and gold-digger slavery). We raved awhile on P D Ouspensky, objective art, esoteric magicians, (dropped Alistair Crowley firmly into the theatrical bum category) and like this we floated across half of Algeria until arriving in Algiers City late at night. Here we encountered a serious change of vibes, which brought us into a crash landing from our previous high altitude. We drove into the city shortly after a coup d'etat had come to a close at sundown.

We had no idea that the coup had taken place while we were driving along the desert roads. Algiers had machine-gunned and grenade blast pocked buildings, deserted streets, most of them blocked to traffic and a general feeling of frightened confusion amongst the few citizens abroad. The Algerian President, Achmed Ben Bella, hero, freedom fighter in the war of independence against the French, was already in jail and despite his popularity amongst most of the general population, this coup d'état was an act of the Algerian military seeking to put in place army general

Algerian Adventures

Houari Boumediene as President and Dictator. Nobody was about to risk his neck to get Ben Bella out.

Most businesses were closed; there were no other cars in sight. Driving along a dimly lit street Nik and I arrived at a hole-shot sidewalk café where the owner, admirably showing faith in Allah and a wish to earn any passing Dinar, regardless of having a street front covered in broken glass instead of having café windows, had re-opened for business as soon as the shooting had stopped. To say that Nik and I were viewed with intense suspicion from the moment we stepped out of the car onto the street is putting it mildly. There was an uneasy silence and aura of tension from the four or five other café clients as we sat and asked for coffee. Anybody looking even remotely French was not welcome here tonight, memories were agitated; French settlers had massacred 6000 Algerians in one weekend orgy in 1958. On top of that, the French Army had killed more than a million and a half in the war of independence.

Our cool amidst all this frigidity stayed reasonably smooth and was surely conditioned by the fuzziness of view brought about by our generous intake of the ball of *majoum*.

The coup d'état was inevitable in that President Ben Bella, an ardent nationalist, had sought to nationalize Algeria's natural gas wells and refineries, despite these being controlled by French companies. Lacking the sole political grip to do that meant he would have had to designate control of assets amongst regional Governors in the territories where the wells and refineries were located. The ensuing dispute over who was to control assets and tax revenues was giving rise in a movement toward an Islamic State. General Boumedienne determined to put it down, deposed Ben Bella, declared himself President, then had Ben Bella executed. Boumediene had the clout to nationalize Algerian gas resources and keep the power to himself. Since that night of Boumediene's ascent in 1965, successive governments have 'disappeared' and murdered over 200,000 Algerian Militant Islamists and 50,000 Algerian civilians have been tortured to death by police and army. In turn, the Islamists have murdered thousands of police and military personnel. Algerian Islamists made up many of the Afghan Mujahedin fighting the Russians and today hundreds of Algerians are fighting as part of The Taliban and Al Qaeda in Afghanistan, Pakistan and Iraq.

There being danger of French intervention should this coup in Algeria not hold, and me agreeing with Nik as having no wish to be trapped in Algeria if more fighting broke out, we decided to start back to Morocco on the following day.

Somehow, and rather stoned naïvely, Nik and I looked for and found a Pension room in the Casbah on a narrow one-meter-wide alley. Although I have lived comfortably at times in Medinas and Casbahs of cities across North Africa and Asia, I have never been in a Casbah as claustrophobic as that of Algiers. The alleys in any Medina are mostly only a meter or two wide and set in defense pattern. The Algiers Casbah is a densely-packed citadel on a sharply steep hill; the twisting alleys are really staircases with houses built haphazardly, one on top of another, forming a maze. Because of the coup d'etat, most citizens were indoors and the alleys and passageways were eerily silent and deserted.

Nik decided he wanted to go out to find something to eat. I decided I was going nowhere until daylight, and then only to walk straight to the car. Having driven all that day and knowing it would take me two days of hard driving even without bad incidents to get back to the Moroccan border, I opted for bed.

Nik went out to eat and instead got mugged at knifepoint by two men in an alley before he even got down to the level of the main streets. On reporting the theft of his wallet and money to a police station the only questions were asked in five languages on a standard piece of paper, which read: "I was robbed. Name? How much? Where? What time?" Obviously, whether or not the police would make any attempt to investigate the mugging, it was sure that Nik and I were not hanging around to find out.

Leaving Algiers in the early morning of the following day and savoring the last of our magic majoun en route, we got to Oran, where, from friendly dock workers we obtained a fine piece of sunny gold to smoke and keep us up and flying along the coast.

The next day, with great relief, we crossed the Algerian/Moroccan frontier at Oujda. We enjoyed driving westward through the Rif Mountains and unwound with a travel break in Tangier. Landing safely

Algerian Adventures

from the Alicante ferry at Ibiza some days later was a distinct pleasure. Our adventure had been exciting, but now we were home. My breakfast at the Café Montesol had never tasted so good

© Neil Rock 2009

Two Magic Rupees and a Space Chillum

12.

Cops and Cobbers

Jack, a summer traveler, and I were on the road from Tangier to Ibiza. It was April 1962, my first trip to the island and Jack's only visit and while he was on a European pre-college tour. I had garaged my car in Tangier, not wanting to pay all the ferry costs. We decided that after leaving the ferry at Algeciras we would have a shot at hitchhiking. Whereas I carried a backpack, in which besides a few clothes I had some Moroccan jewelry and embroideries that I intended selling in Ibiza and Mallorca, Jack toted a rather ostentatious tan colored leather suitcase full of changes of casual clothes and beach stuff. Well, each to his own, and so on. After a couple of rides, we were dropped on a secondary road at a tiny farming community in Andalusia, where our host driver turned off to travel to a Sierra Mountain town further north. Unfortunately, a heavy rain was falling and we had no cover. The place we were outside was a high walled compound with an arched gate through which we could see a couple of old tractors and some compost heaps standing outside buildings around the yard. Obviously, we could not stay in the rain, so we entered the compound seeking shelter. The dilapidated buildings were either stables or closed hay barns except for one barn-like building with wide open doors through which we could see dim lights. Approaching this door, we saw that the building was a bar/bodega with a few rough tables and benches on a earthen floor. Paraffin lanterns revealed that four or five farmers were seated at a couple of tables.

At the far end of the single room, the barman stood behind a rough wood bar. Two large barrels of wine, one of Jerez Seco and one of Vino Tinto, stood against the back wall. These were the only drinks on offer. Jack and I sat at an empty table. We had not eaten since early morning (fried doughnuts) before leaving Morocco, so I asked if food was available. Rough bread and canned sardines were the only availability. So, we had two glasses of Jerez, bread and two cans of sardines. We were left alone; after checking us out when we entered the bodega the farmers went back to talking and drinking. Rain down-poured outside and it was obvious that Jack and I could not move outside until it stopped, so two more glasses. The glasses are medium vino sized so we are taking in four times that of a normal sherry glass.

Through the rain, two Guardia Civil on horseback rode into the compound and approached the bodega. These guys were obviously of a mountain unit, wearing riding capes, thick grey wool uniforms, flat back shiny black hats, heavy-duty knee-length boots and each carrying a short carbine slung across his back. The atmosphere in the bodega noticeably changed when these policemen dismounted then walked their horses into the barroom and tethered them to a bolt on the door. The men took off their capes, placed them open to drip dry by their sides on benches and sat at the adjoining table.

The policemen were surprised to see Jack and myself, but apart from nodding to us and us to them, they then ordered sherry and sardines and sat talking. The farmers kept their heads down and conversation became desultory. After eating, by glances the way of Jack and myself the Guardia obviously were talking about us. Finally, one of the Guardia approached us. Where were we from? Where were we going?

Jack is American, me English, going to the Balearic Islands. Jack is not sure it is good to be American at this time, because the US Air Force has recently had problems with pickets against NATO at the Torrejon air force base in Spain. We are lucky: this cop is from Madrid and has a cousin in the army garrison there who has an American girlfriend. The cop is pleased to meet an American, and—of course—Señor, an Englishman. Drinks are called for, he insists. He goes back to his companion, drinks arrive and we toast each other across the room. Our turn, Jack orders more sherry for us and for the cops. Toast España, America, England.

It was now evening and dusk, still pouring with rain and the ground outside in the compound was a quagmire of hay and horseshit. Regardless, the farmers bade us "Buenas Noches," walked outside, mounted the tractors and left for their village. The Guardia can't leave, Jack or I either. More sherry. By nightfall the four of us were drunk. The barman obviously would have left with the farmers were he free to do so; nobody is coming here through this rain. He can't leave until the Guardia go and he can't ask the foreigners to leave while the policemen are here.

Then, at about 10 o'clock at night, the rain stopped. We get some distant lightning and rumbling of thunder. The Guardia insist that Jack and I leave with them. They will take us to a place to sleep. They are both really drunk, Jack and I are also very drunk and have no choice. With the leather suitcase loaded cross pommel in front of one cop on his horse, Jack is hoisted up behind. Me, with pack on my back am hoisted up behind the second cop.

We rode through the night across the countryside and along the base of a mountain. Jack and I were without protective clothing and were soaked to the skin by mist and light rain. Finally, we stopped at a farmhouse and were lowered to the ground. The fresh air had hit us all and by now the Guardia whose horse had carried Jack was stumbling and mumbling. He hammered on the door of the farmhouse until a light came on inside and the farmer opened the door. He and the cops knew each other. My carrier told the farmer that Jack and I would be sleeping in the barn.

The farmer gave the cops a lantern and went back into his house. The cops, Jack, and I stumbled into the barn. One of the cops kicked some clean hay into an empty horse stall and threw down two rough blankets from a shelf and told us this was where we would sleep. I realized that the cops used this barn for siestas.

Jack's suitcase now became the central piece in this story. There was a roof support pole at one side of the horse stall and Jack was told to lie down with his hand near it. The cop who had thrown down the blankets now got Jack to lie down, then taking a length of chain from a hook on the wall he ran it around the pole, through the handle of Jacks suitcase, and then handcuffed the chain to Jack's wrist. Jack, of course, is protesting but we are told it is for Jack's own safety, this is an expensive suitcase and there are thieves in these hills and Jack's suitcase could be stolen while he and I slept. When I tell you that all four of us were really drunk, I mean weaving, staggering drunk. The police insist the handcuffs are necessary, but if we were to be attacked Jack couldn't defend himself even if sober. Fortunately, we were still reasonably coherent. As the two cops were preparing to leave, I insisted, drumming it in, that they were not to forget to come back in the morning. They both swore it would be OK, staggered outside, somehow got mounted then left.

The next morning at 7 am, sure enough, the cop with handcuff key comes to the barn, groaning, hangover roaring. He unlocks Jack. The three of us look a bit sheepish but then laugh it off. We had all had an adventure. The second Guardia arrives, looks rueful but joins in the grins. Jack and I were once more mounted on the horses and in the early morning sunshine ridden back to the barnyards on the road.

We arrived just as a farm truck was leaving for Murcia. The Guardia secured us a lift and after handshakes rode off on their tour of duty. Jack and I arrived in Murcia, checked into a pension and each with headaches and shakes we slept the day away. Our encounter with the mountain law had been fortunate. If not for the two cops, the bar owner would surely have tossed us out into the night. My thanks to the American girlfriend of the soldier in Madrid.

© Neil Rock 2008

13.

The Great Pyramid

Having long wished to visit Giza and feeling particularly drawn to The Great Pyramid, I took time out on the route of my first visit to India to lay over for a few days in Cairo. What the pyramid would hold for me I had no idea but I had always felt unsure of accepting classic historians portraying it as a tomb. When studying drawings or photographs of the interior I always felt that the building was more attuned to deserving exploration as to it having a use as something grander than merely being a mere burial monument. Several things do not fit the theory that The Great Pyramid is the tomb of King Cheops (also known as "Khufu") and his Queen, including the fact that nowhere in ancient Egyptian writing is there any mention of Cheops or a queen ever having been buried there. No writings exist whatsoever of funeral equipment, coffins or possessions of a king or queen or anything relating to a burial have ever been found there or even anything indicating that a burial of anybody at all ever took place. Nor are there any writings within the pyramid itself. Nothing at all in Egyptology supports the tomb theory. The tomb theory itself solely supports the reputations of historians seeking a purpose for the building.
Determined to obtain access to the pyramid and remain uninterrupted by other visitors while I investigated the interior, I left my Cairo hotel by taxi to Giza one morning at about 6 am. Close to the Great Pyramid, I paid the driver and walked across the plateau, circled around The Sphinx, then walked the remaining distance to the area in front of the pyramid entrance. Two men I took to be Rais (guards/guides) were asleep on the ground and they awoke at the sound of my approach. We greeted

The Great Pyramid

each other and on my production of a US $10 bill and my request to enter the pyramid, one of the men picked up a candle, matches, the key to the grill door at the pyramid entrance and led me inside. As there was no electricity in the pyramid at that time of day, my guide lit his candle to light our way. He explained that I was not to be allowed into the subterranean passageway and chamber as work on the passageway was in progress and materials stood in the way. Some work was also being carried out in the Queen's Chamber, but here, although scaffolding was standing against one wall, the view to the corbelled niche was clear. Two apertures in the walls to the left and right of the wall with the corbelled niche allowed air to flow through the chamber. Later I learned that these were shafts leading to the outer surface of the pyramid and angled to point to the Sirius star system and the star Alnitak in Orion's Belt. Obviously, no purpose would be served by allowing air into a burial chamber. Nor is there any record of a sarcophagus or coffin ever having been in this chamber. Studying the corbelled niche, I became instantly aware that its function was to imprint upon the mind of any individual standing in it the harmonious cosmic vibration of the pyramid as a whole. Regularly repeated use of this standing ritual would reinforce the harmony so that the user could easily and rapidly become attuned. After a few minutes of me memorizing the layout and my impressions of the chamber my guide led me to the foot of The Grand Gallery.

My initial view of the height and ascending length of this gallery was overwhelming. It is surmised by historians that this upward leading passageway was constructed as the route by which the coffin of Cheops was carried to the top and through the entrance of the (King's) chamber. But in fact, to reach the floor level of the gallery from the passageway leading into it from the Queen's Chamber, one has to climb up to the floor level over an 80-centimeter-high solid granite block which was placed wall-to-wall across the base of the sloping gallery. Having surmounted the stone, the actual floor of the gallery is just wide enough to allow passage of persons moving in single file, and even then, up a smooth stone floor. There was no stairway for ascending the Grand Gallery until a metal strip stairway for the use of tourists was installed in the late 20th century. The Grand Gallery was certainly not constructed to allow the passage of a Royal funeral cortege and entourage. There are two ledges each some 80 centimeters high and 60 centimeters wide on either side of the floor area. At the time of my visit the left-hand ledge had a guide rail fixed to the wall beside it and held in place by metal rings. While using the rail for support, my guide and I ascended upward through the gallery with me wondering why this gallery was constructed with such a high ceiling and why a corbelled ceiling which is not required to support the width of the gallery roof? Finally, the Rais and I arrived at the entrance of the passageway leading to the King's chamber. With the guide and his candle leading the way we entered the passageway.

The entrance being only about a meter high, I had to stoop to my waist level to walk the few meters into the chamber.

I was immediately struck by the presence of fresh air in the chamber. On the wall directly in front of me I noticed, as in the Queen's chamber, another small rectangular aperture in the wall opposite the chamber entrance, and a second one in the wall beside me on the right side of the chamber entrance. As with the apertures in the Queen's chamber, these apertures in the King's chamber also have shafts leading through the masonry to the pyramid outer surface and also are orientated to point to Sirius and the star Alnitak in Orion's Belt.

To my right and close to the far wall of the chamber stood the box-like granite sarcophagus.

Instinctively I walked forward to the shaft opposite the entrance and placed my left-hand palm upward in front of it. I did this to test the air current, but the result was quite different. I felt a tingling movement, as if of air, but then without knowing why I walked to the sarcophagus and struck the inside of its stone front wall with the palm of my hand. The sound resonated through the chamber like a bell. My guide immediately withdrew along the passageway leading back to the Grand Gallery, blew out his candle and left me in the complete blackness of the Kings chamber. I climbed into the sarcophagus and lying horizontal in it I made the sound OM at the same pitch as the note resonating through the chamber by my having slapped the stone side of the box. Within a few moments I felt my being exiting the pyramid into deep space, where I found myself without body and seeming to be a spirit with an eye able to see through space in any direction I wished. It seemed to me that I floated for a few seconds while revolving around and through galaxies

The Great Pyramid

before becoming encompassed in a dense all enveloping sulfur-colored fog. Realizing that I did not have the knowledge to explore further, I decided that I must return to the King's Chamber and came to normal consciousness as I still lay in the sarcophagus.

Being stunned by my experience, I rested a few moments to orient myself best as I could in this silent darkness. Then, stepping out of the sarcophagus, I called the guide who replied and obviously had been waiting at the top of the Grand Gallery. A match flared and the guide appeared in the chamber entrance holding his candle. I walked toward him and with me following him out of the King's Chamber we walked without speaking down the Grand Gallery. As we descended, two dim electric bulbs lit up to weakly illuminate our way down. As we came out of the entrance of the pyramid we met another guide bringing inside a column of Japanese people, the first group of tourists of that day. I looked at my watch: it read 9 am.

My guide and I had been in the Pyramid since 7 am and I realized that although I had thought I had been but a few minutes in the sarcophagus of the King's Chamber I had in fact lain there for well over an hour.

There are several written accounts by people having otherworldly experiences in the Great Pyramid and most vary greatly.

As to why I underwent such an experience as I did in The King's Chamber, I have no idea. However, I gave an account of it which was published in the summer edition of *Oz Magazine* in 1968.

A few years later Dr. Selvarjan Yesudian published his book "Stand Up and Be Free" (ISBN 90-202-4077-3), in which he relates having an identical experience as myself in the sarcophagus of the Kings Chamber by following the exact same ritual as I did in the opening of the ways, except where I used the word OM to set my personal vibration in tune with the vibration of the chamber and the harmony of the spheres, he used the word AMEN.

There exists much literature about the purposes and function(s) of The Great Pyramid. With writings varying in avenues of approach from the classic academic, the intuitive and scientific, to the wildly esoteric. The edifice is reported to have many attributes. To Dr. Yesudian and myself and surely to others who made no record of their experience, one of the functions is to facilitate the intergalactic transference of consciousness.

For those seeking more information as to the purposes and uses of The Giza Plateau, I wish to mention here that just as The Great Pyramid deserves more investigation as to its function of accessing the experience of consciousness transference, The Sphynx deserves attention as to its function of accessing the experience of The Awareness of Interstellar Events Through Time.

Even though investigations should and will be made into the purposes of The Great Pyramid and the Sphinx, it should also be recognized that into the future obtaining accurate results might be difficult to achieve. It is probable that the harmonic balances of both edifices have been disturbed through damage done by intrusive work of early archeologists, and now damage by such recent tourism, industry demands and impediments as have been placed upon them.

© Neil Rock 2011

14.

Bombed in Beirut

I was looking for a cheap flight from the UK to India and decided on an Ariana Afghan Airways flight out of Geneva. Although this flight was advertised as departing from London for India, the first leg from Heathrow to Geneva was with British Airways because Ariana had no landing rights in the UK. (Later they did get landing rights, at Gatwick.) Their first allowed flight from Kabul to the UK coming to land at Gatwick overran the runway and plowed into two houses, killing three people on the ground and nineteen of the plane passengers. Amazingly the entire air crew lived through the crash. They were all found on the flight deck in the pilot cabin, probably hoping that instead of seeing brick walls they would get an advanced view of Paradise. Fourteen passengers of the 110 people on the flight were found by British Immigration to be traveling on false passports.

The airplane that I was joining at Geneva was an ancient propeller job flying between Frankfurt and Amritsar. The stopover in Geneva was a hustle. This was because the airport bank at Geneva was the place in Europe where Pakistani and Indian currency could be bought at the highest cut-rate (almost double of the official exchange rates in Asia). In Europe, every week of the year, money to the tune of millions of pounds, marks, and francs had been paid out to middlemen by working Pakistanis and Indians. This money was to be sent to their families back home. Sharks were depositing huge sums of hard currency in Geneva banks on a weekly basis. Contacts in Asia would pay local currency to families at a low legal exchange rate. The money launderers were pocketing fortunes in this scam. When fresh payout money was needed in India or Pakistan, it was purchased at a cut-rate in Geneva and smuggled East. This is still probably true today. I bought some Indian rupees. So did other people from my flight, including the pilot of the Ariana Afghan plane who was standing next to me in the bank, a terrifyingly gin-soaked and tobacco ash-drenched, over-the-hill Englishman in his late fifties. Still, we flew, and he proved his worth. Owing to the plane being really a short-distance hopper and acting like a local bus, it made frequent stops. The route was Geneva, Belgrade, Istanbul, Beirut, Cairo, Baghdad, Kabul, then Amritsar.

We left Geneva on time, and all went well to Istanbul where we were not allowed off the plane and into the transit lounge until five large gentlemen carrying aerosol cans came on board and sprayed us all thoroughly to make sure we were not bringing in plagues of the Frankfurt slum squidges or the dreaded Swiss muesli mosquito.

At the next stop, Beirut, at around 2 o'clock in the morning, we were the only plane and passengers on the ground.

I reckoned that a few minutes of freshening up in the transit lounge restroom would improve my stamina. Accordingly, I was doing deep nasal inhalation exercises in the men's room when the mirror and wall seemed to move, and I thought I felt and heard a loud crump. After more deep inhalations, a minute or two of pleasant reflection, and my antenna not receiving any more tremors, I left to return to the transit lounge. When I exited the gent's, I stepped into the transit lounge and into absolute silence and almost pitch-black darkness. A bulb over an occasional check-in desk provided the only light and the hall was completely deserted. There was nobody in sight. I was mystified as to what could have happened to airport staff, airplane crew, and my fellow passengers.

On walking outside onto the airfield, I could see my plane rolling on the taxiway out to the runway. I started to run. Behind me, out of the darkness and from around the side of the air terminal a guy appeared driving a luggage cart without lights and shouted that I should jump on. I did. We got onto the runway a couple of hundred meters or so in front of the airplane just as the plane was revving up for take-off. My driver frantically flashed the cart lights for a few seconds and drove along the runway straight at the aircraft. As we pulled under the airplane a hatch opened in its belly and a hand grabbed me by the back of the neck and hauled me up and inside. I staggered forward against the torque and the steep angle of the aisle as we roared down the runway to get airborne. I fell into my seat as the plane left the ground and I'm thinking "Wow, what a rush" when the Indian gentleman seated next to me says:

"Oh, sir, WHEREVER have you been? I told them that somebody was missing. I TOLD them that somebody was missing. Oh, my goodness, sir! WHERE HAVE YOU BEEN?" He was stunned when I burst into uncontrollable laughter I was later told that while I was in the transit lounge men's room, the Israeli air force had dropped a bomb on the airport car park. They were having an argument with Syria and hinting that Lebanon stay out of it.

© Neil Rock 2006

15.

Kundalini

Arriving by bus in a misty dawn on the outskirts of a Himalayan foothill riverside town, I had come from another town further down the river where I had slept part of the night in a wood pile. The first person I saw was another young European man dressed like myself in kurta and pajama pants, who like myself was carrying a small cloth-wrapped bundle. My bundle contained my worldly possessions, his, I learned a few moments later, contained chapattis. On my asking what he was doing here he informed me that he was living near this town while studying with his guru and as duty, every day at 7 am he had to feed the local lepers. Would I like to help this morning? I agreed and we walked to the town together. A small milk churn stood outside a building near a jetty at the river's edge. My acquaintance asked that I carry it into the building and down to the basement. In the basement, lit only by dim daylight from grills set high up in the walls, sat or lay several lepers who every morning assembled there to be fed milk and chapattis by this European chela. We set the churn and chapattis on a plank table with several metal mugs on it. After dividing the chapattis and pouring milk into the metal mugs we two Europeans handed the food to the lepers. After they had eaten, we washed the mugs and cleaned the table. We left the building and wishing each other well, we parted ways. I had been invited to this town to visit an ashram on the other side of the river so I waited at the jetty for the first boat of the day to take me across. I was early, but close to 8 am a few other people arrived and when the boat was rowed up, we climbed aboard. Sitting close by me on the boat was a saffron-robed swami carrying a cloth-covered gourd, and who, after our passage over the river as we stood on the riverbank, asked me why I was in this town. I related that I was visiting an ashram. He asked if I had eaten that day and at my answer of "No" invited me to eat with him of food he had in his gourd. We walked someway along a path leading away from the town and in the direction I must take to my destination. We walked between fields and the river until, pointing at a roofed cow byre, the swami suggested we should eat in there. Stooping to enter the byre, I discovered that we were instep deep in cow dung, but there were no animals in the byre. Taking the cloth from the top of his gourd, which was filled with dhal and chapattis, the swami placed the cloth on the dung and the gourd on the cloth and we both squatted opposite each other and ate. After eating, as was the case with the European chela earlier, the swami and I wished each other well and separated.

I still had some distance to go to reach the ashram where I would be staying, and so after washing my hands and feet in the river, I made my way downstream along the riverbank. On arrival at the ashram, I was greeted by a group of people, including my host, who said "Welcome, we hear that you had breakfast this morning with Swami Krishnananda." I was surprised to learn that I had shared a meal with the famous Swami, but how my host knew this I had no idea. Nobody had passed me on the road to here and certainly there were no telephones. I did not ask my host how this information had reached him. But as I discovered, there was more to this town that also could not be understood by me even if it did meet my eye.

Following discussions related to the workings of the ashram, most of us there took a siesta, and following more discussion and dinner that evening we retired early. I awoke late at night. It was a cloudless night, there was a scimitar moon and lots of stars and I decided to go down to the river to bathe. The town, on the opposite side of the river, was completely dark and silent and there were no other people in sight. I felt I should walk back along the riverbank, to the cow byre where the swami and I had eaten breakfast that morning. At this point, the bank of the river was some meters high above the water and a narrow path led down to the water. After stripping to underwear at the river's edge, I walked out until the water was up to my shins, squatted, and thoroughly washed the day's heat and sweat from my body. After washing I stood and remained still and silent for a few moments contemplating the peaceful town and the quiet flow of the river. Quite suddenly I was overtaken by the thought that the peace of this place was maintained by a giant serpent, sleeping deep down on the riverbed. Placing my hands together in front of my face I closed my eyes and asked the river "If this be true, send me a messenger". A few moments later, feeling a touch of something against my right instep I opened my eyes to see a snake on the surface of the water and slowly backing away a foot from me. Amazed at the sight and unable to accept the truth of it having touched me I said to it, "again, because I doubt." The snake slid forward, kissed my right foot again then slid backwards under the surface of the river. Naturally, I was astounded and remained standing in the water for some minutes until finally, turning to leave, my eyes met those of a man wearing a loincloth and who was standing in an arched niche in the riverbank and carrying a pine pitch torch in one hand and a long spear the other. Recognizing that he was a guard of the river at this place I asked, "Is all quiet along the Ganges? And after he replied, "All is quiet along the Ganges." I walked away and back to the ashram.

The following morning, I was to leave this town, so I walked back toward the jetty to wait for the rowboat to cross the river. I passed near the place where I had bathed the previous night. Out in the strong current of the river, there was a sudden flurry on the surface of the water. A group of large carp swimming in a circle, dived simultaneously and with half their bodies and tails still above the surface formed for a split second a golden lotus before disappearing into the river. That a touch of magic had been vouchsafed me in that Indian town is beyond doubt.

And in the almost fifty years since, I have never failed to marvel at the brilliance and wonder of the cosmos and the power that brought it into being.

© Neil Rock 2011.

16.

Riding as the Raj

In a rickshaw taxi on the way to Banaras Airport to catch my Indian Airlines flight to Katmandu, I discovered that my wallet, my return air ticket to Europe, and all my money had gone. Gone also was my plane ticket to Nepal and on to Deli. I hoped that I had lost my wallet in the street and that someone in need had picked it up. In 1967, US $400 would feed a family in India for a long time. Arriving at the airport, I gave the driver all the coins I had in my pocket. I now owned a change of clothes, 2 rupees, and 8 Owsleys.

At the airport, it wasn't so tough to convince the guys at the check-in counter to let me on the flight. First, I told them that I had promised myself to be in Nepal that day to celebrate the Buddha's birthday in the land where he was born. Second, they had my name on the flight list, my passport proved I was me and if they let me fly then nobody else could use the ticket. Good intentions and logic were accepted, and I landed in Katmandu later that morning. After riding the airport bus into the town it was obvious that I would need some cash if I wanted a place to park my bag and to sleep. I walked into a tailoring establishment (a tent with two Sikhs in attendance, a few rolls of cloth, a coal heated iron, an ironing board, and a hand-crank sewing machine.) After taking off my English shirt and shoes, my Levi jeans, and digging a new English sweater and another pair of jeans out of my bag, I was measured, treated to chai while waiting for my new drag, then walked out onto the street with 50 rupees and wearing a quickly run up cotton kurta, pants and sandals. Things were looking up. Seeing a sign reading Blue Tibetan Café, I decided on a tea with a paratha breakfast. A young Tibetan, also having breakfast, asked me if I had anything to trade and told me that he was looking for anything useful, but particularly his family wanted warm clothing. OK, first finish breakfast then I tell the Tibetan I will be back. I took a short taxi ride to the USA Peace Corps office. Inside the office, I look around, sight a floral-shirted sandaled beard, and call him over. We talk, he goes to the storeroom, I leave and go round to the back door. A couple of minutes later he has 6 Owsleys, I have two army kit bags, one full of US Army cold weather clothing and the other full of snow boots. The beard and I are extremely happy. Taxi back to the café.

The Tibetan trader and I decide on a deal: part cash, part goods for me and for him, all goods. He got 4 padded US army parkas with 4 pairs of matching padded pants, 4 pairs of woolen gloves, 4 pairs of wool socks, and 4 pairs of snow boots. I got a carved silver Dorje and matching bell, a bag of turquoise beads, a Neem seed mala, a nineteenth-century Nepalese Tanka, and US $30. Having now enough money to live well for a couple of weeks, also some trading goods for later, it was time for me to take a real vacation. I got a room in the house of a Nepalese family and spent my days sightseeing. The Stupas in Nepal are beautiful and Swayambunath is still active; the statues of the Buddhas in the forest are very aware on reckoning your karma. Short local trekking around Katmandu is comfortable. The Nepalese and Tibetans are mostly wonderful people and the muggles of course transmogrifying. End of money and Nepalese vacation. Coming back to planet earth after a couple of weeks of being beautifully stoned and vaguely aware that another reality was waiting for me out there somewhere, I dug in my pocket and paid my room bill, and discovered that I still had 20 rupees, (at that time—US $2). The next day at 8 am, I paid 8 rupees for a madcap rapid 2-day truck ride down through the Himalayas to the town of Chapra on the Indian Border near Patna. About twenty Nepalese people were also on the truck and we shared laughs and being scared shitless while hurtling 'round countless hairpin bends. The air at high altitude looked like drifting smoke until about noon on the first day when the clouds parted in the mountains, and between other peaks, I got a magnificent view of Annapurna imprinted on my brain forever. At night we stopped at a chai house built across a waterfall and 2 rupees each got us all chai, dal, chapattis, and a place to sleep on the floor. The waterfall roared and pounded down the mountainside. I slept like a stone.

Riding as the Raj

From Chapra to Patna I took a bus ride that I paid for with 2 rupees and a Woolworth's propelling pencil. Arriving in Patna I was faced with somehow getting to Delhi—a few hundred miles to the west across India. With only 8 rupees remaining to see me through until Delhi—where I could count on more trading to pick up some cash—setting out hitchhiking for a few days didn't seem like a viable option, so I decided to do it in comfort. By now my kurta and pants although daily washed are looking a bit worse for wear, BUT I was after all, a leftover member of The Raj. And I know well that the lunatic eccentricities of The Raj are regarded as being deeply mysterious, often tolerated, sometimes respected, and permanently imprinted on the minds of generations of countless India Railways Wallahs.

So, first off, I walked to the railway station and spent 2 rupees buying a Times of India at the newspaper kiosk. Next, newspaper in one hand and 3 more rupees in the other, I bought a first-class ticket to the nearest station up the line. I repaired to the first-class dining room and spent my last 3 rupees on a meal of aloo mutter and chapatis, chai, a packet of Char Minar cigarettes, plus two bananas in a bag for the train ride. Next, I got my head down in a first-class waiting room and enjoyed a comfortable, air-conditioned afternoon sleep until nightfall arrived and the Patna to Agra/Delhi whistle-blowing night train departed. I nipped sharply into an empty first-class carriage and pasted on an Imperial Persona Glower for any unfortunate soul foolish enough to want to share my compartment, The Raj being recognized as most famous ass-kickers. I remained alone. We were barely rolling up to speed when the ticket puncher arrived at my carriage. Without lifting my eyes from where they are buried in The Times at the all-important virgin girls arranged marriage page, I casually feel for my ticket (placed strategically on the seat beside me) and nonchalantly hand it over. Ticket punched; Raj left in peace. After the next (and my ticketed) stop, I am again ready and waiting, still deeply ensconced in The Times, and still with my ticket resting on the seat beside me when the ticket puncher comes round again. Sure enough, Raj is remembered, first-class ticket has been punched before, destination has been forgotten and ticket wallah sails along the train corridor straight past Raj and on to the next carriage. Raj pulls down the compartment blinds, settles down for the night, and only opens the

81

blinds once between now and Delhi; this is as the train arrived in Agra so I can get a beautiful moon-glow view of the Taj Mahal. The train arrived spot on time next morning at Delhi Railway Station

My friend Brice provided me with his air ticket back to Europe in exchange for my wandering sadhu clothing and a promise to rescue him later, and then strolled off on his own adventure to the Himalayas. I flew to Ibiza. All difficulties resolved by non-acceptance of any problems pretending to be existing. I had done the remaining Owsleys somewhere around Swayambunath and Annapurna. Fun was real vintage stuff that year—and let's face it—The Buddha gave a really GREAT birthday party.

© Neil Rock

17.

Jasper and Mataji at Varanasi

Fond Memories. In the late afternoon of my first day in Benares during May of 1967, I met Arthur, Pete, and Jasper at Sanskrit University. At my wish to visit the bathing ghats, Jasper guided me through the city and down to the river. Hundreds of people, healthy, fit, deformed, diseased, and crippled were congregated, praying and performing puja on the burning ghat steps and in the water. This being the holiest place on India's holiest river, I gave my thanks for living to all of India's gods, dropped my kurta and lungi on the ground, and like the uncountable millions before me and undoubtedly many more millions since, walked directly down the steps, into the water, immersed myself and began to swim. The first thing that struck me was the pure taste of the water, the density of grains of sand moving in the current, and the obvious skin scouring and cleansing properties. Jasper surfaced beside me in the water, suggesting that we see the town from across the river, so we swam together to the sandbank on the far side.

Jasper had presented me with a rare gift. No other city I have ever visited has impressed itself so clearly in my memory as the view of Varanasi at dusk from across the water. The riverside buildings, their cupolas, minarets, and the ghat steps all glow golden in the light. The myriad colors of clothing and the swirling movement of worshippers and bathers, the brick pyre platforms, and the curling blue smoke rising from the embers of the fires of the dead, all provide a scene that looked destined to be there forever.

When Jasper and I returned to the ghat, we met a female sadhu. She joyfully frizzled obeisance at the sight of Jasper, who bowed to her in deep respect. Introduced as Mataji, I came to know her later as a rare person who owned nothing but wisdom. A most exuberant spirit, she neither lacked nor wanted more than body fuel. Once, bathing in the river and close to the burning ghat, I was contemplating a previously unnoticed dead body floating beside me. Thinking about the mixed karma in the death of this man: how fortunate he had been to die in this most auspicious of all places of Hindu worship, how unfortunate that poverty or solitary existence had made wood unavailable for a pyre, how such was the holy cleansing power of the water here that it would probably break down his body within three days, I saw Mataji approaching me. I started to comment on the corpse, but she halted me by crying out "You are here, he is gone, alive or dead we are all small matter." Swift truth. Inviting me for chai, she wind-milled her arms, jostling our way through the throng on the steps, shouting "Make way for the foreign saint, make way" and leading me to a table in a curbside tea stall, she banged on the table shouting to the proprietor, "Chai, for the foreign saint, you must give him chai!" Regardless of the outrageousness of her unfounded claim as to my spiritual station, the chai was brought, jeldi, ai! Paisha nai! for both of us. Thus, she had fulfilled her intention of the first place. Me? I was her choice of route that morning in the everyday struggle for free-of-charge fast-breaking. Jasper and Mataji were both bright souls, each helping to make Varanasi enlightening.

Neil Rock 2009

From a letter from Neil:

Hello Susan, I wrote this story for Brice in memory of two very impressive people in my life. Jasper Newsome was a Brit (an Irish lord) living most of forty years in India. He spoke fluent Sanskrit and was a fully accredited and respected member of a Saddhu religious sect. He died in 2004 shortly after I visited him at his England home in Oxford.
Mataji was a female Saddhu, lived on the burning ghat on the Ganges at Benares, spoke excellent English and was greatly revered amongst the foreigners living in Benares from 1966 until her death a few years ago.

18.

Two Magic Rupees and a Space Chillum

Strolling around Connaught Circus, New Delhi, following siesta and shower from the heat of the day. Ladies and little children under the arcades selling necklaces of Jasmine and Night Queen blossoms, roasted cashew nuts, pistachios, strong scent of incense. All together wonderful; breathe in, ahhhh, lovely. There are thousands of walking, talking, hurrying and sleeping-on-sidewalk people, buzzing rickshaw scooters, truck and car horns blaring. This is a normal evening in New Delhi's Connaught Circus. My appetite is good and I am looking forward to curries and puris, gulab jamun, a bidi, enjoying a pleasant after dinner cool night stroll. A middle-aged smiling gentleman in a bedraggled double-breasted jacket and pajama pants steps in my path and says—" Excuse me sir, I am a man of God, but not being him and being just like anybody else I have to eat. For four rupees I will tell your name, your date of birth, your mother's first name and the first name of your girlfriend."
Interesting, yes?
So, I reply, "Just like you I am a man of God and just like you I am a man of few means. I have four rupees for my dinner, but I will share it with you if you think you can get my dossier from God for two rupees, I would like to hear what you say, then, we can both eat dinner." My money is safe. I know that at least I have him on the girlfriend bit because I don't have one.
The magic man steps back, sizes me up and then accurately gives me my name, my date of birth, my mother's Christian name.
Just for good measure and to let me know that he really knows his way through the pearly gates, he gives me the name of a young lady who I

Two Magic Rupees and a Space Chillum

with dad (James Rock)

with sister (Susan) and mom (Hilda Rock) 1947

with Susan

as teenager 1950's

with Davey Graham 1960's

busking by the Seine, Paris 1960's

dancers at "The Mecca" Leeds, UK 1950's

Two Magic Rupees and a Space Chillum

Beatles arrive USA, NY 1964
(Paul McCartney holding GONK toy)

Mirror newspaper clipping (Paul McCartney owns a GONK)

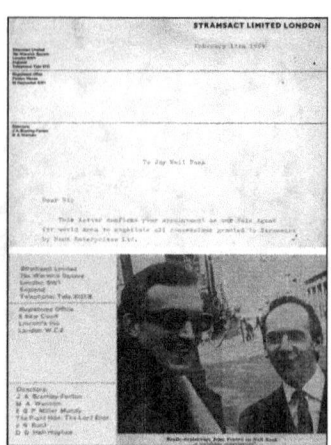

Stramsact ltd.
licensing correspondence

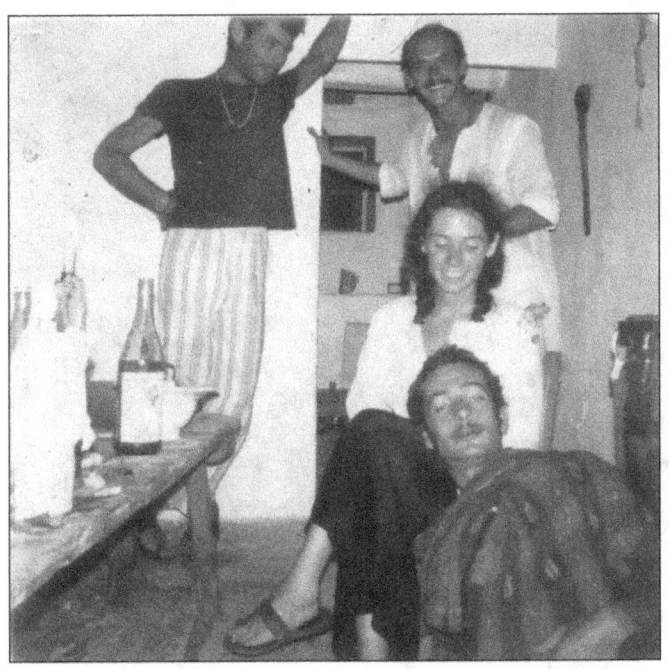

With Wolfgang, Mary, Brice at "Casa Patatas"
Cap Berberia, Formentera 1968

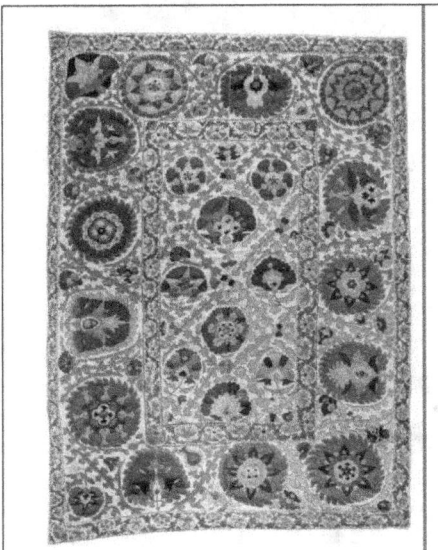

Wall hanging BUKHARA

The super trader with
Zeus, the white Shepard Dog 1970's

In Kabul, Afganistan, 1970's

with Barbara 1970's

In Ibiza 1980's.

Neil 1987 Calle Miranda apartment Ibiza
leather working artisan mode

Left to right, Neil with Terrance Mann and Juliette Bora from the cast of CATS, Broadway award winning performer Andre DeShields and Brice, on New Years Eve, 1985.

had met by accident the previous Friday afternoon in London, and who, prior to our most enjoyable weekend together in her apartment, I had not seen in about three years. I cannot speak, so I gawp, shake my head to clear it—and hand over two rupees.

A burst of laughter comes from knee high nearby. Another man, chuckling, nodding his head at me and obviously my memory reader's guru, comes out from where he is squatting under a sidewalk table, smilingly touches my elbow and both men disappear into the crowd. Two rupees well spent, another piece of goody I tuck into my amazement bag.

A Space Chillum

One winter day, walking in Haridwar, Northern India, along the bank of the River Ganges. I am watching pilgrims lowering themselves into the rushing torrent while holding onto stout chains bolted into the steps of the bathing ghat in order to safely submerge their heads while making Puja. Ganges Carp, huge, fat, glowing golden fish bigger than you or me are stretched out and basking amongst the people on the steps of the Ghat, the tops of their heads and back of their bodies out of the water while people feed them bright colored flower petals. Crowds of people lining the riverbank are sitting on cloths, on charpoys or the ground, praying, eating, chatting together. All these people look different of course, but also, they all look the same. Peace is with us.

My thoughts turn to Astrology, for why I have no idea, not at all my subject. I find myself thinking that as we have twelve astrological sectors and signs of the cosmic orange delivering to each of us some recognizably distinct characteristics, is it possible that each season as a functioning period in the essence of the All is in any way delivering to us quarterly traits as well as those of the monthly planetary and stellar influences? Of course, this would mean us being possibly governable by the seasons also- according to our own birth dates—and would add to the forces influencing our behavior.

As I am mulling this over a hand is raised in the air by a saffron-robed Sadhu beckoning to me from where he is seated on a charpoy in the crowd and amongst his friends, some fifty or sixty meters in front and over to my left. I nod my recognition of his signal and thread my way

Two Magic Rupees and a Space Chillum

through the throng to join him. When I arrive at his charpoy, he, myself and three other people around the bed all nod to each other. He has a goolie and a chillum. Do I have a cigarette? When I hand him a Char Minar, he breaks it open, warms the goolie by rolling and squeezing it between his palms and mixes in the tobacco.

Working the mix into the chillum he gestures for a light. I pass him a lighted match. We all smoke and reflect on good fortune while watching the people, the fish, the rushing river. We smoke some more until the chillum is empty and then sit comfortably taking in the air and the river scene for another fifteen minutes or so.

Apart from the Sadhu having asked for a cigarette none of us has spoken. I stand to leave, make hands together and bow my thanks for the smoke. The Sadhu nods back and says—"There are only twelve distinct astrological changes, each according to the powers in each month. You are on your last change now, go with God."

So, I am feeling very comfortable with the day and my inner debate on cosmic influence is solved for me in two sentences from a stranger.

The point of these two stories is that truth is often told in humble places. I will bet a hundred bucks you couldn't get stuff this good, this accurate, for any amount of money from famously fancied gurus, or anybody even with a crystal ball and a Ouija board.

© Neil Rock

Two Magic Rupees and a Space Chillum

19.

View from the Howdah

Waking up some time after midnight on a December night at my hotel in New Delhi I suddenly had a yen for an alcoholic drink. Having not even seen alcohol in many months, never mind drinking any, and there being no pubs or bars (and—I do not have a permit to buy alcohol from a government liquor store even if they were open this time of night) I gave in to the urge and took a motorcycle rickshaw to the Oberoi Hotel. Outside is a Rolls Royce Silver Ghost with chauffeur polishing brightly. In the bar, the only other drinker there greets me and introduces himself as the Maharaja of Jaipur. He looks the part, sort of rotund, short, Brilliantine, Bridge Rubbers and Lawn Croquet. Well polished. He surely cut his teeth on Aspreys, made Oxford Firsts in high denomination banknotes and Brazilian/South African mineral deposits, has a couple of horses that won the Grand National. He is on double Remys and already twinkling pleasantly, suggests it would be nice that we toast each other for Christmas. OK sounds good, I'm for it too. I order us a couple. Him being already well oiled and a gregarious and amiable chap he tells me that India has gone to ruin since the British left and that he has been seriously over taxed by the Congress Party politicians, who are all very common fellows. The Maharaja's friends are all annoyed at having to cut back to under 200 house servants—and well, he still has an adequate few, but only 82 for his wife and kids, plus 24 gardeners, and 8 grounds sweepers. And being forced to pay Bills for 'things' from suppliers. Hasn't been allowed to put cheeky retainers to the thumbscrew or rack, not even once for old times sake. Can't use dead farmers anymore for fertilizer. Degrading life style fall, I should come and see for myself.

View from the Howdah

It really is an unfortunate truth that the Congress Party politicians are very common fellows, but they are also very aware of and very familiar with the significance of a very important Indian number –420- (which is the number for the crime of cheating in the Indian criminal code of 'justice'.) Cheating is so common that every Indian citizen in the country who is over three years old knows this number. A short pound of sugar or flour is sold to a housewife and she will say it is 420, an overcharged taxi ride or overcharged anything else is 420. If the police find any cheating you ever did they will bring 420 criminal proceedings against you and find some way to cheat you,—big time—and if you did it with anybody else, then it is 420b,—Conspiracy to cheat. The 420b will cost you at least three to four years inside and as much of your fortune as your molesters can squeeze out of you—before you are even charged with anything, Police Superintendent and Tax Man steadily getting rich and with feet comfortably on desk with criminal case for life. To the outside world India is known as The World's Largest Democracy, inside India the country is known by its own people as The Worlds Largest Hypocrisy. Bells, bangles, beads and Karma Sutra make great PR.

" Exceedingly common fellows" says the Maharaja. His foot treadles up and down as he seeks for the bar rail like he is operating a spinning wheel. He waves his glass around. With foot treadle and hand wave it looks like he is in a beginners weaving class at the Gandhi Ashram. We drink. I order us another round of double Remys. Now, the Maharaja is holding onto the bar top like he hopes it means something. "Would you believe the crudity?" he asks. " The ignominy." His Palace was searched and his wife was body searched in her apartments—by Government Fiscal Inspectors trying to locate her collection of diamonds. They found nothing.

Although already the taxmen had several other Rajas in the clink and were sucking them dry, they possibly considered it a bit over the top to charge a Maharaja and his Maharani with 420b conspiracy to cheat the taxman without any proof. But, knowing she must have diamonds, she has worn them often enough, the courts left him alone but fined her anyway for failing to declare a tax return for an unknown quantity of wealth. In other words, they don't know how much his wife has got— but whatever it is -they think she's got too much. They even put the news in the National Press. (The Maharaja is telling me what I had read earlier in the year in The Times Of India). Maharani replies to charges, letter to The Times. Sulks and tells India she is absolutely distraught at thought of parting with her last hard earned paisha, might even have to pawn a Swiss bank or two. Maharani totally miffed by body search and massive fines, threatening to resign, wants to wind back karmic clock, wants to be back in finishing school. Wants her Montreaux swimming pool filled with Krug again and playing Dietrich at undergrad pajama parties.

Nobody cares anymore, sigh, shrug, shrug, suitable Prime Ministers are So hard to find these days, etc.

I remark on the Boss Raja's Rolls Royce transport at the front door and comment that at least he can still socialize and arrive in style. Knocking back his double Remy, stiffening his shoulders somewhat and calling for us a round of two more the Maharaja tells me with some disparagement toward the Oberoi that there was a time when he wouldn't even think of coming out for a drink to a place like this without being accompanied by at least six elephants. Six elephants!

This guy knows Really ALL about putting on the style.

I must say that the Maharaja warms my heart, he really is Pukka, to the Palace born. I commiserate with him on his fallen fortune, death and taxes, etc. A Rolls Royce is second rate? This is indeed Royal Chutzpah! And, just to be sure, the chauffeur and Rolls would have gone ahead to the hotel with his own chef to whip up a small banquet snack just in case he got peckish.

I was figuring Oh Wow! the lowdown on government thugees and minor misdeeds from the seraglio, we are soon getting to the good stuff, which eunuch strangled who on Diwali Night, etc. Alas, not to be, Raj got a bit foggy when he ordered another round; the Maharaja was now feeling for the bar foot rail like he was trying to stay afloat or kick start a Harley. Realizing that His Highness has gone to sea and is floating on a dangerously volatile tank, the barman stopped the fun by leaning on the bar and checking the Maharaja's eye level, his eyes were far from level. The barman must have been informed that the Maharaja was staying the night when enough was enough, coz after speaking on the blower the barman flicked room lights off, room lights on, the bar lights out, looks at me, hint, hint. The barman himself signs the Maharaja's tab, I am invited to pay mine. 420 is written big on the bottom line. I pay rather than have the Maharaja charged with 420b conspiracy to condone nonpayment of a total stranger's drinking bill. The Maharaja and I clink last glasses, slur 'Merry Christmas, Goodnight' to each other. The chauffeur and a hotel doorman came to ease Jaipur on his way through the swaying corridors. When I left the hotel the Roller was still parked in the same place, but with a wallah parked asleep at its side.

All in all, my trip out on a whim had provided interesting entertainment. I had thoroughly enjoyed the drinks and the company. The Maharaja obviously never really intended to extend me an invitation to visit—it had just sort of slipped out with Christmas cheer. He never sent even one elephant to fetch me. I never sent a notice of imminent arrival. Ships that pass in the night.

© Neil Rock

20.

Dead Elephant

Once, driving on the Delhi to Jaipur Road, seeing police vehicles parked on the roadside and a large crowd standing around a house garden and looking at a dead elephant, I thought the scene looked passive? I parked the Land Rover and joined in. The cops and health department officials were seriously overwhelming some poor bewildered guy living in the roadside house and who had woken up that morning to find the dead elephant in his garden and which elephant he didn't know when alive, or recognize now when dead, had never heard of or seen before and knew nothing about anyway. The elephant not belonging to this Householder, he had seen it, ignored it as a mirage of Samsara, or thought the owners would remove it and had gone to work as usual so as not to lose his job for bothering his boss with reasons of being absent from work because of irrelevant chiff-chaff.
A Superintendent of Police having checked that the Householder is not of higher caste than himself, and thus, avoiding being reduced to toilet paper by Brahmin priests from Householder's local mafia temple, has dragged this guy home from his place of employment and, heedless of his feeble excuses of innocence, now charges him as a criminal.
Instant court proceedings before the gathered onlookers result in Police Superintendent's assessment of a traffic violation by illegal parking of a vehicle, no paperwork and no tax disc. Householder gets dizzy.
The screw is then further tightened a major baksheesh notch by a Health Department Inspector doing a reshuffle upward—to a more serious additional charge of harboring a public health hazard.
King Solomon couldn't have done it better. Much hand wringing and wailing prayers, pleading and promises to the entire heavenly pantheon.

Dead Elephant

No go, the bribe is already in, paid up to date, bread-buttered and all Gods are working for the sticky men. Householder shaken.

The villain's landlord arrives and is amazed at seeing dead elephant. Arms waving, eyes rolling, slaver down shirt, staggers, fakes a heart attack. Scribble on paper, immediate estimate of damage cost for dead elephant crash landing on garden fence. Bill for broken fence must be paid, NOW, otherwise Householder to be evicted forthwith and police enticed to bring charge of encouraging vandalism.Householder frazzled.

The Onlookers express satisfaction with the show so far but are not quite sated yet.

It is now another turn of the Health Inspectors. The sun is at hot noon and it is pointed out to the miscreant criminal by the health department boss of fumigation—that somebody, if he wants off the health hazard hook, is going to have to pay to have his house fumigated and every other house nearby—before nightfall. Householder drops to knees, grasps Fumigator's ankles, kisses Fumigator shoes, tears not crocodile. Fumigator not having any and wants a most sizable backhander from Householder or Fumigator will gas everybody—in every direction—for at least three miles around.

Householder is now clearly approaching a state of panic, pleads sick wife, is supporting useless younger brothers, gaggle of sisters in law, backyard cage full of second-hand kids, fifteen shrunken arthritic grandmothers, etc. All no go, the Health Doc has got the teeth sunk in, several tons of dead evidence is spread out all over the front garden.Health department and Police agree that it is cough up or go down.

Brief pause, while Householder makes a quick abacus reckoning of his life since his first birthday. Finds nothing. Not even failing to vote for Indira Gandhi could have brought this on. Householder searching karma, if in past life shot dead elephants great, great stepmother? Cry of bitter anguish, tears, tugging at hair, lose driving license, lose job, lose house. Total misery. Hit with big stick

The crowd is growing larger every minute. A guy in a nightdress and pushing a soft drink trolley arrives and sets up business. A small boy turns up with a tray of cigarettes and matches. A woman selling salted sugar cane. This is show business. I am surprised that the police have not cordoned off the house in order to sell entrance tickets and commercial concessions.

Left-Wing troublemakers in the cast of onlookers urgently wanting progress in the case, now suggest Householder pay up. Want to see somebody with money, anybody with money, getting Shtupped, thoroughly drubbed and wrung dry.

The Press arrives, photographer and intrepid reporter. Serious doings have drawn The Times of India.

The dead elephant might not be as important as an atomic bomb, but it is definitely bigger. A good picture is worth a thousand words—and a blow up of this will fill across a few columns.

The Superintendent and Fumigator go to smirk beside dead elephant. Photographer hugging limelight, waves hand around like Bollywood film director, supposedly getting correct light reading, shuffles round head cop and the gasman. Thumb up, OK on final position of sun and subjects in heroic stance.

It is clear, the Times reporter thoroughly knows His job when he throws in a superb piece from the Sunday quiz crossword puzzle and asks the Householder—WHY has the dead elephant picked HIS place to die in? Householder is speechless that his life should end like this.

Two photographs, quick shorthand, and press races away to meet deadline and catch Pulitzer Prize.

Householder is now near to state of utter exhaustion. Almost demolished, he casts a last appealing glance at dead elephant, wails final wail of no money and makes ultimate bid for reprieve by claiming that neglect of spiritual duty has resulted in Lakshmi wearing earplugs since 1953. Health Doc also is not listening, threatens to add charge of illegal business operations—speculation in meat dealing without a license. Householder stupefied at being crapped on by Vishnu in chariot from such great height.

No question, says a crowd member, sticking in the boot—easier for the 200 or so direct relatives to have a whip round.

The householder obviously not having the wherewithal to pay off the police and the Health Department, the Cop Boss and Fumigator retire to roadside chai house to decide jurisdiction of the case. Like how will whatever loot be divided? Tea is served, bank account numbers exchanged, tea is drunk, the authorities return to the crime scene.

Stunned Householder, now incoherent, is handcuffed to a police minion. It is sure that his family will be bludgeoned for boodle from Cardiff to Calcutta. Resigned to fiscal inquisition, the criminal is placed in Police jeep to be taken to a dreaded fate. A Health Department guard is left with elephant. All other officials exchange handshakes and leave. Police driver whisks Prisoner away to Police Station, while Householder screams and kicks jeep as final curtain closer in response to the Landlord firing last venomous shot of crane costs, towing charge and undertaker bills.

More people drift away now than arrive. Crowd being left without action gets bored of looking at the dead elephant, me too, time to leave.

Next day I read an item in the Times of India suggesting that the owner of the dead elephant might come forward and claim it. Fat Chance. The cops might identify the owner of a nighttime roadside dead elephant found in West Texas, but not here in India.

© Neil Rock

21.

Rollin' with the Rabbi

Mike the Rabbi and I met in a London Casino on Christmas Eve. I was in London on a short trip from India to sell hippy Indian paraphernalia and in the casino with a girlfriend who was playing dice, making enough to cover her rent. Mike was on a sabbatical away from his Rabbinical duties in Brooklyn, NY, and in the casino also on the ivories while waiting for a connection to a smoke. Recognizing we were kindred souls and having good luck, we pooled some of the winnings, scored when Mikes's man arrived, and lit out in a taxi for Mikes's pad to spend a leisurely night. In the morning as the girl and I were splitting Mike asked where I would be on January 14th. I told him that for sure on that date and in the evening I would be relaxing on the roof terrace of the Palace Heights Hotel in New Delhi. January 14th, I am with my best friend Brice, and taking tea on the terrace of the hotel in Delhi when here comes Mike the Rabbi and sits with us. After a while, a young American guy sits at the next table. He hears us talking and casually asks if we would like to share gasoline on a ride in his VW Camper to Bombay, where he is heading for the next day. Why not? Mike hasn't seen Delhi yet so we go to Old Delhi, eat some good food, visit the Red Fort then a dragon who lived in a back street courtyard off Chandi Chowk. The housemaster can't possibly believe the intake capacity of Mike. The guy is worried, then astounded, relaxes, and just grins and he grins and he grins. Anyway, next morning, Brice, Mike, and I are rolling down The Grand Trunk Road with the American in his VW.. After a stop in Jaipur to see the sights and visit a former Formentera friend, Faith, now married there and living in the city, we motored south. A couple of nights later, somewhere in a Gujarat jungle, we saw a tiger on the road devouring a cow it had killed. The tiger ran off as our headlights lit it up. For sure it would have returned to feed again after we had passed. As we are talking about the tiger, we round a sharp bend on a downhill run and see in front of us two soldiers armed with rifles standing at ease outside a hut at an Indian Army Check Post with a striped pole barrier across the road. An army officer is waving us down with a flashlight. "Shit" says our amiable driver, " I've got 32 kilos of hash built into the bed." The adrenalin rush was so strong it was almost worth having. We could have cut the terror in blocks and sold it to the Kremlin. I am swearing to Shiva and Shakti that I will never be a bad boy EVER AGAIN, Brice is flashing on karma and Mike The Rabbi is saying Kaddish for himself. Our driver then proved his smuggler credentials with a brain of ice-cold steel. As we roll up to the barrier our driver flicks all headlights and fog lights full-on, blinds the army guys in front, then lowers his window and in an impeccable Sandhurst Officer And A Gentleman accent screams at the top of his voice at the Indian army officer trapped in the blast of the lights: "What the hell do you think you are doing man? What the BLOODY hell do you think you are doing? Open the gate, man! OPEN THE BLOODY GATE!" Memories of full-throated British Officers giving furious commands are long. No matter that those days were long gone and this is 1967: Whan! Zoo! Schree!—Program IN! The soldiers sprang to attention, stamped boots, and presented arms. The officer saluted, leapt smartly forward, and swung up the barrier. Like the Fabulous Furry Freaks in a nightmare of being accidentally overdosed on out of date psychedelics by Fat Freddie's cat, we cruised smoothly through the checkpoint and down the hill in a cloud of chattering teeth and frozen funk. Arriving safely in Bombay we dumped the idiot and VW immediately, not too heavily, after all as Mike The Rabbi coolly said, "Be generous—it's Shabbat."—and we'd safely made it.

© Neil Rock 2007

22.

Girls in Goa

My friend Alejandro and I were in Raj-style relaxation having breakfast on the terrace of The Royalty Tourist Hotel, at Calangute Beach in Goa. We were dressed for the weather in tangas and straw hats and were about 40 meters back from the shoreline. It's around 9 am on a fine warm winter morning, the coconut trees blowing from an offshore breeze. A half dozen European naked nymphs jumping up and down in the choppy waves; nobody else in sight and no guests were staying in the hotel. Peace all around, what more could we want? In February 1968 there was a total of 32 foreigners wintering on Calangute Beach in Goa, we all knew each other, and calm reigned. The one and only beach hotel was where my friend and I were treating ourselves to breakfast that day.

Quick sound of a jet airplane engine—and over the hill at the north end of the beach comes an Indian Air Force Hawker Hunter fighter plane. The pilot sees the naked girls in the water, drops down to palmtop level to get an eyeful, buzzes the girls then roars off in a left-hand climb toward the village of Mapsa. Peace descends again, the girls continue playing and Alejandro and I go back to our tea and toast.

Again, the sound of the plane as the fighter comes over the hill at the north end of the beach, and once more the pilot drops down to about 20 meters above the waves. The pilot flew the plane along the shoreline toward the girls then, unbelievably, he turned the airplane upside down to make a roll so he could see the naked girls as he flew over them. Because he was flying so low the pilot was unable to get the plane to roll over from belly up and after traveling some fifty meters beyond the girls the fighter passed directly in front of Alejandro and I and crash-dived upside down straight into the sea. Airplane and pilot hit the water at 200 miles per hour about 10 meters offshore. A big explosion took place, but with most of the sound and most of the smoke being stifled by the sea; stunned silence from us on the hotel terrace and the girls in the water. No sign of the airplane, it is as if it had never been there. Within a few seconds, the sea had settled back as if nothing had happened. I say to Alejandro "Wow! What a show" Alejandro said, "Yeah man," sucks on the spliff and rings the bell for the wallah to bring more tea. The girls resume funning. Nobody on the hotel staff came out to enquire about the noise or what had happened, our tea wallah stayed zipped up also. Because of this cooled-out attitude Alejandro and I decided that the occurrence was none of our business. The vibe drifts back to normal, more tea.

Later: New sound. This time there is a heavy offshore rumble. Alejandro and I plus a few foreigners who are now on the beach, look out to sea to find what's up. A naval motor torpedo boat followed by an Indian Navy Destroyer appears around the southern headland. The destroyer stays offshore and in comes a bunch of naval guys in the torpedo boat. Three officers transfer from the torpedo boat to a rubber boat and pull up on the beach. The officers pass by the few foreigners on the beach, mount the steps onto the terrace of the hotel and after walking past Alejandro and me with eyes averted from us and tangas, they go into the hotel without saying a single word.

After about five minutes the officers came out of the hotel, took off in the rubber boat, then back to the Destroyer in the torpedo boat. The rubber boat came back from the torpedo boat and deposited seamen with diving gear on the beach. The Destroyer then split the scene. Neither Alejandro, me nor any of the girls or other people now on the beach had been questioned as to our being potential witnesses to the crash. I never heard any Goan local mention it.

Next morning, I caught the early morning bus to Panjim and bought that day's issue of The Times of India. A few words in a single paragraph on page two told a story that the day before, a Hawker Hunter belonging to the Indian Air Force had exploded in midair while on a training exercise over Calangute Beach in Goa. The pilot had been killed. The cause of the accident was thought to be a faulty fuel line. Further investigation was underway. What was not written was the truth and the newspaper also missed reporting that despite navy divers searching the sea in front of the hotel for hours the previous afternoon, all that was found of the pilot was a piece of rubber tubing from his helmet. Sharks got the rest.

© Neil Rock

23.

Even More Elephant

Arriving at a Rishakesh ashram where we were staying for the weekend my friend Nick asked the keeper where were the toilet facilities. Directed to the jungle outside the back fence, Nick was warned to take care as elephants frequently came to break down the fence and raid the ashram cabbage patch. Nick should move away if any elephants should come. So Nick is squatting contentedly amongst large plants, trees and vines when a lizard almost as big as he is comes up from behind and puts its head on his shoulder.
Nick was back in the ashram faster than a fly, pants still held up in one hand and a severe case of the blocked shakes. From then on whenever Nick saw or heard an elephant his pipes blocked up again.
One time, got constipated in Cambodia for a week.

© Neil Rock

24.

Tihar Prison

Eight months in Tihar, one of India's largest prisons, this, from my entrapment on a hash possession charge was uncomfortable, but, hey, if you get trapped but are guilty in the first place you can only really get pissed off at being caught.
I was on a trip to buy clothing and jewelry in India. While standing next to my Land Rover in New Delhi, and paying a carpenter for the making of a wheelchair type shoeshine stand, (a gift from my friend Brice to a legless beggar), two guys I knew casually from sharing an occasional joint at black-market money changing shop, came across the road and the youngest told me that he had to visit his brother in Old Delhi. He asked me if I was driving over there that morning and could I take him and his pal. At my reply of, "Yes" he asked also if I had a joint on me as he owed his brother money that he couldn't pay but at least an offering of something might help. OK, so I give him a small piece of hash from my pocket and while finishing business with the carpenter, the older of these two guys says he must go over the road to his office and pick up his briefcase. Coming back with the briefcase he and his pal get in the rear seats of my vehicle.
And away we go. I am taking the usual traffic and fume-choked route down toward The Red Fort when the young guy tells me to turn right as he can show me a much faster road. Following his instructions, I find myself in a quiet tree-lined residential street confronted by two police jeeps and some excited armed cops spread across the road. Somebody held up a hand and stopped me. When I turned to question the guys in the back, they are busy weighing a chunk of hash on a grocery scale

taken from the briefcase. It turned out that the older guy is a cop, the younger a fink, and I have been set up and busted. No way out, I know that the laws will strip my vehicle and find my own personal half-pound of Afghani, as having broken off a piece the night before I had stupidly not re-sealed the stash where I kept it. And even more serious, I need let them know I have a pistol before someone thinks they have got John Dillinger. An American friend, Jerry, and I had both bought guns legally from an arms company in London on the strength of each traveling alone overland to India. Stopping the Land Rover on the edge of a lawn, I took the gun from its pocket in the doorframe and dropped it onto the grass. Immediate idiocy from the cop in charge as with no idea of what he is doing, he scoops up the pistol and tries to get the ammunition out while holding the gun horizontally and pointing it toward a line of people at a bus stop. Thankfully an assistant takes the gun and unloads it correctly. The two guys from my vehicle are now busy searching it with other cops and there is a shout of joy as someone finds my stash. With much excitement and my vehicle full of cops, I am forced to drive to the local police station. I asked the cop who was weighing the dope in my van, and who I knew for years as a black market money changer: How come he had an illegal money changing business? And he replied, "The police force and the treasury work very closely together". In other words, he and treasury pals had a money exchange rate scam. I also asked him: How, as he knew me, could he smoke a joint with me nearly every time I gave him dollars for rupees and then bust me? To this, he coolly answered, "It's all in the job".

Things got a bit flat for the cops when, while examining my passport and other papers, they found in my wallet a copy of the British Board of Trade export license for my pistol and my end-user permit. I took the opportunity to tell the head cop that I had other copies back home. Just in case these papers 'got lost'. Delhi police humor did pick up again at the thought that at least they had me on smuggling hash into India and failing to declare the pistol at the border. The ace I had on this I decided to keep until the smuggling charge came up.

After spending a night in the cop shop lock up, next morning was a photo opportunity and cop brag time for the news media. I was then handcuffed and driven to Customs and Excise headquarters. On arrival there I was whisked up eight floors in an elevator and brought face to face with Delhi chief hash-smuggling-stopper, The Right Excremental Mr Khana, a five foot two inch Adolphe Menjou type, complete with patent leather hair, pencil moustache, gray plaid tie and jodhpurs. His first words were to ask me my astrological sign, and on my telling him I am a Gemini he replied, "I'm a Scorpio, you won't jump out the window, will you?"

Getting straight to the starting gate, Mr. Khana told me that he would get me two and a half years for smuggling hash, and eighteen months for not declaring my pistol at the Furozepore border post. Four years at least, or maybe more if he got lucky.

Things swung my way as I thought they would when I laid my ace: namely, that although hash possession looked good for the police, there would be nothing for him on smuggling. It would be difficult to stick me with the smuggling charges because on this trip, I had crossed from Pakistan just as the Indian border post was closing for the night, so the Customs Chief had foregone questions and a vehicle search, but asked me for a lift to his home, from where after a cup of tea and best wishes from his wife, I had departed for Delhi. As to the hash, well, I told Khana, I had bought that on the street in Delhi from a British hitchhiker I didn't know and who was heading south. Khana rightly scorned the story of buying the hash on the street but was stopped in his tracks and almost green with envy at the story of tea with Mrs. Customs in Furozepore. After all, HE had heard everything in his time and had made up his own giant whoppers, but he knew that he could not beat that I had the Furazpore Customs Chief bang to rights. I knew the customs officer's name and could describe him, his wife, and the house to anybody. This interrogation in the Delhi Customs and Excise office was taking place on Friday morning. Khana left me sitting in front of his desk while he went away for three hours until office closing time. This guy really thought he was hot evil that day, he got his kicks by handing me a bucket, then locking me in a three feet wide by six feet long office closet in the empty building for the weekend. This gave him time to check my story at Furazpore and decide what to do about it. Two Delhi customs officers brought in cooked food at mid-day on Saturday and Sunday. On Monday morning with a big smile, Khana let me out of the closet. Obviously, he had checked my story with Furozepore, because he informed me that no smuggling charges would be brought against me. I thanked him for a wise decision, told him that he had proven to be a gentleman after all, and he turned me back over to the police.

Taken straight to court I was surprised when no charges were made. It was alleged by the cops that eight ounces of hash had been found in my possession and I was to be held, 'enquiries pending'. Nothing at all was mentioned about my gun or about the guys weighing hash in the Land Rover, in fact, those two guys were never mentioned at all in the case, then or later. I was told by the cops to pick a lawyer (any lawyer) from a long line of scruffs standing alongside papers and pens on tables or fruit crates at the courthouse door. I pointed at one. By the fact he was dressed the cleanest, I should have known he would turn out to be the biggest crook there. After telling me all would be OK, (he would fix things) this legal eagle confirmed that the police would forward my money and possessions (less gun and hash) to the British High Commission. He would arrange the release of money to me from the British Consul and asked if I wanted anyone to know of my arrest. I wrote down a couple of addresses, gave them to him, and after being held again in the police station cells, I was transported a couple of days later to Tihar Prison.

On arrival at Tihar, the first thing I was told was to strip from my street clothes and was handed a pair of raw beige cotton pants and matching shirt. I was then shown The Times of India newspaper with my photo on the front page and a story that because I was light-skinned and wore a Karakoul cap, the brave inspector of police who had arrested me had in fact been following me for days in Delhi as he had suspected me to be a Pakistani Kashmiri spy. The arrest for hash was incidental to the crap about being a spy, but I must admit that the whole story made the inspector look good.

The next thing I was shown was a message to me from Brice telling me that he had been contacted by my lawyer and asked to send to the lawyer all the money he could raise to help with my defense. I sent a message to Brice telling him to pay nothing. I had a lot of his money with me in India anyway.

The next morning my lawyer turned up at the prison and informed me he had obtained 1000 rupees from my money at the British High

Commission, and also told me he would need a lot more as my defense was sure to be very costly. He handed me 10 rupees for cigarettes from the 1000, said he had to keep the rest for immediate expenses, at which I blew, said I already knew about his attempted scam on Brice, and told him to fuck off or I would have him inside with me, charged with extortion and fraud. I fired him on the spot.

Tihar wasn't too bad for ferengis. Myself and thirteen other foreigners were designated as "B-Class" prisoners (Educated), and housed in a dormitory with rope charpoys, no sheets, but mosquito nets and a blanket. We lived inside a high-walled and guarded garden surrounded by—but separated from—"C-Class," the general prison population. We were free to move at will inside the garden, had our own showers and even our own cook, who I swear was the spitting image of Little Richard. All the B Class foreigners except two (a Tibetan awaiting trial for murder and an English guy on currency smuggling charges), were in for smuggling hash or possession of hash. A dozen or so Indian B-Class prisoners included a bent police superintendent in for kidnapping, a wife poisoner, and an accountant who had cut up his nephew, stuffed him in a trunk, and thrown him in the Jumma River in the hope of thieving the kid's inheritance. The rest of the Indian B-Class were in for fraud or theft. Another inhabitant in our garden was a Mongoose who lived amongst some bricks in a corner. He was most welcome. We never got snakes.

In the garden were also three A-Class prisoners (Educated, and Wealthy,) living in private rooms for which they had to pay rent. These guys were two plump middle-aged Jain brothers, and a slim, rather sleek, and well-dressed Pakistani, all inside now for over two years and still awaiting trial for conspiracy on gold smuggling charges. Indian justice being what it is, these three could be many more years waiting for trial while systematically being milked dry.

One offer from the authorities to speed things up was that the Jain brothers should build a house near the prison, live in it while serving their as yet undetermined sentence, then turn it over to the prison governor. I was told that this was a common way of doing business between prison authorities and wealthy A-Class prisoners.

In the meantime, while the Jains were still in the prison, two house servants of theirs lived in there with them, in an adjoining room to their masters and were at hot and cold running beck and call for everything and anything day or night. Iqbal, the Pakistani, was alone, far from home, and knew that for him there was no hope but to sit it out while the fuzz tried to skin him, and then to fight a trial stuffed with prefabricated evidence. He was a professional big-time gold smuggler and stock market manipulator who wasn't about to give up friends or a few million dollars. He expected ten to fifteen years. The Jains expected eight to ten. Iqbal took to me and helped a lot. Somehow my mail moved in and out of the prison unopened and uncensored, cigarettes were dropped on my bed by a night guard whenever I handed over money for them. Once hash appeared at my request. The hash was the pits though, it looked suspiciously unlike hash and it tasted like I was smoking tarred cork or a soup cube, maybe I was. I didn't get a buzz, so I threw it away and I didn't order more.

After I had been in Tihar about a month I appeared in court once more, yet again without being charged with anything (Fuzz still making inquiries). Iqbal and the Jains were at court the same day and they invited me to chai on the courthouse lawn while waiting for the last prisoners to come from court and be loaded into the prison van. The Jains and Iqbal traveled in convoy with the prison van, but in a car. As we drank chai, a prison minion was rounding up the driver and guard of the car in which these gold smugglers traveled to court and back, and in which for once I would travel with them.

On the way back to Tihar, Iqbal told me that I would have to get myself charged. This seemed a new twist in the arm of the law, but Iqbal explained it as follows: All the cops wanted were the drug bust and a payoff. They would not charge me in court until I came through with an offer. If I wanted off easy it was up to me to fix it. Iqbal further explained that the cops could not charge me exactly as the arrest went down as they would have to admit entrapment. If I tried to use this to get off, they would most likely pay some poor fink who they would claim to have uncovered 'during inquiries', to say I had tried to sell him my dope or pistol. On charges of trying to sell half a pound of dope or a weapon, the judge could hand me at least two or three years. My best way out was to get a new lawyer who could talk to the police inspector in charge at my arrest and who could then ask for a court hearing where I could admit to possession and be so charged and immediately sentenced. Iqbal offered me his lawyer and seeing as I knew this guy was straight enough and good enough to have blocked all attempts to get at Iqbal's money or business for the past two years –I accepted.

Some days later, the lawyer, whose name I was never told, and never asked, came to Tihar and laid it out. Four hundred dollars for the judge, four hundred for the head cop, four hundred to himself for making a single court appearance and he would guarantee me six months on a sole charge of possession of the hash. I arranged for money to be drawn from my cash at the British High Commission and on the day of my next hearing, the lawyer and myself huddled outside the courtroom. I handed him three envelopes. My hearing was about five minutes in court, where the judge asked why I was there. I told the judge I had half a pound of hash –for personal use. I admitted it. The head cop of the case confirmed it, the lawyer swore I was a good man and it worked out exactly as promised. I had been in Tihar for two months and now had another six months to go. My life changed somewhat after sentencing. I continued living in the garden but was marched in a column of general prisoners to work six hours a day, six days each week making cane chairs in a huge compound containing several hundred prisoners. Caning chairs peels the skin off your fingers and for me like the other prisoners was back-breaking work as we had to stand to work and bend over the chair frames for hours every day. Although I got quite good at caning, I never attempted doing it again after leaving Tihar.

There were four of us foreigners being marched to work and back in the prisoner column every day, and one morning on the way to the compound, the column passed a guard standing over an Indian prisoner sprawled on the ground and the guard jabbing the prisoner with his rifle butt. An English guy named Nick calmly stepped out of line, snatched the rifle from the guard, and struck him on the head with it, knocking him unconscious. Nick then dropped the rifle on the ground and stepped back in line. The column of course had stopped and our own guards, armed only with batons, panicked and began lashing out at anybody who moved from the line. Many Indians in the column flipped out even more and were screaming at us foreigners and at Nick in particular. Luckily before a real fight started, a prison sergeant with a drawn revolver, ran up and halted the problem by threatening to shoot. Nick was led away but was back in the garden that night with a few new cuts and bruises. For some days after this event, some Indian prisoners and guards in the column who were scared shitless by what had happened, took to insulting and threatening the foreigners. On top of this, a few days later, the nephew killer, doing life, lost his appeal and was sentenced to hang. He went completely berserk for about ten minutes, smashing up the dormitory and attacking anybody he could get his hands on. The guards quickly got hold of him before he maimed or killed anyone and carried him off to the hospital kicking and screaming. I decided to make sure I was not bothered by anyone.

The foreigner's diet differed from the food provided for C- Class prisoners. We ferengi were fed whatever curries our cook could come up with from such rations as he was issued, rations included by edict, sliced white bread. It was useless to say the bread wasn't wanted. White men ate Roti. The prison rules said so. The C-Class prisoners lived solely on brown dal and chapattis. Amongst the C-Class prisoners in the work compound was an enormous hulk of a man, the largest guy by far in the prison and doing life for seven murders amongst his in-laws during a family spat, and for which he would never be released. Hulk was a calm enough guy, but most prisoners and guards were wary of him. If he blew, they would be dead and he had nothing to lose. He hung out in the work compound with a crowd of other murderers and badmash villains. He was easy-going, but not very bright. I picked him as my protector. One morning I took my bread ration to work and started to eat near him at break time. Sure enough, I got his attention and he eyed the bread. I offered him a slice, he grinned, nodded, and accepted. He offered me a chapatti, I grinned back, nodded, and accepted. We smoked a couple of beadies together and as soon as I knew the guards and some prisoners were watching this, I offered to exchange my bread ration for his chapattis every day. He swelled up even larger at this and smiled a big smile. For sure he had never before been given white bread in his life. I doubt he had ever exchanged words or smiles with a European. From then on as soon as I arrived in the compound each morning, I went to where Hulk worked and handed him my bread ration and a beadie or two in exchange for his chapattis. Everybody in the yard saw this daily ritual.

No guard or prisoner ever fucked with me. Are you kidding? I was the Hulk's friend of his life.

A small incident led to serious later repercussions for me although the rebound didn't show for a few more months: A mango tree grew in the garden, and one day seeing the fruit was ripe, I picked one and started to eat it. A guard went immediately ape-shit, screaming at me that the tree was the prison governor's, and only the governor could take the mangos. I told the guard to piss off, at this, he shouted for another guard to go tell the governor. Sure enough, five minutes later here comes the man himself with two bodyguards. The governor asked why I took the fruit. I explained that it was on the tree, it was ripe, nobody had told me not to eat it, and that this place wasn't Eden. There were a few laughs at this from foreigners standing around, but the governor stayed cool, looked icy, told me not to touch the fruit again, then just turned on his heel and left trailing the guards with him. Of course, I didn't eat any more mangos, neither did the governor, the fruit just rotted on the tree and got eaten by foraging jackdaws and insects.

The authorities could be mean in their frustration at having to deal with Europeans and Americans they could not really dominate, and this showed up in petty ways like guards walking mud into the dormitory and shouting for it to be cleaned up, or turning off the water in the shower as people came back from work. Banging on the wall or floor near a foreigner just to see him jump was a favorite sport. A certain sergeant just loved to scream at us. Just once did some of them get the chance to really let go with mindless venom.

Late one night there was the sound of horrible screaming and singing and mad laughter coming from somewhere behind the dormitory and outside the garden wall. In this raving I several times heard my name called out. At dawn, the screaming was still there so an American and I slipped a buck to a guard for him to take us to the origin. We were led inside a totally bare and walled compound, in the center of which was standing an iron cage with a completely naked and raving young English boy inside it splattered all over with shit and blood. I reckoned he was in his late teens, didn't know him but got him calmed down enough to learn that some English guy outside had told him my name as being a guy inside. Just street talk.

This kid had got on a bad acid trip, freaked out, and run naked along Jan Path in New Delhi. Unable to get any sense out of him the police had simply clubbed him, driven him to Tihar, and the prison guards had whipped his arse, beaten him with Lathis, and thrown him in this cage. He had been calling my name in the night hoping somebody, me, anybody would hear him and tell him that all this wasn't a nightmare. My appeals to the guards to get him into the prison hospital fell on completely deaf ears. Nobody would take any responsibility. The American and I did fork over money to a guard to get the kid a blanket, and we gave money each day for a guard to take him food and water. He was left in the cage for days. After a week or so a Canadian guy was freed and we got him to phone and report what was happening to the British High Commission. They got the kid out. I later learned he was hospitalized in Delhi then flown back to England. The incident of helping this young boy did my psyche some good and took the edge off my nerves, as after the previous few months I was as capable as anybody else of losing my cool at anything at all.

Sometime toward the end of my sentence, a notice appeared on the dormitory wall advising that a blood collection vehicle would be in the prison on one day that week. What's more, two weeks' remission off time would go to anybody who gave blood. Me—I'm in. On the given day I walked to a hospital vehicle parked outside the garden and was surprised to find that I was the only person there, later some Indians told me that on their diet they could not possibly spare blood without collapsing so they never gave it. An even bigger surprise was a most beautiful Indian girl dressed in a sari and sitting inside the van to take the names of donors. She was more surprised to see me than I was to see her. She turned out to be the prison social officer, knew nothing about me, and told me that she had never even been informed that there was a foreigner in the prison. On my telling her that there we are a dozen of us there at that time, she was totally shocked. She had graduated university the previous winter with a degree in Sociology, some family connection got her this job. She thought it crazy that people were in jail for possession of hash. This was as much a result of all her life having seen hash being smoked by wandering sadhus, and by the ambiguous laws on the selling and possession of hash in different Indian states. (for example: in some cities you could buy it in government-owned shops). She was confused by the fact that not a single Indian in Tihar was imprisoned for possessing or selling hash. She was intrigued at meeting a foreigner in the jail, wanted to know more about me. She insisted that she send for me to visit her office later that day so we could talk. Sure enough, that evening I was marched to the office block and turned over to her.

This scene was truly amazing because she had that afternoon demanded of the prison warden why she had not been told of foreign prisoners and had been told to mind her own business. She had told the warden that I and any other prisoner was her business. I warned her that having me visit her could cost her job. She insisted that things couldn't possibly be that way, then phoned the guardroom for a Fanta for us. For me this was a treat even if it was a soda, this was the first time I had drank anything but tea or water in six months. She and I got on well. We talked about travel, religion, philosophy, food, anything. She fixed it so we got a couple of hours to chat twice a week. It helped me unwind as her office was the only place in the prison where I was not constantly uptight and wary of the guards.

She told her parents about me and other foreigners being in jail for having hashish and invited me to her home for dinner on the day I was to get out.

I accepted.

And here is where the prison governor got me for the mango. My release date came and went with no explanation as to why I wasn't leaving. A week later I was still trying to get to see the governor, my friend tried too. She could not find any paper saying I had the two weeks remission for giving blood. Finally, she got to see the governor and asked him about why I was not released, and really was told she would lose her job if she didn't stay out of it. I told her not to worry and that I could handle a couple more weeks. In the end, the governor let my release date slide a week over my actual six months to be served, then one morning I was told to split.

And that was that.

She was at the guardroom as I left and reminded me, I was eating at her home that night. She would phone my hotel. Dinner at her parent's home was a bit stiff for conversation and a neighbor was also invited to witness that everything was Kosher and so not to give other neighbors anything to gossip about. It was obvious that her parents trusted the judgment of their daughter and they allowed that she and I would meet here and there for tea in New Delhi and continue to talk about everything under the sun. One afternoon she told me she had handed in her resignation to the prison service, having admitted to being naïve to the corruption when she joined. Her parents weren't happy but were satisfied that she had successfully applied for a job as a social officer at a hospital. I really respected her and her folks for that. I enjoyed one rare and brief moment of Karmic reward on the morning I went to pick up my passport and car papers from the court offices. The young fink who had turned me in eight months before, now with cuts and new bruises all over his face and shaven head, was being dragged almost unconscious a few feet in front of me toward a cell by two uniformed policemen.

I stopped them by putting my hand against the fink's chest and told him, "Namaste" then stepped aside so they could lock him up. He was in no state to really recognize me, so I thought better of the Namaste as they put him in the cell and looking straight in his face through the bars, I told him "Fuck you", then walked off to pick up my papers. That brief encounter really gave me a boost.

Justice after all.

My friend and I remained in contact until the day I drove out of Delhi bound for Europe. We both knew that we wouldn't be taking our friendship further, or even ever meet again. She had shown me great kindness in a place where kindness was needed to heal me. I had helped her to gain an insight into the true nature of those in charge of her work position. As I left India, she gave me a framed small watercolor she had painted of herself kneeling by a stream and washing her hair. I still have it, and She remains a brave pure soul in my memory. Tihar prison wasn't too tough on me, but it did leave its internal scars, even though I have visited friends in jails in Afghanistan, Turkey, and Spain where I admit the conditions were very much worse.

The three weeks drive back to Europe cleaned out much of the hatred I had for those who trapped me, but not quite all is gone even today. Although I got through the whole experience still in one piece -enough was enough- on further visits to India, I took great care never to give reason to ever be arrested again.

© Neil Rock 2010

25.

The Bamiyan Buddhas, Ali's Dragon, Kohr-i-Baba Pass

On an Autumn morning of 1968 in Afghanistan, two friends and I set out from Kabul in a Land Rover to spend a few days visiting the statues of Buddha in the valley of Bamiyan in the Hindu Kush Mountains.

The road out of Kabul is the same road leading over the Salang Pass and on to the town of Tashqurghan, where it forks left to Mazar-i-Sharif and Uzbekistan, right to the towns of Faizabad, Kunduz, and up into Tajikistan and China. Traveling north from Kabul and some kilometers before the Salang Pass there is a dirt track leading off west from the village of Pul-i-Matak, it leads to Bamiyan Valley, on to the Band-i-Mir lakes and Maimana in the region of the Hazarat. Although this is the main route from Kabul into the Hazarat, this dirt track is strictly for animal caravans, trucks and other four-wheel drive vehicles; it is the only road stretching across the center of Afghanistan, and only open from April to October. The drive from Pul-i-Matak to Bamiyan is some 150 kilometers through gorges and valleys and takes several hours to negotiate.

A hotel sits on a hill outside Bamiyan Village, a simple and welcoming government-managed hotel and mainly used by archeological teams, historians, or the rare tourists like us who visited the area. It gave a wonderful direct frontal view of the adobe-built village on a poplar-lined river and on to the 55 meter and 38 meter standing statues of Buddha, which stood in niches carved from the sheer rock face of the base of

121

the Hindu Kush Mountains that rise behind them. From this position, the statues appeared to be holding up the mountain range. The entire history of Buddhism is encapsulated in the atmosphere here, as it was here that Mahayana Buddhist teaching was developed from the tenets of King Ashoka, and from this point that Mahayana Buddhism spread to India and onward to China and the South East Asian world. The wonderful Standing Buddhas were later destroyed by the religious intolerance of The Taliban. In 2006 a team of archeologists began examination to view the possibility of re-creation. Rebuilding would be necessary as there is nothing left to restore.

My first morning in Bamiyan, awaking early and after breakfast in the hotel, I decided to walk to the Buddhas and make some exploration of the caves (monk's cells) that are carved into the rock walls surrounding the statues. Arriving in front of the largest statue I was met by a Hazara Tribesman who offered to guide me around the cave complex. On my acceptance, we set off through a series of caves and ancient cells of former monks, until having climbed a steep rock staircase cut deep inside a cliff we emerged onto the top of the head of the Buddha. From here, standing on the head of the Buddha we were facing south into the jagged mountains of the Kohr-i-Baba Range, beyond which to the south lay Kabul. The mountains seemed impenetrable and I commented on this to my guide. He replied that this was true except for the Hajigak (pilgrims) Pass, open three summer months and leading from Bamiyan to Ghazni. He mentioned another pass through the Kohr-i-Baba mountains, down to Istalif, toward Kabul but that this latter pass was a track usable only by walking men and animals. The Hazarat part of the range is regarded as not being accessible from the south by vehicles except through the Pul-I-Matak and Hajigak summer passes. Some mountains in the Hindu Kush rise to 23000 feet, many are snow-covered year-round. To the east, in the adjoining Pamir Range are mountains over 24000 feet high and known to the nomad transients as The Roof of The World.

From the top of the Buddha where we stood, I could also see a hill in the center of Bamiyan Valley on which is the ruined town of Shahr-e-Gholghola (The City of Screams,) so named because the grandson of Genghis Khan was killed here in battle and Genghis beheaded the entire pop-

The Bamiyan Buddhas, Ali's Dragon, Kohr-i-Baba Pass

ulation. Other names of some places in Afghanistan reflect a harsh land with a lurid past. Besides Shahr-e-Gholghola, there is Dasht-e-Margo (The Desert of Death) and the Hindu Kush Mountains (The Indian Killers) in which I now stood, so named for the countless soldiers, traders and adventurers who have died in them on this part of the Silk Road track to the trading centers at Samarkand and Bokhara.

North of the Hindu Kush, through Alexander's Pass and some hundred or so miles northwest of Balk, in ancient Bactria, is a region of unmapped territory where oil bubbles out of the ground, still untapped when I saw it in 1970. The town of Shibergan is nearby, and where author Jason Elliot mentions in his book 'An Unexpected Light'. Not discovered and unearthed until 1979 were over 20,000 artifacts of gold buried in the graves of Kushan kings.

Some regions of the Hindu Kush have an obscured history. One example of this is the remote 200 feet high Minaret of Jam. Built in 1194 in the Hazara district of Ghor, it was only first discovered by the western world in 1866. Twenty severe passes, each of about ten thousand feet above sea level on the road from Bamiyan to Maimana must be negotiated to reach the minaret. Nobody knows why at its hundred feet high mark the minaret bears a verse in Arabic celebrating Mary and the Virgin Birth of Jesus, or who were the people buried in a twelfth-century Jewish cemetery nearby, or why there are ruins of forts for more than twenty miles around.

After my guide and I descended from the head of the great Buddha and down through the rock staircase to the ground level, we came out of the caves and onto the track in front. I told my guide that I would like to visit the smaller of the two standing Buddhas, so we walked east along the track until arriving in front of the 38-meter statue, which rose above us in its' niche on a steeply angled shale slope.

When I told my guide that I wished to walk up the slope to the statue he replied that this Buddha really did not like being disturbed and had been known on many occasions to throw stones at inquisitive visitors. I told my guide that all I wanted to do was walk up to touch the statue. He told me that I was welcome to try but that he was not going any closer than where we stood. I thought then that he did not want to climb the shale hill. I started up the slope and got about 50 meters from the stat-

ue when a whirring noise caused me to stop and listen. I was suddenly aware also of a crackling noise like small arms fire and that stones were flying out horizontal from the cliff face surrounding the body of the statue. The sounds I heard were of stone separating from the rock face and whizzing past my head and body. I turned and ran back down the slope with stones of a size from peas to pigeons' eggs shooting past me like slingshot. The hail of stones stopped as I neared the guide on the track. I interpreted the event as being that my approach to the statue had set up a reverberating vibration, which had bounced off the face of the cliff and loosened stones around the statue. I was surprised when my guide, (a Muslim,) replied that the statue was benign but very powerful and that the people in the valley never disturbed this Buddha. I was forced to recognize his sincerity and to realize that the stones around me had not been falling from high above the statue, they were shooting out horizontally. My guide told me that this statue could only be closely approached safely from the side; he told me also of a third carved stone Buddha named The Sunburst Buddha, to be found in a cave in the entrance of the nearby Kakrak Valley.
Later that day I set out alone to find the cave of the Sunburst Buddha and after some searching in the entrance to the Kakrak Valley, discovered the cave hidden behind boulders and bushes in a narrow gully leading off a goat track. This Buddha is in perpetual shaded silent retreat in his shallow cave, the figure and the surrounding sunburst are carved directly out of the cave's rear wall. The rays of the sunburst stretch floor to ceiling to floor around the statue and it is as if a message of peace is radiated from here to the rest of the world. I made my sincere respects to the people who carved this figure and to their intent that all who would find it can appreciate its' aura of harmony and calm.
The day following my visits to the Buddhas, over curds and kebabs in the village bazaar chai house, a local man told me the story of Ali's Dragon. Hajrat Ali, the son-in-law of Mohammed, The Prophet, may peace be on his soul, was said to have fought and bested a dragon which had been terrorizing the people of the Hazarat. The dragon lay in the hills close to Bamiyan Valley and still cried with shame for it having been beaten in battle by Ali. The village man explained to me where to find it. Some kilometers beyond Bamiyan in the direction of Ghor and Maimana,

The Bamiyan Buddhas, Ali's Dragon, Kohr-i-Baba Pass

two red hills that I had been told to look for to the south came into view. Driving off-road along a desert defile I came to a valley between the two red hills and found a track running near them. Leaving my Land Rover, I walked on the track and rounded the hills. Facing me was an ancient frozen narrow strip of volcanic rock flow some 250 meters long that had formed along the spine of a ridge running to the ground from the crest of a hill. The shape of the lava flow is that of a dragon crawling tail to head down the hill. It is of white and yellow rock along its entire length. I climbed the hill and walked back down slowly along the back of the dragon. This rock formation is truly the most amazing rock formation that I have ever seen. When the volcanic explosion had taken place, the ground had opened up and an underground stream of water had been released to the earth's surface. The water had broken through from under ground at the same time as the lava flow and resulted in the water cooling the lava, shaping the dragon and splitting open the beast along the length of its' body. Jets of molten lava were thrown up from the split, caught and cooled by the exploding water, so that water-cooled rock formed huge spines, rising some 1 to 2 meters in the air along the length of the dragon's back. Deep inside the split shape were tall vertical rock striations blasted into forms looking like giant organ pipes in the dragon's bowels and as ribs in its chest cavity. As the lava and water had flowed down the mountain the lava slowed, expanded and set into the shape of a bulbous head some 10 meters long and 8 meters across. A two-meter single Rhinoceros-like horn of volcanic rock rises straight up into the air from the tip of the dragon's nose. In the side of the head, I saw a slow drip of water was running to the ground from a fissure shaped as an eye. The dragon really cried: And I am still truly amazed. My friends on this trip had also spent their time exploring and walking around the area. Meeting at the hotel in the afternoon of the second day of our visit we were warned by the management that snow was forecast for the next day and that we were advised to leave at first light, if we did not, we could be snowed in for days or possibly months. If the track back to Pul-I-Matak had closed, we would be stuck. I asked about the pass from Bamiyan that leads through the Kohr-i-Baba mountains toward Kabul and was again told—as my guide of the day before had said—that it was a caravan track for walking persons and animals only.

Later that afternoon we were again warned of snow and that it might come that night. We decided to leave immediately. Knowing that the longest drive -in terms of kilometers to be covered- would be to Pul-i-Matak then down to Kabul and that we could not reach Pul-i-Matak before dark, we decided to try the Kohr-i-Baba caravan track going south from Bamiyan. Our reasoning was that we had a Land Rover good for rough terrain and if the track was wide enough for pack camel or donkey caravans then it would be wide enough for our vehicle. We were assured by the hotel manager that other Land Rovers had been in Bamiyan Valley before, but also that he knew of no motor vehicle of any kind that had ever tried to drive out by this route.

The pass started as a dirt track at Bamiyan Valley floor level and about three meters wide. Then the track climbed into the mountains and narrowed to become a ledge about 2 meters 50 centimeters wide and running along a cliff face. Soon we were driving along this ledge at about half a kilometer high from the floor of a gorge on the right-hand side of the vehicle. It was clear we could not turn round or reverse back down the mountains and if we met anybody coming the other way, then they or we could not pass each other. It started to snow and dusk set in. We were at a height of about 12,000 feet above sea level and still climbing. The mountain wall was ice-covered and the wet cold air was painful to breathe. The Land Rover engine changed tone as it labored in the thin air. Night fell and we feared sliding into the chasm. To put snow chains on the vehicle two of us had to get out and fasten ourselves to ropes around the wheels while we hung over the abyss and attached chains to the tires on the right-hand side. There was not enough space between the left-hand side of the vehicle and the cliff face to attach chains on that side. We drove with chains on one side until we came to a place wide enough to open the driver-side door and crouch with back against the mountain wall while fastening chains on the left side wheels of the vehicle.

The drop from the ledge to the gorge floor was so deep that although we knew from hearing torrents of water tumbling down the mountainside that there was a river below us, we could not see it. Our flashlights couldn't reach down the chasm and there were no other signs of tracks to possible villages below. We drove along this ledge for a couple of hours, switch-backing up and down along the mountain face, the Land Rover so close to the edge that stones moved by the wheels were tumbling into the abyss. We crawled along, all the time realizing the danger we were in and that we could do nothing but continue. The night turned pitch black with nothing to be seen in our headlights except the mountainside and the blowing snow. Suddenly the ledge we were on stopped dead at the edge of a deep crack crossing our front. Between us, and the continuation of the ledge at the other side of this crack was a gap about 4 meters wide. Spanning this gap were two thick sawn flat logs laid side by side for animals and men to walk across the terrifying deep gorge. The three of us got out of the vehicle and two of us walked across the logs over the chasm and with the aid of flashlights spread the logs apart on our side while at his side of the chasm our friend at the vehicle guided the logs until we had spread them to the width of our vehicle's wheels. Using the flashlights to illuminate the scene we got the Land Rover up onto the logs and inched it across the gap. We had started driving along the ledge on the mountain face again when our lights showed that the ledge we had been on had ended, and we were ascending and driving along the sheer face of the mountain on a shelf made of a bed of packed dirt, pebbles and stones resting on tree branches spread between crude hewn wooden stakes driven into the cliff face at an angle of 60 degrees. Only the stakes held everything in place over the emptiness below. We were fortunate that the dirt surface was not completely frozen over, so we did not slide. Our chains and tires gripped the stones and the spread branches. This track hanging on the mountain edge and held up by stakes was several kilometers long and at no time were our outside wheels more than 50 centimeters from the edge of the chasm. Finally, the cliff edge ledge appeared again, after which we started winding downward on a track through the mountains.

About 2 AM, after a seven or eight hour drive it had taken to cover some two hundred kilometers, we descended into the town of Istalif. Although nobody appeared on the single town street as we drove through, the people who wakened must have been surprised at the sound of a motor vehicle engine coming out of the mountains. Lights appeared in houses as we passed.

On exiting the town, we could see through a gap in the mountains the glow of the Kabul Street lights below us. We were home within another hour.

It is difficult to imagine now how we were so fortunate as to have crossed this pass safely. I think it probable that at least until that year, 1968, no other men in a motor-driven vehicle had ever traversed it. If any of the hotel staff we spoke with in Bamiyan had known what was facing us and told us, then I do not think that we would have tried.

Remembering this adventure even all these years later brings a heady rush of fulfillment. I visited all three Buddhas at Bamiyan, I walked in amazement on Ali's Dragon, and my friends and I drove an animal caravan track through the Kohr-i-Baba Range of The Hindu Kush Mountains. It still feels like I just drank a glass or two of heady champagne.

Failing memory caused me recently to investigate Google Earth 5 to determine the name of the pass by which my friends and I left Bamiyan Valley in November 1968. It does not appear on the maps, has no name, probably being to the mountain people merely "The way to Istalif"

Those of us who lived in Afghanistan during the 1960s and early '70s were fortunate to explore in a land of spectacular beauty and to share an exhilarating adventure.

Thirty years of horrific war and mindless destruction came there after us.

Afghan army soldiers now guard the hill of Shahr-e- Gholghola against public incursion because it is sown with Russian land mines. Bamiyan Village bazaar was destroyed in the 1990s by fighting for territorial gains between rival warlords. Recently I learned that The Sunburst Buddha in Kakrak valley was dynamited along with the Standing Buddhas of Bamiyan. The spines and rhinoceros-like horn have been smashed from Ali's Dragon

The hidden agenda of the current war since 2002 between the Western Countries and The Taliban is that of the multinational industrial conglomerates continually buying privatized control and exploitation of Afghanistan's substantial wealth of precious metals, gem- stones, minerals and natural gas. Bamiyan Valley is a UNESCO Heritage Site, but in spite of the efforts being made to revitalize tourism, it is targeted as

The Bamiyan Buddhas, Ali's Dragon, Kohr-i-Baba Pass

a multibillion-dollar industrial development. Bamiyan is situated on a huge coalfield and the surrounding mountains contain the second largest iron deposits in Asia, the richest in raw ore and one of the most valuable sources in the entire world. The valley is destined for desolation by large-scale coal mining and iron smelting operations. Sad.

© Neil Rock 2009

26.

Tribal Cues

A 2 AM burst of light machine gun fire and the crack of a couple of rifles had both Barbara and I sitting up in bed immediately. This was July 17th 1973 and on the street outside our house in Kabul changes were taking place. "It's OK" I said to Barbara. " Probably a coup d'état and we will hear about it in the morning." Safe behind our fourteen feet high and three feet thick garden wall and secure in the knowledge that whatever it was had nothing to do with us—and that in this country I could legally shoot anyone trying to get into the property, we both promptly went back to sleep. Sure enough, it's a coup d'état. At 7 o'clock our two batcha brothers were in the living room when we came in for breakfast and rather shakily informed us that it would not be wise to go outside the walls just yet as we had a dead policeman in front of the garage door and there was another one dead on the sidewalk across the street. About 10 AM a helicopter roared in and clattered over our garden and landed in the garden next door, where the Afghan President lived. His son, who, we learned later that day had shot the policemen laying outside, was hauled off to jail. (Two days later a car brought him back in one piece and nothing was said about his slight infraction of the law ever again.) About 12 o'clock noon some guys with a handcart came along the street and picked up the bodies and I took this as a sign that I could go into the city.
Shit! I mean on main city crossroads were modern tanks, armored troop carriers and soldiers with modern weapons, none of which I had ever had an inkling existed in Afghanistan, having seen only road check scruffy looking conscript soldiers carrying old model bolt action rifles. On this day mobile cannon, machine gun half-tracks and other

military stuff had appeared from nowhere. Before this, the only really sharp looking military uniform that Barbara and I had ever seen in this country was on our landlord, an army general, when he personally came to our house in a jeep with driver and armed escort to flush the toilet on word of his Aide de camp receiving a message from Barbara that the toilet wasn't working. Jeep driver, the general's bodyguard, adjutant, house servants and Barbara and I were required to observe the general pulling on the chain until he determined that a plumber was needed. The Aide de camp, an army captain, was officially designated my contact to the general for all house hassles from then on. As the military left the bathroom, our youngest Batcha, to show his worth, nonchalantly cleaned the toilet bowl with Barbaras face cloth and put it back on the drying rack.

Anyway, so on the 16th of July, 1973, the King had gone to his lapis lazuli pillard villa on the Cote d'Azur to see his optician and get a new pair of glasses, (so the world was told), taking his wife, half of sons and all his daughters with him.

His nephew, a bad guy named Mohammad Daoud Khan killed or captured the remainder of the family and some other people left in the palace, knocked off the country and declared it a Republic with himself as President. He had held the post of Prime Minister in a previous government, when he had caused drought and famine in the province of Herat by selling the border river water rights to Iranian crooks. The fruit trees of the orchard city of Herat almost died in entirety until he was sacked. He was not popular.

I immediately contacted every Afghan I knew in Kabul and Kandahar, congratulated them on being alive and wished them well. This was a time to be remembered and well thought of as a friend.

A few days after the coup a connected Afghan friend informed me that one of the first decisions of the new government was to find out just how many foreigners were in the city and who we were. Foreigners who had been in the country for more than two months were to appear in front of a judge and show cause for being in Afghanistan. Having been in and out several times during the previous year I had no problem, but during my trips abroad Barbara had stayed home in Kabul and had by now been in the country for almost a year without leaving. On my asking that something be done so as to avoid Barbara having to show up in court, some feelers were put out by my friend.

I was informed that the chief of police could 'fix things' for me but wanted to see Barbara in his office to 'examine her passport.'

Well now, Barbara, then, was a twenty-one years young and good—looking girl, so I guessed that he felt he had to try. I replied by sending my friend back to the police chief with a message telling him I would shoot him in the leg if he even attempted to speak to my wife. I figured that him being a Pushtun and respecting tribal law he would easily appreciate my position. He did. Back came a request for two bottles of vodka instead.

So, a very dodgy situation of uptight soldiers loose on the streets in a country where possession of alcohol is forbidden, being drunk is an absolute no-no, and I have been challenged to show my mettle.

This called for a measure of appeal to macho romantics. I wrote a violin-string-sugared note to an acquaintance at the Italian Embassy, his wife defensive hormones were immediately aroused and the Charge´ d'affaires was subsequently informed of my stance with the police chief and advised that this is really how Romeos with Juliets should treat all villains. The Charge´ thought this over, reminded himself of his young daughter safely protected at school in Klosters and the key to the embassy wine cellar was quickly and quietly provided. Two bottles of Russian pepper vodka landed in our kitchen the same day and I sent them on in a police jeep to the cop shop.

The police chief kept his word, and on Barbara's entry papers into the country miraculously disappearing from files in the Ministry Of The Interior and new ones being later discovered in their place, and also her passport suddenly bearing brand new entry stamps into Afghanistan dated the previous month, all was solved.

When Barbara and I left Afghanistan that year we were driven to the airport by our connected friend and cheerfully accompanied by the chiefs of customs and immigration, each smiling widely and nodding advisedly at passport inspection and baggage searching staff. The parting handshakes from the director of the national airline cooled the military security guards. Our luggage was even loaded onto the plane in the seats behind us and we zoomed away to Europe. It was Definitely the way to get safely through a military/political upheaval. Although the days since the coup had sometimes been difficult, I can truly say I had not even a moment of real worry.

Afghan friends are really friends, tribal affiliations are all powerful and nothing can break the ties. Even the police chief laughed with us as he waved Barbara and I off at Kabul airport.

I really do love the inherent honor, sense of humor and mischief in Afghan stand-up people. But then, honor, humor and mischief is to be expected. After all, in Afghanistan, Mullah Nazruddin is almost a national hero.

© Neil Rock

27.

Room in the Bin

In the late1950s the first paved road in Afghanistan was built across the country. It is a road with one lane each way running East and West between Iran and Pakistan and links Herat, Kandahar and Kabul. From Kabul a spur several hundred kilometers long runs North to Mazar-i-Sharif then curves back West along the Steppe to serve the towns along the northern frontier with Uzbekistan.

Half this road was built by America, half by Russia. About 50 Ks out of Kandahar toward Kabul the Russians threw in an extra goody in the shape of an intended western style hotel. It had a broken and unreadable name sign on the roof; I remember it as Hotel Kandahar; no sign on the road advertised its' presence. I had passed this hotel several times while going one way or another across the desert on this road over the 60s and early 70s years and had never seen a single person or vehicle anywhere near it. It was a lone gray building out in the desert. Set back from the road, it had a dirt driveway hemmed with stones, no fence, no trees, no garden; three floors of brown plastic curtained windows, a glass front door and nothing else.

I was on the desert one autumn evening while driving from Kabul on a buying trip to the Kandahar jewelry souk when my VW van air-cooling system started to overheat near this hotel. I decided to stop until the next morning and then check out the cooling problem.
I would treat myself to dinner and a room.

On entering the building, I found myself in the hotel foyer, dust, sand and scattered bits of paper littered the floor. The décor was Central Asian no paint rough cement, with genuine watermark art and running crack design in walls and ceiling, plus empty plastic tubes sticking out of the walls and obviously intended for light fittings. It would soon be dark—outside and in—the hotel had no electricity. Afghan friends in Kabul told me later that the connection to electricity was to be paid by the Afghan Government who had ignored this.

A fly-specked glass case holding a variety of dead moths, some rat invaded biscuit packets, some miniature tinfoil pots of jam and half-empty packs of Bulgarian cigarettes topped the reception desk. A cardboard box with dusty bottles of brightly colored Russian soda pop in it topped the glass case. Not a chair, table, sofa or lamp in sight. No staff in sight either. I shout, "Hello," nobody answers, I shout again, nobody answers.

Leaning against the back wall of the foyer and opposite the glass front door was a sheet of corrugated asbestos covering the empty doorframe of a doorway leading outside. Moving the sheet of asbestos aside I was standing at the unpainted cinder block rear wall of the hotel; before me, an unpaved area led directly onto the desert behind.

A few chickens scratch at the sand in a tin-roofed wire pen and a bacha is asleep in the open air on a broken divan beside a smoking small fire. An axe on a block nearby, some feathers and wood chips on the ground convince me that I know where the chickens go and where the reception area furniture went.
I shout, "BACHA!" the bacha stirred, opened his eyes and exploded into action at the sight of this western apparition.

Bacha jumps to feet, rushes past me into hotel, goes into toilet set in wall behind reception desk and shakes awake Manager who is asleep on a mattress on the floor and covered by a chapan and a kapok-filled blanket. Glimpse of a teapot on the crapper lid, a transistor radio and a pile of chair leg firewood beside a petrol tin stove having pipe to a wall ventilator is proof that the toilet is manager's home. (He wasn't so dumb either, he had the best room in the house, as you will find out later). The manager wraps himself in the chapan and with sleeves and shirttail trailing to his knees walks to the reception desk and beckons me before him. With kohl round his eyes and a flurry of eyelash he tries to look coy. I glance at the bacha who imperceptibly jerks his head and shoots a "not me" look. Actually, the manager looks like a cross between Genghis

Khan and WC Fields, so I figure to obey. I approach the desk.

We go through the customary pleasantries: Is my health good? Is the health of my wives good? Is my house in good condition? What about my goats? And are my sheep and children free from the croup? Are my stones not grumbling? Did I pass smoothly this morning? Allah be Praised!

When asked what is my sincere desire I reply that it is a room. Hand washing, head nodding and lip smacking—Certainly, sir, and which one of the twenty empty rooms on each of three floors would I like? Hotel front? Hotel back? Oh Sir! back sir, back! It could be most peaceful as we could expect noisy rush of at least four trucks passing on busy desert highway in front during the night.

But—then again, at back,—well,—also might be disturbing is early morning raucous screech of back yard rooster fucking next day lunch. I ponder. Manager makes an eye-down smile and glances suggestively at his boudoir toilet. The bacha shuffles his feet.

After stating that any room with bed and shower would do, I was escorted by Mr. Manager and batcha up a dim flight of concrete stairs to the second floor, walked along a dark empty echoing mildewed corridor lined with unpainted metal doors on each side then halted before a door which I thought I was being taken behind for interrogation. I was ushered into my front hotel room with bed and shower.

Unfortunately, I had neglected to mention that it would be nice for the bathroom to have a door, some shower taps, a flush handle for the toilet—and a sink instead of a hole in the wall leading through to the bathroom next door. I now told the manager this.

Doubt from manager. Why bathroom door? Who I hide from? Nobody else live in here. And besides—not cold, -and no place in room to light fire. Shower taps? Flush handle for toilet? A sink? Why ever for, sir, when bathroom have no running water? I remark that this is not quite up to the standard of the Dorchester. Sharp defense from manager: "But, sir, this IS a room with bed and shower!" I agree, and mention that a mattress and a repair to the rat chewed holes in the no sprung rope bed would be nice. Mattress for The Illustrious Visitor? Certainly! How many? Only one? He has 20!

Room in the Bin

Special Occasion Past Purchase: Hay stuffed flour sacks brought at great expense by truck all the way from Kandahar for crazed French overland bicycle team all suffering red hot raw ass while pedaling madly to Thailand two years ago. Repair rope bed? Certainly. DIY. Bacha would bring me a piece of string. Unfortunately—repair not done before—owing to interference from will of Allah. THIS manager knew HIS way around the block.

A few millimetres of sand on the floor, torn curtains hung up by nails banged in the wall and absence of any window glass assured me of a cool and dusty night. Still, this palatial habitat could be mine for 30 Afghanis,—money, not people,—37 cents US per night. I paid my money, it disappeared faster than a donkey into a Magicians hat. The manager twirled a gesture of acceptance, pointed to the seven-meter drop outside the window and assured me that I was safe. From the outside, possibly yes, I am two floors up from the ground. From the inside I didn't believe it,—Doctor Fu Manchu's chief torturer would trail the steaming entrails and quivering gristle of the bacha through my bathroom doorway at midnight for free.

The manager scratched in his armpit, pulled at his baggy pants' crotch to free a few fleas and asked just how long did I intend to stay in residence? "Well" I reply, "Oh, pardon me, please, pressing business in Kandahar with a man about a dog prevents me from taking extended pleasure of your hospitality with a delightful sojourn in such relaxing surroundings; unfortunately as soon as I sort out my van I will be forced to split".

I knew I had over done the Afghan graciousness bit when the manager positively screamed at the bacha not to be lazy bacha, but to be hot and cold running bacha, to be the maid and get Great Khan's room floor swept, then being the parking attendant and guiding The Honoured Lord and his Motor Chariot to the back of the hotel and after that being the porter and bringing up First Chief's bags, DIY bed string, mattress and a candle. And after that being the cook and waiter and seeing that The Mister Governor Of Europe got chai, nan and apricot jam for first-class dinner. And in the meantime, he should heat water for shit, shave and shower and bring it in a fire bucket to Highly Gentleman's room.

And tonight, he would be guard and sleep in the back yard by Foreign Caravan Master's treasure and get his ass broiled and kicked all the way back to the Hazarazat Mountains if he didn't. The manager was putting it on a bit strong for my benefit but believe me, the officious prick meant all this. After smirking in my direction, the manager retired to repair his eye shadow and the bacha did everything asked of him and did it for me with smiles.

After all was done by the bacha and I had fixed the hole in the rope bed, eaten my bread and jam dinner and smoked a relaxing joint I ran the bed up against the room door and settled down in my sleeping bag.

That night the wind howled and wailed off thousands of miles of endless empty desert. I had a coat of fresh sand on my bed, piled clothes and shoes.

In the morning the bacha knocked on my door and woke me with fresh chai and more hot water for face washing. Before he left my room, I gave him a pack of Marlboros, knowing that they were worth a month's wages and if I gave them in front of the manager they would be had at knifepoint the moment I was out of the hotel.

I fixed the cooling system in my van (a loose tube connection) and left to wishes of "A pleasant journey, may Allah guide you, and Come Again. Tell your friends in London. Let me know when they will arrive. Send advance message for chicken dinner." from the shuffling crotch roiling manager as I tipped him a couple of small coins.

The bacha walked out to the road ahead of my van and we both said "Salaam". I nodded back toward the manager and said to the bacha" "Gearbox Harabas" which is a universally understood commonly used expression amongst Afghans meaning, "Broken brain. That guy is crazy." The bacha started to shake, hugged himself, tried uselessly not to look at the manager and cracked up laughing as I drove away.

© Neil Rock

28.

The Northwest Frontier

After traveling east from Afghanistan, through the wild frontier tribal town of Landi Kotal, the Khyber Pass and on to Peshawar, there is a road leading into the Tribal Territories of North West Pakistan. To the North is Afridi tribal territory, with since the 1970s, a military road leading in from China. To the south is Waziri tribal territory leading to the Afghan tribal territory of Pashtunistan. Afridi Tribal Territory, which only recently has come under partial Pakistani Government influence was once made up of a dozen independent small tribal kingdoms, Swat, Chitral, Hunza, Dir, Nooristan and Kafiristan being among them. There is still a strong society of tribal life here and the incursion of Pakistani Government is regarded, correctly, to be an instrument of intended control. Up and until at least the middle of the nineteenth century The Rulers of these kingdoms maintained their royal position by dint of goodwill from their peoples, depending on their ability to keep peace with tribal enemies and by maintaining good relationships with the crop fairies believed to live in the King's gardens. If the King was seen to be not friendly with the fairies (bad crops, etc,) then the tribe fired him. (Was failure to buddy up with the crop fairies the reason that Danny and Peachy really couldn't cut it?) At the entrance to the Tribal Territories is the former Maidan (military barracks) of the elite British Indian Army Regiment of the Northwest Frontier Guides. Now, the barracks are occupied by troops of the Pakistan army. Here on a mountainside is also one of my favorite billboards of the world, *"Hotel Maidan—Best Worth Seen In Swat. Fifteen Miles From Mingora With Flush."* So, supposedly, the Tribal Territories are under Pakistani rule of law; this is really not the case as the Government has no control. The absence of roads, except the military road, plus thick forests in mountainous terrain, make troop movement and any control very difficult. That there is no control is exemplified by the fact that when any foreigners enter the tribal area they are halted by Pakistani Frontier Police and required to sign an exit book exempting Pakistan from any responsibility if anything amiss should happen to them. Anything bad happening to anybody is very unlikely unless to Pakistan Police or Army Personnel who could reckon on the possibility of being shot for committing the slightest infraction of tribal law. Even today as Pakistani army troops seek Al Qaida and Taliban fighters in the Waziri Tribal Territories, they are not allowed in without first acquiring permission from tribal leaders. Although no travelers now move through Waziristan owing to it now being the Al-Qaida stronghold, foreign travelers still recently moved around in the Afridi tribal areas and I was told in August of 2007 of a Swiss guy still running a hotel in Chitral.

In 1968 after an attempt to gain a surrender of small arms from the tribes and having made a two months armistice time for collection of guns, the Pakistani government issued a Rawalpindi saying they were convinced that 2 million pistols and rifles were still in the area. They were probably correct as then, even in Peshawar city, it was considered normal to openly carry weapons. Since the occupation of Afghanistan by Russia and the conflicts from then until now, the number of arms in the Tribal Areas must be much higher and the types more modern, military and varied. Directly above Maidan is the tribal area of Swat. The first police post built by the Pakistan Government in Swat was in the central village of Qasakela at the close of the 1960s'. It was razed to the ground and all policemen shot on a Saturday afternoon by an angry group of villagers after a very stupid policeman had taken a bundle of firewood from an old man and told him that he may not any longer gather firewood from the forest. This, mind you, while Pakistani logging companies with backing from crooked politicians were stripping the forests and shipping lumber to the Bhutto family-owned paper mills near Karachi.

Many of the people in the Northwest Frontier Provinces area have light skin and green eyes. They also have mixed Indo/European facial features and can be recognized as descendants of the army of Alexander

The Northwest Frontier

The Great. The physiognomy is evidence of part of Alexander's army settling here after failing to reach India. The Greek presence here can also be recognized in the archaeological finds of the classic Greco Buddhist bronze sculpture known as Gandhara; probably the best-known example of this being the statue of The Starving Buddha in the museum of Lahore. The decorations on carved wood used in construction of houses and on the tables and chairs in the houses also denote members of Greek civilization having once been here. Olive trees, some much older than a thousand years grow in Swat. Remnants also of the Greek culture, though the people do not know the use of olives as food or oil for themselves, this knowledge has faded, they do know that olives can be eaten by sheep and goats. Once, traveling with a Greek/American friend who explained to villagers about uses of the fruit, we were asked to stay and even an offer to build us a house was made—so my friend could teach them about olives. We were told by a mason that a granite stone two-roomed house with attached animal stable would cost us a hundred dollars and if we left a deposit of ten dollars with the reader at the local Mosque then the house would be ready and waiting for us the following year. No doubt it would have been if we had accepted, for even though we declined, on meeting us the Mosque keeper welcomed us to his village, gave us lunch, invited us to visit tribal dignitaries, assured himself that we had our own weapons,, then strapped on his own automatic pistol and he and the builder escorted us in our Land Rover for days through the valleys in the region and introduced us to many fine local people. Hospitality is the first tribal law. Any foreign visitor once invited to share food with a local is completely safe. Vengeance is the second tribal law and woe to anyone who incurs it. The law of hospitality is so strong that a murderer of any member of a family can seek sanctuary of that family and live with them in their home in complete immunity until he should stepoutside the house, when he will be immediately killed.

Another great example of hospitality is that of my friend EL Z, while ina tea house in Mumbai (then Bombay) one spring mentioned to a friend that he would be traveling with me through Swat in the following autumn. An Afridi, overhearing the conversation asked that a letter be delivered to a village where lived a brother he had not seen or heard

141

from in sixteen years. El Z and I delivered the letter to the village. An interpreter/translator was rustled up, the letter was read aloud to everybody from miles around and El Z and I were feted like beings from a far planet. The entire village contributed to make us a feast, AND, Paradise NOT Lost, all the paths and lanes through the village land were lined with wild ganja plants. Maybe thirty or more people accompanied El Z and I on an after-dinner stroll along a riverbank while we sampled the fine and fresh local cigars. Roll over Kipling and Raj tea parties.

Another friend, Alan Zion, once told me a wonderful story of his meeting with the Walhi (The Tribal King) of Swat. Alan was resting on a riverbank along a dirt road when he heard the sound of an automobile engine coming from around a curve in front of him. As at that time there was no paved road and only dirt tracks in Swat, Alan expected to see a four-wheel drive pick-up; instead a1920s wicker-bodied chauffeur-driven Rolls Royce open-topped touring car appeared. The person in the rear seat was as amazed to see Alan as Alan was to see the car and its occupants. The King, such was the passenger, ordered the chauffeur to stop and introduced himself to Alan in impeccable Oxford English and invited him to "A spot of fishing and a picnic, old chap". After a few fly casts into the river, the chauffeur erected camping chairs and a table, laid linen and silver flat-wear. A Harrods picnic hamper was produced. The King explained that he had a standing order for such a hamper full of English canned and bottled goodies to be flown out to him from London to Rawalpindi every couple of months and trucked up from there into Swat. Alan told me that he had not eaten or seen anything more interesting than stringy mutton, dusty rice and flatbread for a couple of weeks. On being invited to sample everything, he went through the hamper like a piranha. The King, realizing that Allan was short on calories invited him to stay at the Palace (a large wooden house in a compound) for a few days. Alan was treated like royalty himself and left after a weekend of being fed everything that could be crammed into him.

On one trip to Swat with my girlfriend, (later wife) Barbara, we several times heard of a young Danish girl who had lived in a village with her boyfriend for almost a year. She had seen a small boy picking at a sore on his scalp and had stopped him, taken him home to her hut in the village, and smeared on ointment. By the next day every mother in the village with an injured child was at the door. Realizing that there were no medicines or other treatments available the girl caught a ride down the valley on a jeep to the Maidan military barracks and spent all her money to bribe army medics for a medicine chest of emergency supplies and boxes of penicilin powder and tablets. She treated children for months and when leaving Swat, was asked for a small photograph by the village chief. Many copies of this picture were made in Peshawar. Almost every man in the area carried a copy in his pocket; Barbara and I were shown dozens. Unfortunately, charity did not always begin at home. A local silversmith told us that a previous village chief was a greedy bad guy who would order things to be made and then collect but never pay for them. He helped nobody. He got shot somehow. This chief was referred to in conversation as The Cheap. From the nineteenth to early twentieth century two tribes from villages in adjoining valleys in Swat fought a running war over many years. Eventually, tired of needless killing on both sides they hit on the solution of having a shootout party. Tribesmen from each valley faced each other from mountain tops at a safe distance of a mile or so and banged away at each other for a few hours (hitting nobody) then all the people from both villages got together for a full blast feed and party for the rest of the day. This mock war and party is still celebrated every summer. In the past, other Hatfield/ McCoy situations have erupted here and also lasted for generations. Although every man up here is customarily armed, it was very rare in the mid 20th century that anyone was killed over private issues.

Kafir in Parsee means unbeliever and Kafiristan (land of the unbelievers) is a tribal area that never converted to Islam and is still, "primitive". Sometime in the 19th century, one half of this country converted to Islam and became known as Nuristan (Land Of Light). Both Kafiristan and Nuristan officially belong to Afghanistan, nobody quite knows the Afghani/ Pakistani borderlines here, and both territories were still inaccessible by vehicles in the 1960s. No roads, but only trails and paths make traveling possible. Eric Newby›s wonderful book *A Short Walk In The Hindu Kush* portrays the difficulties of moving around in this area. During their occupational war in Afghanistan, the Russians did their best to halt all traveling in both Nuristan and Kafiristan. The tribal areas became staging areas for Afghan guerrillas and some villages became war refugee centers. Millions of anti personnel Sicamore Mines were dropped by aircraft all through both regions, making it impossible for people to move about without having a heel or whole foot blown off. At that time there were no hospitals or medical services within a hundred miles. The Russian action was State Terrorism at its worst. Kafiristan was particularly difficult to enter by vehicle from the tribal territories up to the 1970s owing to only having two access points, one a track from Chitral, the other a bridge crossing a river from Dir. A Dutch priest living in Peshawar for almost thirty years told me that he had known an American couple working in the American Embassy at Rawalpindi who, in 1956 had made a dirt track journey by jeep through a valley close to Swat. The couple got as far as a footbridge giving access to Kafiristan. When their vehicle was at the bridge some people coming out of the forest on the Kafiristan side of the bridge cut branches from trees and threw them in front of the jeep for it to eat. They had never seen a motor vehicle. In 1972 a friend and his wife, while visiting Barbara and me at our house in Kabul, decided to make an expedition to Kafiristan, which they entered from Chitral. Even at that late date, they had to buy 19th-century Indian silver rupees in Chitral owing to Kafiris still being far enough removed from civilization to not accept paper money. Silver only could be used. Kafiristan, like the rest of the Tribal territory north of Maidan, is heavily forested. The houses of the Kafiris, unlike some in parts of Swat are not intricately carved, but the Kafiri houses have huge carved wooden eyes, painted in bright colors and several meters across in size mounted on their roofs and looking directly upward. Everybody is obviously thinking of traveling onward someday and on the lookout to be collected. Graves of ordinary villagers are earthen space ship-shaped mounds with flat stone slab fins at sides and tail. People of rank are buried under life-size carved wooden statues of crowned men sitting on horseback.

The Tribal Kingdom of Dir lasted until the 1950s. Sixty miles long and some twenty across it was ruled by a King who made a living by charging nomad gypsies a fee for crossing the land with their herds of sheep on their way to summer and winter pastures either in Afghanistan or Pakistan. Kuchi gypsies had used this route for millennia until passage into Pakistan was finally forbidden by that government in the 1960s. Dir has

The Northwest Frontier

only one village consisting of a small caravan Sarai, a shop, and a few houses. The Royal Family lived in a wooden fort surrounded by a spiked palisade. The country is only accessible to motor traffic from the end of May to the end of August, (and even then to 4 wheel drive vehicles only.) The rest of the year it is snowbound. Since the partition of India by the British in 1948 the Pakistan Government has been trying to gain control of the area. They finally succeeded to some extent at the close of the 50s by bribing a son of the King to convince his father to accept a state visit from Pakistani dignitaries. A helicopter landed outside the fort and when the King emerged he was kidnapped at gunpoint, flown to Rawalpindi, and jailed. He died in prison. The son was rewarded for his treachery with a lifetime stipend, a home in Karachi and an honorary Generalship in the Pakistan army.

In 1972 my Greek American friend and I managed to get into Dir with Afridi tribal guides. We were hoping to get through Dir and into Nuristan from there. Unfortunately, that year early in August, snow had closed the pass from Dir onward. On arrival at the caravan Sarai in Dir village, we met a terrified Pakistani official who had been sent from Rawalpindi to Dir as a population census taker. He had not managed to realize any figures. The remnants of the tribal royal family wanted nothing to do with him and had refused to receive him. He was in fear of his life and waiting for a jeep supposedly coming to take him back to Peshawar. On leaving Dir after a stay of a couple of days we wished this unfortunate gentleman well and left him in the caravanserai pining for his transportation. Being a Pakistani Government representative he was anathema in the tribal areas. Honor of independence was alive and well in the regions of The Northwest Frontier tribal lands.

What happened to change The Northwest Frontier Tribal Territories to a region of millions of war refugees and tens of thousands dead and war wounded during the period from 1970 to now can be regarded as the result of historical continual political interference in Afghan tribal affairs by the British and Russian governments over the last three hundred years, plus the uncaring incompetence of successive Afghan governments, the land encroachment by Pakistan and the territorial designs of modern Central Asian and USA business interests. The repressive regimes of The Taliban and Al Qaida are crystallized in the person of yet another interfering foreigner, Osama Bin Laden, (A modern, yet this time dishonorable Saladin) and the opium warlords in the region. The destructive policies, absence of the principles of freedom and decency, and the adherents of these regimes are now infecting the tribal peoples and constitute history's most damaging wound to date in the tribal soul. In my visits to the Afghan/Pakistan frontier tribes, I was always conscious of being a welcome guest. The region truly was The Last Frontier. Many ills of so-called "advanced civilization" lay in wait for a justifiably suspicious people. Sadly, because of the incompetent political administration, and now the spreading of religious intolerance from ignorant manipulative preachers, I will most probably never visit the region again.

© Neil Rock

29.

Naked at Night

One October on the stage of the Afghan road from Herat to Kandahar I was traveling with my wife. Tired by the heat of the day we stopped for a tea break and a short sleep at the Southern Fried Chicken Caravan Serai. This stop delayed our arrival in Kandahar until after nightfall. It was customary for overland travelers stopping at hotels in Afghanistan to sleep with their animals or vehicles in the hotel garden if they wished. So, arriving late at night in the city I parked my van in the nearest hotel garden and my lady and I went to bed. We were just getting cuddly when there was a single knock on the sliding door and a voice said "Mister—Hotel." Figuring this was the bacha telling us we should check in, I shout "Tomorrow". Silence, OK, back to pleasure. Two minutes later knock, knock "Mister—Hotel—All Go". Somewhat pissed off I again shout "Tomorrow". Again silence. Two minutes later: another knock on the door and "Mister—Hotel—Go—Saturday". This time mystified, seriously coitus interrupted, thoroughly disgruntled and completely dishabille I leaped out of bed and threw open the door stark naked while shouting "Fuck off" at the top of my irate voice into a flashlight held by a uniformed policeman. Boy, was this cop cool as a cucumber. He shines his flashlight at my crotch, the boarded-up windows and doors of the hotel, looks at me and shrugs. "Hotel all go Saturday" He is telling me that the hotel went out of business and shuttered closed, the week before. I leapt starkers out of the van, ran round to the front, jumped into the driving seat and with my wife rolling around with laughter in the back of the van I drove naked and shivering through Kandahar until I pulled into the garden of another hotel and promptly went back to bed. We slept. She had lost it and couldn't stop giggling.

© Neil Rock

30.

Buzkashi

One winter while living in Afghanistan I took a few days' trip north from Kabul to watch a game of Buzkashi being played on the Uzbek Steppe near the town of Andkhui close to the Amu Daria Bridge over the river of that name which is the frontier with Uzbekistan. Here the Steppe is flat desert stretching from horizon to horizon and it is possible to ride a horse in a straight line all day and night on the level plain without seeing a single rise in the landscape.

Buzkashi is the original and primitive form of polo. It is played on horseback without a mallet and, instead of hitting a ball, the rider, called a Chapandaz, uses his hands to pick up the dead body of a goat and carry it to the goal line. The game is reputed to have been developed centuries ago on fields in the mountain fastness of Hunza. Any number of riders can participate. The action is expert riding, thrilling and brutal. There are no teams, competition is all on all and all on one. In a major game, there can be fifty or more competitors from towns and villages spread over hundreds of kilometers. The winner gains great pride and honor for himself and his community.

The riders mostly wear thick fur jackets over padded coats, padded quilt trousers, high leather boots, and chin-strapped fur hats; this clothing is worn for protection in the struggle against other riders and their horses. The audience, usually observing the game at a guessed safe distance from the action will run to one side if in the way of approaching galloping horses, although are sometimes injured in the heat of the battle.

To start the action, two Chapandaz, each carrying a lance bearing a small triangular flag on the butt, ride in opposite directions across the Steppe for any distance they wish to up to a kilometer or so. They plant the lances in the ground to designate the winning posts then return to the starting point. The competing horsemen all take out money and slowly parade their horses in a circle while shouting the amount of money they are holding in their hands. They show the money to the audience then hand it to the game-master. These bundles of banknotes are money they are placing as bets on themselves and their mounts. Local landowners and other wealthy backers of favored horsemen also hand prize money to the game-master. The game-master then excites riders and audience by announcing and showing the total amount of prize money that will go to the winner. He exerts the audience to make personal side bets then carries the dead goat into the circle formed by the riders and throws the animal on the ground. He retreats quickly. The horsemen then furiously vie for possession of the goat.

To win, a rider has to scoop up the dead goat from the ground, or forcibly take it from any other player who holds it, then tuck it under his thigh and hold on to it while riding and fighting his way through biting and kicking horses and the melee of whips lashing, and punching and kicking opponents. He must carry the dead goat to either of the lances. The riders gallop back and forth across the Steppe as the goat is fought for and changes hands. There are no rules except that no knives, guns, or clubs are permitted to be used and make sure you arrive with the goat at either winning post. The whole pack of opposing horsemen continually fight for possession and mercilessly ride down and attack whoever holds the goat. The game can last for hours. I saw an Uzbek horseman riding toward me at full gallop fall full length and face down to the earth from his horse after being lashed across the face with a leather and iron quirt. As he fell our eyes met from where I sat watching from the roof of my van. This man hit the ground so hard he actually bounced on it when he landed amongst dozens of stamping hooves. With blood pouring down his face and with utter scorn for his torn cheeks and other injuries he stood up and while looking me straight in the eye, shook himself like a dog, and raised his hand in the air as a signal for another horse. Tougher, more courageous and arrogant horsemen than the Chapandaz don't exist.

Chapandaz are taken very seriously as supreme lords in the Hindu Kush Mountains and on the Central Asian Steppe. Whole town markets up here have their stalls laid out with goods displayed at saddle level for the convenience of horsemen who can choose purchases without having to suffer themselves the indignity of having to dismount. Mere walking men have to stretch to view the goods. The Chapandaz rules. His horse is worth much more than a house. An example of the true worth of a Buzkashi horse is that an American friend of mine owned a magnificent dappled gray stallion named Shah Ruba (King of Foxes). Once, two men tried to steal this horse on the Steppe near the town of Balk where my friend was camped for the night. A pistol fight ensued, my friend won. As it was known that the horse was his, no questions were ever asked.

The game of Buzkashi I saw that winter weekend was a major event and serious business, with gold coins and thick bundles of banknotes waved about by the game-master and on offer for the winner. Hundreds of dollars and many goats and sheep were also won and lost on side bets. After a two-hour tournament in which the goat was reduced to a ripped inside-out steaming bundle of rag, an Uzbek rider from Bokhara was the winner.

© Neil Rock

31.

Afghan Road Cuisine

The stretch of road between Herat and Kandahar is 250 kilometers long without a single village anywhere in sight. Until and throughout the 1960s the only gas pumps along the road were two five-hundred-liter fuel drums for emergencies: One drum of gasoline and one of diesel stood at the side of the road 125Ks from each city. The fuel was guarded and served by an Afghan conscript soldier who lived in a 3 meter by 2 meter shed situated alongside the drums. On the other side of the road was a caravan serai with a courtyard for camels and a chai house with dirt floor covered with carpets for desert travelers to sleep on. This chai house served tea and bread. Huge hand-painted green, red and yellow flowers climbed the outside of the building from the ground up and covered the walls and the wooden window frames. Obviously, a traveling and flat broke hippy had stopped here and, probably in exchange for food and a place to sleep on the floor, had offered to increase the chances of the place attracting customers.
Across the twenty-meter-long façade of the roof, large psychedelic multi-colored letters advertised: FINGER LICKIN' MOTHERFUCKIN' GOOD SOUTHERN FRIED CHICKEN.
The itinerant artist surely made it safely eastwards across the country as there was a caravan serai near Jalalabad at the entrance to The Khyber Pass carrying on its façade, paintings of lots more flowers, knives, forks, a picture of a giant burger and the legend: FAR OUT MEAT BALLS. KFC and McDonalds in the making.

© Neil Rock

32.

Drive from the Steppe

My friends Ali and Gulam and their families had hotels (and connections to other hotels) all the way North, East, South, and West across Afghanistan and on through Pakistan to India. These kinds of extensive links are not uncommon amongst Asian hotelier and food catering families. The largest percentage of Motels in the Southern United States are operated by Indian immigrants who know each other, and so are train station candy/ magazine stands all over the UK for that matter. You want fresh flowers and groceries at 3 am anywhere in New York or New Jersey and the guys in the shop are surely Korean.

One December weekend I had driven from Kabul to buy tribal jewelry in Acha, a village near Balk, the Central Asian capital city of Alexander the Great. I was in a jewelry dealer shop when a caravan of Kuchi Gypsies leading sheep and camels passed along a desert trail near the town and a man from the group came to sell some practically worthless silver beads and bracelets. To my surprise, the dealer accepted a kilo or so of silver, a few good small pieces, but mostly broken bracelets and necklaces. After the Kuchi had left I asked the dealer why he had accepted scrap quality jewelry. He took me into his warehouse and showed me several tons of broken silver jewelry in zinc boxes stacked along the walls. He told me that the gypsy tribes were steadily becoming poorer as restrictions were put on their cross-frontier marches to grazing pastures in Central Asian countries and that flocks were dwindling because of this. He explained that most of the jewelry I was buying was from stock that had been mostly purchased by himself and his father more than thirty years before. Some was recently smuggled in by dealers from Bokhara,

Samarkand, and Kiev where there was no market owing to those cities being inaccessible to foreigners because of being Russian-dominated Communist territory. Most of what the dealer bought from gypsies in recent years could only be resold as melted-down silver ingots. His most profitable business came from illicit trade with the workers in the ruby mines and Lapis Lazuli mines in the Wahkan Corridor of Badakhshan close to the Chinese border. He felt obligated to buy silver from the gypsies as long as he could afford it as he had had years of good profit and did not want to see them starve. He felt there was nothing else he could do. I marveled at the integrity of this business effort and could not see such an effort being made by a dealer in the West.

After business, I passed the night at Mazar-i-Sharif fortress, in the yard of a caravan Sarai serving worshiping pilgrims at the Mosque of Ali, son of The Prophet Mohammed. An English friend, Clifford Smith, had worshiped here also, was given the honor in the mosque of reading out a Sura from The Koran and is entered in the mosque book as an honorary citizen of the city of Mazar-i-Sharif. Thirty years later this resting place was the site where the American, John Walker, was discovered by a unit of US special army forces while he was a prisoner amongst 7000 Taliban who had surrendered in the battle of Kunduz. General Dostum's Muhajadeen army locked 4000 of these prisoners in container trucks in the desert and shot them at random through the truck walls while they were locked inside the trucks on their way to prison in Sheberghan. They were buried in graves bulldozed in the desert. The night I slept there I met another traveling Englishman at the caravan sarai. He was aiming to catch a truck ride north-east to the city of Kunduz, then, walk overland to the Lapis Lazuli mines in Badakhshan. I figured that as my friend and world-class roadrunner Blind George had made it alone through the roadless rock maze of Badakhshan—then Maybe,—but Just Maybe, this guy could do it. We shared a lamb kebab and tea supper wrapped in kapok blankets, swapping road stories and smokes with a group of pilgrims from Samarkand. It was a freezing cold night, a new moon, and the stars hung like flashing ice in a black sky. Even around the fire, we could see each other's breath in the air. We stoked the fire with camel dung and settled down in sleeping bags. In the morning we all visited the mosque and parted after wishing each other Peace. Having filled my fuel tanks from cans I bought in the market town of Tashkurgan, I set out south through Alexander's Pass on the 10 hour drive through the Hindu Kush mountains to Kabul.

Some Ks south of Bagram, (later, a town with a Russian-built airbase—and now in the hands of the US military), is the Salang Pass. This pass is the only paved route from China, Uzbekistan, and Tajikstan to Kabul, and to the Khyber Pass, and across the Balochistan desert and the Spin Boldak route to Pakistan. Vehicles traveling south through the Hindu Kush Mountains must climb this pass, as must vehicles heading north from Kabul. At a height of 16000 feet above sea level and with mountains rising to 20,000feet on either side, it is the highest pass in the world that is accessible to motorized traffic. It is a very dangerous proposition to cross this pass in winter and guards are posted at both ends to ensure no vehicle attempts it without being in good condition. No vehicle can be allowed to traverse the Salang Pass without being equipped with snow chains. On all large trucks, summer and winter, a man rides outside clinging to the back of the truck while standing on the rear fender. These men are invariably mountain men, Hazara tribesmen, and known as the Daid Panj, or Fifth Gear. The job of the Daid Panj is to jump off the back of the truck to jam large wedge-shaped chunks of wood under the wheels if the truck should commence to slide toward the sheer cliff edge of the mountain. Overloaded falling vehicles are not unknown, as on one winter's day some years before, I had been forced to retreat backward down the mountain in neutral, and using brakes for steering way on the ice to escape a runaway truck as it slid backward and sloughed close to the edge, only just failing to push me over.

This day it was snowing heavily as I approached the northern entrance to the tunnel leading south to the Salang Pass. Russian engineers with giant bulldozers, snow ploughs, and heavy heating generator trucks refused me entry and told me I must turn back and not make another attempt for at least two days. OK, back to Bagram the nearest mountain town and try to get shelter. My only concern was that although I had a full tank of fuel, I had nothing but a few coins in my pocket, having spent a lot up in Acha on beautiful gold and silver Turkoman jewelry.

I turned around and drove back through the icy mountains to Bagram, found the only hotel in town, and told the hotel owner that the pass was closed, that I had no money with me, that I was a friend of Gulam, owner of the Gazni Hotel in Kabul, that I was in need of a room for at least two days, plus food, water, candles and a stove with wood. I told him that the day I arrived in Kabul I would arrange with Gulam to have the money sent to him the following morning on the first truck coming up from Kabul and through the Salang Pass. Upon offering him my pistol and ammunition belt as security, the hotelkeeper shook his head and didn't even ask to see my passport. A room was provided, stove fired up, a kettle, tea leaves, water, and cooked food brought to me three times a day. I was given the rare winter treat of a mud-covered wicker ball, which when broken open contained a bunch of grapes picked in September and kept fresh by being suspended on a string inside the airtight mud ball until December. As the date was the 20th of December the hotel owner presented me with the ball as a Christmas present. Three days later the owner told me that the pass was open again. I thanked him, drove to Kabul, and gave the money to Gulam. The money was paid out at the hotel in Bagram on Christmas day.

There is no doubt that without this tradition of hospitality I would have frozen to death or been killed that winter on the Salang Pass. Trucks stranded in storms or broken down up here in winter are often awaiting help or storm clearance for several days at 40c below zero and Force 6 to 10 gales are the norm. Drivers and crews wrap in layers of sheepskins, coil up with their mastiff dogs and keep gas burners blazing around the gearboxes to avoid gears freezing and snapping like sticks. More than a few heedless truck crews have died frozen in their vehicles and are buried in graves of stones and snow on the Salang Pass. Bandits sometimes get to a truck and load before rescuers arrive. A VW camper containing the bodies of four shot young English hippies was dug up from the ice in the spring of 1971 after being buried there for two months. The British consul in Kabul told me that the youths in the van were unidentifiable except by number plate and paperwork. The inside of the vehicle was a stinking mass of rotting jelly.

I can truly say that in my years spent in Afghanistan I experienced the example of a proud culture and its hospitality to foreigners at its very best. Considering that twice the British invaded Afghanistan and twice the Afghans drove us out, they had no reason to love us. In the last British/

Afghan war only one English soldier escaped alive from the massacre of the entire military and diplomatic staff stationed in Kabul. The Russians didn't win there either and I predict that neither will the American-led coalition. As in Korea and Vietnam, the defeat will be sugar-coated in publicly palatable phrases. That the Afghan tribes cannot agree on a ruling person or government is beyond doubt. Regretfully, western forces must be there. A deal to post UN forces must be brokered somehow. I love the country and most of the people I know there. I owe my friends there much more than the tip of a hat.

As is the case in the North-West Frontier Province of Pakistan, one only needs to review a short 300 years of recent history to realize that the interference by "The Great Game" of empire as played by foreign powers in Afghanistan, and the internal mismanagement by a succession of careless rulers, warlords, and now the rise to power of the fanatic extremist Mullahs, has led to the final collapse of the country. The Russian 1979 invasion and the resulting rise of the repressive Taliban regime being the latest horrors vented on a wonderful people. In the 1990s while reminiscing with an Afghan-American friend, he pointed out that the Afghanistan I had known was dead and forever gone.

Note, for anybody interested: The scenes of the deserts and mountains, the portraits of the people of Afghanistan, and predictions for the future of the country as described by James Michener in his 1963 book "Caravans" are accurate and the closest that could be got to this country and its culture as it was before 1973 and the coup d'etat, which changed the status quo. The book has good information for anyone wishing to view the country without traveling there. The CAUSES of the current American-led military intervention in Afghanistan can be found in the book of author and Times of India reporter Achmed Rachid—"Afghanistan: The Taliban And Oil".

© Neil Rock

33.

A Short Real Glasnost

I had a job with Friends Of The Earth in which part of my campaign work required me to visit and monitor the Tourism Fairs in the capitals of Europe. While traveling in this job I met a most remarkable lady. In November 1989, close on the heels of the fall of Communism, some USSR private tour operators seeking clients from Western Europe made their international sales debut at the World Travel Market, Earls Court, London. At the Russian display stand I stopped and leafed through a couple of brochures of city hotels and excursions. Amongst some of the usual dowdy female middle-aged communist party functionaries at this stand was a very healthy, pacing, red haired young lioness from Saint Petersburg. This girl came over to me and asked if she could help. I enquired if she offered any wild life tours. She thought for a moment, puzzled, then burst out laughing, shook her head at me, put her hands to her throat and astounded -asked -"What?!" I said "You know, do you do wild life tours?" She hesitated, looked at me sideways, cracked a grin and asked " You like wild life tours?" "Yes, I said." She wrote on her business card, handed it to me and said: "That's my hotel number, phone me tonight, I'm leaving back to Russia tomorrow morning."

© Neil Rock

34.

Donkey Doings

Driving through the Pyrenees Mountain Range in Spain, close to the pass at Isaba, and stopping overnight to service my van before crossing into France. When I had arrived at this quiet back road forest campsite in late evening there was nobody in reception. The bar outside had a few people in it, so figuring the boss was there and I would catch him/her later I drove past a few RVs and tents into a corner by a river and picked myself the corner spot. Beautiful, completely shaded and the river rushing over rocks a few meters away. A fence next to my spot cut me off from a field next door. Under trees in the field, I could see two or three animal stables. A farmhouse stood some short distance further away from the animal shelters. After checking the van and getting myself settled in I walked to reception and found the boss inside his office. To say this guy was drunk is a downsize lie. This guy was Stiff. So stiff that he did not seem to be able to move body or even eyes and sat with his arms splayed open on the desktop to maintain himself sitting upright.

"Buenas Tardes" Says I.

" Ocho euros." Says he.

When I put coins on the desk his arms opened like mechanical sweeps. His eyes never left mine. His left hand moved to open a drawer in his desk, arm back to original support position. Right hand swept the money across the desk and into the drawer. Drawer closed and right arm back to splayed support position. Work over.

" Buenas Tardes" he says. I went back to my camper

It being dusk and chilly now up here at 2,800 meters, I put on a sweater

159

and decide on some barbecue from my fridge. For my dog and me, I grilled a treat of some lamb chops with veg, a half bottle of Rioja for me and prepared for bed. As I am washing dishes in the river a few camping vehicles bearing German number plates pull off the southbound lane of the outside road and into the campsite.

Kids spill out to play by the river, folded chairs opened and beers for the folks. I read a book until the mommas had cooked and the kids quieted down to eat supper and were then packed off to bed. Me too, river rushing by next to my head and I slept like a log.

Early morning, I was wakened by a screaming honk so loud I thought someone had let blast with an air pressure horn beside my van. It changed to a bray, which I recognized as the scream of a donkey. Opening the curtains of my van I see beside me and just across the field fence a mountain honeymoon couple. A male donkey is mounting an exited and yelling female.

This taking place at about 8 AM some other campers are up and kids are running around again.

More screams from the female as she pulls away. Teeth bared and wrath from male—really loud braying "Submit or die!"

Kids came running to see the show and immediately some red face hausfraus swung into action and were hot in pursuit. A blonde eight-year old freckled Heidi, arm stiff out front, finger pointing straight ahead has only time to let out amazed shout "Look Mutti, it's black" before being whacked by an arm three times the size of a Christmas bratwurst and the smack sounding like a car crash This was followed by a Heidi scream so loud that the reverberation was probably recorded on the Richter scale in Barcelona. Male donkey screams nearly as loud as Heidi. Heidi dragged off and incarcerated for life sentence of celibacy in RV clothing cupboard. Many distraught mothers descended on the scene like barracuda and kids were scattering like a shoal of sardines. Mothers were casting sly glances from under eyelids when thinking nobody is looking The donkeys are now enjoying themselves regardless of Teutonic upheaval. At least six hefty huffing and puffing Puritanical Muttis were outside my camper windows and shouting, trying windmill arm-waving and shooing exercises to frighten away the rutting animals. No way, the male was adamant and going nowhere but in, his girl friend having decided

Donkey Doings

she liked it after all. More roars and really stuck into it, women shouting louder, bitching, some, moaning also. All this Mutti hysteria is three feet from my head so I shout through the window "Shut the fuck up!" at the top of my lungs. The women freaked. Wild-eyed and hairclips falling, red faces turn to me, turn purple with embarrassment. They had No clue what to do; the kids were enjoying the show from a safe distance. Wake up from one Mutti, shouts at pinafore barbecue breakfast husband to get his dumb ass in gear and DO something. More Muttis shake up more Pappis from stupor. Fishing rods dumped, beers dropped, van beds suddenly not good for sleeping in, Dortmund Dagblat is Later Dagblat. Kids rounded up by instant storm troopers and interned in RVs for the duration. Pappis join Muttis.

The donkeys took a break. Male eye gleaming at Muttis and Pappis, this is groovy and fuck you too. Nobody is having to ask "How's it hanging, Pal?" Most wives turned away and the Pappis were instructed by the female Obermeisters to get a move on and make a report to the Campsite Boss. Several men hastened to the reception office and went inside. About ten seconds later the Reception door opened again and the men came back outside carrying The Campsite Boss, still totaled from last night plus this morning intake and suspended like rag doll between two very irate Pappis. Campsite Boss dragged to the farmyard boudoir of amour.

Some BIG brays at Campsite Boss from male donkey, the show must go on. Donkey do or die! The Alcazar or death! Continues making new donkeys. RV curtains being parted by junior voyeur Hansels and Gretels had mothers in a flip over how to control the situation. Shouted threats of smacked bottoms, ripped up toy train tracks and no new doll dresses had no effect. Men now being present, most of the women went back to their RVs, pretending to cry, sneaking looks and secretly wishing they had picked up the camera.

Continuing donkey doings. The Campsite Boss was shaken from his alcoholic coma, but was incapable of action and could only mutter the name of the campsite cleaner. Two Pappis went to the bar and found the cleaner, who luckily was sober. Being told what was happening at the far end of the campsite he rapidly got on the phone to the farm next door. The farmer arrived on a Quad with a large fertilizer sprayer filled with water and a hand pump attached. He drenched the donkeys in the right places, the female tried to split and was reined in by male teeth. The next drenching and some eye squirting did it and the animals parted with much more angry screaming. The male donkey was thoroughly pissed off while showing off. Eyeing the donkey's doer and warily eyeing the donkey kicking shit out of the wooden fence, the Boss minders dropped the Campsite Boss on the grass for the cleaner to sweep up and stepped back, ready to run. The male donkey turned away from the fence and attacked the Quad with a furor that caused the farmer to do a runner double-quick. After the male donkey had reduced the quad to recycling junk, he suddenly turned calm and he and the girlfriend left for home. The cleaner arrived in a 2cv and carried the boss back to the bottle.

I open my vehicle door and step outside to go shower and shave.

One sniveling fat-rolled Mutti, still present amongst the donkey audience mutters to Hubby and sneaks a glance in my direction. Der Englander swore at me Hansi. Hubby looks at me, is stupid looking and big. I keep a large hickory axe handle clipped inside the van door just in case of any intruding idiocy or villainy. I put my hand on the door, close to the axe handle. Little does Hansi know all I have to do to get really uptight is even think of Adolph Hitler and I will cream Hansi's cobblers permanently back up into his youth movement. Hansi will never be able to do his fatherland duty or think of anything but donkeys ever again. He sees the "Don't do it" in my eyes and turns his attention back to consoling Shatzi.

The remaining women went back to their RVs. I could hear children being chastised as Muttis found it hard to cool down from the flummox. All the men returned to their recreations and chores. There was a lot of moaning from the barbecuing, van-polishing and fishing Pappis about vacations are ruined by no nookie for at least another fortnight. It is for sure that after that there will be six months of purgatory as the totally dissatisfied hausfraus fondly reminisce on action and angles.

Thoroughly satisfied with my cheap accommodation and entrance price to the entertainment and the show being over, I showered, shaved, and packed up to leave. Breathing deeply of the exhilarating mountain air and thinking happily of a promising soon-to-come enjoyable shopping trip for wines, terrines and cheeses I drove onto the Saint Emilion road.

Donkey Doings

I didn't bother to check out. What for? The boss hadn't bothered to check me in.

© Neil Rock

35.

Communist Constrictions

At the time of my first visit to Lithuania the country was still not in the European Union and the government authorities there were not welcoming any foreign visitors except commercial traffic. But, I wanted to see the Baltic States so had got my paperwork together to transit from Poland to Finland through Lithuania, Latvia and Estonia.

After traveling through the beautiful forested and lake-filled district of Mazarian in Eastern Poland and passing through the town of Suwalki I arrived at the frontier with Lithuania. The border crossing was in a stretch of open flat country with not a tree in sight. Barbed wire fences surrounded the frontier buildings on the Lithuanian side of the border. Some ideas of what difficulties were to be expected at the frontier had been brought home to me by passing a seventeen kilometers long tailback of hundreds of trucks waiting in line to enter Lithuania. Drivers told me that for them a wait of three days to one week was normal. Two Lithuanian number-plated cars passed my van as I was speaking with truckers, so I followed these cars to the frontier. There were three entry lanes, one for trucks, a lane for speedy nonstop access of official VIP vehicles and one for private cars. On the Polish side of the border was a single customs and immigration office where I was waved onward after a cursory flick through of my passport. So here I was waiting to enter Lithuania at the barbed wire fenced-in buildings. Leaving Poland had been simple, but the other side of the frontier was an entirely different matter of an armed and fortified paranoid military complex.

On seeing my van approaching, a machine gun-toting guard in a sentry box at the roadside picked up a telephone to a guardroom, from which

Communist Constrictions

a uniformed young woman officer stepped out and directed me to pull over out of the traffic lane and to the side of the road. The uniform of this grim-faced young woman frontier guard, from gold-braided, sand-colored, high-topped peaked hat and same colored jacket and skirt to pistol belt and jackboots, signaled Banana Republic Ridiculous to Concentration Camp Evil and I was immediately on guard for being turned back to Poland or search and seizure of anything in my vehicle deemed to be illegal.

My passport and car registration papers were taken from me by the female frontier guard, glanced at and handed to a male officer in the guardroom. He perused the papers and handed them back to the jackbooted woman, who now informed me that my international insurance had no legal standing in Lithuania, but I could buy either transit insurance which only allowed me forty-eight hours to drive straight through the country or I could buy two weeks insurance that allowed me to stay that period if I wished. My insurance papers read that they were legal in Lithuania, but I did not argue. To be sure of no hassle should I get stuck in the country for any reason, I bought the two weeks package. This purchase took half an hour.

Then, the female guard studied my vehicle registration papers and put the information into a computer. A so far unrecognized by me mistake of a letter in the vehicle registration papers, not quite coinciding with my vehicle number plate, cost me another half-hour delay until I thought to show my vehicle road test papers which coincided perfectly. On this paper being accepted and passed it was obvious that this woman was not reading information other than matched numbers.

I was then instructed to zigzag drive between concrete block road barriers to another guardroom. My passport and vehicle papers were passed to immigration officers who went over my passport by computer scanning and a National Immigration Ministry check. Then through another concrete block maze to a third guardroom where state police did another passport check. The jackbooted woman now handed me my papers and curtly said Goodbye in English. I replied just as curtly. A barbed-wire barrier was now pulled to the side and my vehicle and I were now in a Customs shed where I waited while inspectors searched the vehicle. I was surprised that all my canned food, bottles of wine and

165

alcohol, music cassettes and a box of videotapes were returned intact. Another barbed wire barrier was pulled aside, I exited the Customs shed and was halted again at a military check post, where once again all my papers were checked, this time by army officers.

On being released from the Army check post I was now on a one hundred meter length of road with scattered cobbled road risers that allowed me to snail pace to a blockhouse with a machine gun pointing in my direction and a guard peering through a viewing slit. An automatic across the road pole blocked my progress while I was observed from the blockhouse and my new insurance papers and entry stamps in my passport were checked by a soldier. The barrier lifted and I drove some two hundred meters to a final sentry box with barrier where another armed soldier phoned back to the frontier and gave my passport and vehicle numbers to check my clearance.

Finally, I was released to an open highway with a row of peeling paint money changing offices all with identical rates of exchange and topped with a billboard in about twelve languages telling me that I was, "Welcome to The Democratic People's Republic Of Lithuania." All in all, I had gone through three hours of waiting at seven checkpoints to enter this Communist, "utopia." Luckily, I was not driving a commercial truck.

I drove toward the regional capital, Kaunus, on the finest stretch of four-lane highway I have seen or been on anywhere in the world. A two hundred Kilometer engineered marvel of asphalt-covered billiard table with not a single tremor. Built with EU development funds it was Russia's first warning that things were falling apart for them in Eastern Europe, and to just to rub it in, all other roads were left to be the usual cracked concrete slab military roads. Passing through the town of Marianpole it was obvious by some shell damaged buildings and bomb craters that few repairs had been undertaken since WWII.

I stopped and slept in my van by a gas station on a garbage strewn highway truck stop. Pathetically, young farm boys and girls dressed for Saturday night out came from the countryside to the gas station and gathered to talk around the soda vending machine. There was nowhere else for young people to meet until cafes in Kaunus, 60 Ks away. At five o'clock in the morning, a police truncheon rapping against the side of the parked trucks and on my van alerted drivers it was dawn and time to move.

The landscape seen from the road was flat, dull, uninteresting and like all the North German Plain, there is hardly any terrain worth calling real hills between Hamburg and Moscow.

This country had once been half Prussia half Poland, open land, difficult to defend, easy to invade, borders had shifted with wars of many centuries. The housing in Kaunus looked the same as that in Bucharest, Belgrade, Sofia and the rest of the peeling concrete apartment block cities I had seen in forty years of passing through many countries of, The Workers Paradise, where huge painted numbers on high rise outside walls identified buildings. They were not dignified with names. I drove straight past the city.

Out on the highway two young girl medical students hitching from Kaunus to Vilnius with intent to visit a flea market were thumbing for a lift. The youngest at seventeen spoke excellent English, her friend of eighteen years spoke not a word of my language. The young one had learned English from an aunt who had lived in London during WWII and who had hopefully and foolishly returned to be trapped in her Russian occupied country. The purpose of the younger girl to learn English was to get out to the UK as soon as she had her medical degree. I was told that the parents of both girls and many friends were worried that the Russians would re-invade the country now it was obvious that Lithuania would be joining the European Union. I had to present a breakdown of the political situation currently existing between Eastern/ Western Europe for these young people to understand and pass to their parents.

E.G. The cold war had forced Russia into massive spending on military weapons development and stockpiling. Russia had gone Bankrupt because of its economy being completely war based and supporting huge military forces throughout the vast USSR and it's satellite countries. The Communist bloc had no world trade. There had been no money and no commercial skills in Russia to develop the vast natural resources into a consumer based economy, either there or in the satellite states, and now no money to further support even military presence in the Eastern European Communist states. The Warsaw Pact was disintegrating. The post cold war Russian economy was to be built as an industrial producer/

consumer economy on sales of oil and gas and other natural resources to Western Europe. This meant that there was no choice for Lithuania and all other Eastern European countries but to sink or swim alone in a free market. Western Europe would have to foot the initial bill to help these states become self-supporting. Supportive infrastructure for labor and business would grow together. This situation meant that European East/West peace was assured for well into the future unless destabilized by outside intervention. It was strange to be discussing economic politics instead of pop music fashion with two teenagers.

I had Miles Ahead playing on my box. The non-English speaking girl had never heard of jazz music, didn't know what it was. Both girls looked at my car fridge, automatic cooling fans and other electrical appliances as things from a far-off heard of but so far unreachable land. I switched the cassette to Roxy Music. There came a sense of lightness into the atmosphere. Both girls were obviously pleased to have met and spoken with a foreigner and to have heard forbidden Western music, but I could recognize also that my presence had heightened their sense of isolation from real freedom.

After dropping the girls in Vilnius I drove northward on backcountry roads, really just cruising around while loosely heading for a campsite marked on my map. On a single-lane country road, I came across an elderly man outside a run-down but picture book country cottage. He was sitting by the roadside at a table bearing small hand made reed baskets filled with strawberries and raspberries. By his clothing of a threadbare suit, ancient collar and tie and polished shoes it was obvious that he was somewhat of a gentleman. His city dress in the countryside interested me enough to stop and speak with him; I thought to buy some fruit.

This man looked at me curiously as I approached him. At my words of, "Good day," in English, he sat back surprised, blinked, looked puzzled and replied haltingly in English, asking, "You are English?" When I replied, "Yes," he asked in amazement, "Really English?" I again replied, "Yes," he asked, "But whatever are you doing here?" When I answered that I was traveling through his country now that it was permitted his face lit up in wonder and he again said, "English." He smiled and his life poured out before me. He had been a professor of chemistry and biology at Vilnius University. The Russian authorities had retired him early many years ago because he could not lecture in Russian when teaching in Lithuanian was no longer permitted. He was banished from the city to his cottage in the countryside. His wife was now dead. His only son had moved away, married elsewhere, didn't visit anymore. The Professor had a pension, equivalent of twenty US dollars a month, was selling his homegrown fruit to earn a bit extra.

Did I play chess? Would I give him a game? He had no one else to ask. I told him regretfully that my game was unsure and that I had not played in many years and could not possibly give him exercise. He looked downcast, then brightened up when saying he would make us tea and we could talk together. He went to the house to make tea and I wondered what would occur and what would be made of me by any other traveler coming down this country road and stopping to buy fruit. In many countries I travel in and where communication becomes necessary, if I know nothing of the Language I claim to be deaf and dumb. (Except with Authorities). It works great for shopping, done it for more than fifty years. Signs and signals raise immediate sympathy and clarity of understanding every time. Communication becomes easy and you don't need even a structured hand language. I had once lived and traveled a lot in North Africa with a Berber mute and we used descriptive sign language every day, even once had a whole sign language conversation on the origin and nature of diamonds. So, I would be deaf and dumb if anyone should show, but nothing, not a car or cart came in sight.

The Professor and I had tea by the roadside. He expounded about Paris where he had once been on vacation as a youth before WWII. He had walked in La Grande Jardin de La Tuilleries; just imagine, he said, flowers growing there since 1665! He had strolled in Le Bois de Boulogne, visited Versailles and had seen the Mona Lisa and the Monets in The Louvre. Did I not just love the Sacre Coeur and Notre Dame? And the Eiffel Tower! What a miracle of engineering! An identity icon landmark that revealed Paris to be the leading cultural city of the world! We drank tea, enjoyed the bridges on the Seine, recalled the Champs Elysees.

Wasps buzzed around the fruit on the table and we occasionally lazily waved them off.

The Professor offered strawberries from a basket and asked how the fruit was named in English. If Lithuania was to be free, he said, and if visitors were coming, then he would make a notice board naming his fruit in as many languages as possible. I spoke the word and wrote it down on paper for him and asked how it was called in Lithuanian.

He looked blankly at the ground, hesitated then told me what it was called in Russian. When I asked why he told the name in Russian he slowly stood, his hands hanging loose at his side, shuffled his feet together to attention in the grass, still looking down at the ground, shook his head repeatedly from side to side and said pleadingly, "No, no, I am a good Soviet, I am a good Soviet." I was appalled at this transformation, his condition was pathetic. I almost burst into tears. I took his hand and drew him to sit again. My only thought on this, then, as now, is that whoever had done this to him should be shot. The Professor rubbed his eyes, sighed and sat quietly. I was sorry for him but felt that I needed to get away before becoming further involved and possibly coming into trouble, so I said I must leave, as I wanted to be at a campsite before dark. He wanted me to stay. He needed somebody, anybody, to talk with. I could not stand the pathos or face possible danger. I thought of the previously unknown fault in my vehicle registration, imagined authoritarian problems. I just had to leave.

I bought a basket of raspberries and the professor insisted on giving me an added gift of a basket of strawberries. I was shaking with anger at imagining the Professors tormentors as I drove away. My mind in turmoil, I was so upset that I headed straight back to Poland. I would transit the Baltic States in some future and free year.

Again, I slept in the truck park. Next day, and after waiting in line three hours while six cars in front of me were cleared at the border, a young guard officer in a ridiculous sky blue and obviously fortune costing hand tailored uniform more like an airline captain than a border guard bid me a smarmy "Goodbye" in English. He hoped I had had a good stay in Lithuania. I could not help replying that I looked forward to Lithuania joining Europe and to visiting again when the people were free and the frontier open and when, fortunately, HE and his regime companions would be out of a job. He frostily handed me my passport and waved me across into Poland. My stay in Lithuania had been less than 48 hours.

Communist Constrictions

I stopped at a cafe inside the Polish frontier, realized that I was exhausted by tension, and pulling into the parking area I got into bed and slept like a log through the entire night.

A couple of years later-on visiting a newly independent Lithuania to explore further and now breathing the clean air of freedom I drove in one minute straight through an open no razor wire, no customs, no police, no immigration, no army, no cobbled road risers, machine gun or barb wire barrier checkpoints—across an open and now normal European Union country border.

The truck stop was cleaned up, even had a barbecue and picnic area, music in the gas station shop. I drove the road from Kaunus to Vilnius while thinking of the hitchhiking girls and hoping they were progressing in medical studies to help in Lithuania or to reach England.

I spent a whole day driving around country roads trying to locate the cottage of the fruit seller Professor. Looking forward to seeing him I had even brought gifts, I searched carefully, but I never found him again, I could only hope that some kindness from elsewhere had come his way. After some days spent exploring the countryside, I headed north to Latvia and Estonia.

© Neil Rock

36.

The Latvian Law

Well, here I am, early evening, driving through the mud streets and clapboard house suburbs of Daugavpils in Latvia. I've already done the main entertainment tour to the newly opened supermarket and looked at all the Western European gourmet cat food and Mars Bars unaffordable to anybody except the top five percent of the national population. There's not much else but the supermarket to see in Daugavpils except a smashed up some kind of former Russian Government owned factory. Seven storeys high and a hundred or so metres long, hundreds of broken window panes on every floor and gaping holes in the roof testify to the truth that during 45 years of military occupation the Russian Communist Regime was not loved for being here. The factory looks nineteenth century in design and condition, but a plaque set in the brick wall reads that it was built in 1983. It lasted six years, then, about two minutes after the Russian army left, a very resentful population attacked and destroyed it. It's the same with most Russian government installations in all the former Communist dominated Baltic States, commercial and military ruins can be seen everywhere. So, now I'm on my way out of town, heading north-east to drive up alongside the Russian/Latvian frontier and up along the Russian frontier at Lake Luga in Estonia until I get to the Gulf Of Finland. I want to hop a boat across to Helsinki and drive up through Scandinavia to Cape North at the top of Norway.

So, meanwhile, still in Latvia—I'm just thinking to myself how fortunate the Latvians are to finally have freedom from the Communists when out from a clump of bushes at the side of the road a cop leaps toward me waving a Speed Reader Baton. Hand up in halt position he signals me to stop.

Communist Constrictions

This policeman is a lost remnant from another day. His uniform looks like it is made of raw sheep wool and recycled weed fiber, style of Moscow Tram Driver, Circa 1922, broken cardboard peaked cap and all. The only difference between the cop and the tram driver are the ID badges on this man's shoulders and cap, and he has new bright boots and a nice shiny gun. Anyway, I'm nicked.

The next thing that happens is that the nose of a patrol car pulls out of the bushes and the fuzz partner driving it blocks the road in front of my van in case I try to split. The cop standing in front of me (looking at my number plate) realizes he doesn't have clue one about where I'm from and is thinking hard about communication. He walks up to my camper, then points with one hand to the Speed Reader held in the other, it reads 40kms per hour, he then points to a rusting road sign half hidden in the bushes, it reads 30kms per hour. There is nothing beyond the bushes but open country.

Cop to attention, thumb in belt loop, idiotcracy to the fingertips—signals me to leave my van. I get out of the camper. My dog, (Pekay) a Tibetan Spaniel, eight years old, the size of a ladies handbag, no teeth, growls at the cop, the cop steps back one pace in case of rabid assault, hand on pistol holster.

My vehicle papers are Spanish; my passport is British. Ivan Kojak has no idea what languages he is looking at and the only thing for sure is that he is certainly not reading them. For good measure I hand him the dog travel papers as well. The idea of the dog having his photograph and his name in his own Spanish issued European Union Canine Passport almost blows the cop away. He does a double take then peers in round the van windows to make sure he got it right and that the dog really isn't somebody else hiding in the back. He walks to the patrol car to show his mate the dog picture. The two cops look suspiciously at me, then at my dog. Am I possibly a western spy? Is the dog a spy dog? Maybe this dog could even be a secret police dog? Why not an Asian Secret Police spy dog? He does have a Chinese look about him. Hmmmmm?

Car phone picked up and a call made to the local Lubianka. A cop dressed up to kill in black leathers and with a white neck choker, blue smoked aviator glasses and looking like a TV Movie version of a Spetznaz Commando rides in as fast as a genie out of a bottle on a

173

BMW motorcycle. He is a tough looking character who peers at me through his eye mirrors and examines my papers. It takes ten seconds flat for this specialist to determine that the van has Spanish registration papers, my passport is British and the dog is a dog; he is back on the bike and gone.

By now passers by are coming along to watch the show. A toothless, white haired sprightly looking grandmother wheeling a couple of baby girl twins in a weather faded vegetable box pushcart with solid rubber tires stops to take in the action. A scabrous-headed six-year-aged junior punk in baggy pants, cracked plastic sandals and a Heavy Metal somebody or other tee shirt rolled up to his belly button and with a finger poked in his fly front stops by on the way home from school. Two iron-faced elderly farmhands who look like they haven't laughed since Stalin died come out of a field and lean on a wooden fence which immediately collapses and drops them onto a grass bank, they shuffle around to get comfortable and lie there unfazed.

My friend (and yours) the Moscow tram driver cop comes back to me at the van, hands me my papers, hitches up his pants. The punk kid admiringly takes in the gun, shiny belt and boots and is wondering how much money he can make on the take from a police job when he grows up. Glaring at me, this cop is now really pissed off. He has been seen by the citizens as Lumpenkopf by not being able to read the papers from me, van or dog and having had to send for an expert. Behind this I can see in his eyes that he is not getting any from his wife and won't get any either until he turns over two years pay to get her a color TV from Germany and a perm at the newly opened Coiffeur Pariski down by the community sewage plant. Besides this he is eyeing my vehicle and I realize that he is really torn up that I have a camper van for only me and my dog, while at home he and his wife have four kids and a second hand 1919 Siberian made three wheeled, two seater, coal fired Klutzmobile.

Taking out a pencil and paper from his breast pocket the cop spits out a stream of hick dialect Latvian for the benefit of the audience and writes on the paper for me to read—10 Euros—(US $15) The punk kid groans and salivates in ecstasy at hearing the power of this job, which can command a month's wages from any western born sucker on wheels. A Soft Shoe Shuffle and vague whistling of Latvia Swannee drifting from the kid as he contemplates floating on the future in a hedonistic Miami Vice lifestyle. He shifts finger from digging in fly front to digging in nostril and looks in total fascination at both cops, their car, and again at the shiny boots and belts. He definitely wants to be baptized as a capitalist lawman. The two farmers on the grass bank mutter, then, they shut up as the patrol car driver looks their way. The grandmother, more brave, aware that the Russians have gone home and that she is now in the free world clears her throat and lets loose fifty years of Communist gagged frustration in a blast of umbrage on the cops that would have withered the ass off Laventry Beria. My roughly synthesized phonetic understanding was: " Ten Euros? You said Ten Euros! Shit! That's four and a half zillion Latvian Sludgeniks! Don't you ex-KGB slobs realize that such sleaze could cause the Government to fall? President Thiefski Putz and his entire Government Cabinet are all in the cement business and have bled the entire country dry to raise money to meet transport development subventions coming from the European Union. We're building new roads for Marxs' sake! It's pork barrel heaven! We're joining the European Union Common Market so that we can import Mercedes Benz cars, Westinghouse Fridges and export Latvian fish food and grass seeds—and dumb foreigners will come here looking for Latvian Utopia! We pay taxes so you idiots can watch out for our economic interests. Instead of laying out red carpets all you do is joy ride around stealing large lumps of foreign exchange and frightening tourists away! You Morons from Minsk, you. Nobody, but nobody from the money-drenched west will ever come here again! I'm reporting the both of you to Moscow Center. If you carry on like this, Russian gasoline sales will fall through the floor and Czech concrete mixer shares will go belly up in a week". Etc,etc. The cop at least has the grace to look down at the ground, then, he quietly shushes her by patting his hand on the air.

But—he is adament -10 Euros.

In the vegetable box pushcart one of the baby girl twins farts, the other one farts, nobody appears to take any notice, except my dog starts barking. I crack up, I can't help it. I'm red faced and near tears at the side of my van. Pekay is barking his head off. The cops have registered what happened, my response to it, are nearly apoplectic with anger, and

I'm trying to cool it. The Grungehead Kid looks appealingly at my cop, urging him to do something in the name of the law—like shoot me. The farmers at the fence start to laugh then think better of it and disappear into the distance like Harry Houdinis. The cops writhe a bit then make effort to cool down. Grandma pats each baby on its head. Kojak glowers at me, looks threatening, I pay over a 10 Euro banknote. Kid Junior G Man gasps hoarsely at the sight, shifts finger from nostril and buries it back in his fly front, he almost swoons into shock and coma. He has a Big dilemma of whether to make his first fortune in the tourism business as a Highway Robber or make it in the police as a Master Traffic Sergeant. Common sense wins, he chills out after deciding that stealing through a cop job is more rewarding and more secure.

Rapid promotion and more loot as a cop is certain, he can already see the color he will paint the wall of his office at the Riga FBI.

Grandma cranks up again, waves her hands about and pours out more scorn and insults about police thievery. She is ranting again about the enormity of a 10 Euro fine and is demanding that an armoured Brinks truck be sent to collect the money. She nudges the cop to give me a receipt. To my surprise he writes me a stamped traffic violation ticket. (Later in the year when I got back home I managed to partially decipher this paper and it turned out to be a parking ticket, real fine value about 40 US cents.) I framed the ticket, hung it on my kitchen wall, it is still there. I predict a prosperous future for the young punk kid.

Cop pockets loot and gets back in the car. His partner pulls the vehicle back to hide in the bushes and wait for the next victim. I'm free to go. I drive past the half hidden 30 kilometre road sign and no further than five metres more along the line of bushes when in the foliage I see two more rusted traffic signs: The first shows that I'm leaving Daugavpils city limits, the second tells me that the speed limit from this point is 80kms per hour. I look in the rear mirror and see grandma smiling widely and giving the cops a sly finger as she trundles the twins away—and I swear I could see the Fingernose Kid boldly handing the cops a pencil and a scrap of paper and asking his heroes for their autographs.

© Neil Rock 2008

37.

La Maison Perdue

Summer had arrived and I was on my way from Spain through France to Italy at the beginning of a round Europe driving and camping trip. After driving through the Pyrenees in Aragon and Catalonia I crossed the border into France one morning at the medieval town of Bourg Madame. This is a beautiful walled town of stone and slate houses built on the side of a hill; it has strong redoubts, a drawbridge, gate towers, a double turn entrance sleeve and is only marred by the bottom of the moat having been concreted over and now being used as the town car park. Inside the walls are one cobbled circular inner street and two more parallel cobbled streets cut through the circle down the hill from top to bottom. Bourg Madame boasts ornate cast iron street lamps hung with baskets of geraniums, apron-wearing housewives scouring already spotless doorsteps, sidewalks you could eat off and baby perambulators as the only traffic. There are three bar/cafes, a vegetable/grocery store, a bow windowed bread/patisserie, a butcher/charcuterie, a small clothing store and two souvenir shops, anything more is to be searched for elsewhere. I walked slowly through the town streets, soaking up the atmosphere, my head filled with images of mongols, catapults, knights on horseback, swordsmen, pikemen, archers, tunnellers and siege towers.

Standing with fields behind it at the very top of the town is a tiny lace-curtained and gabled house with a swinging sign jutting out above the door reading "Gendarmarie". In the front window a hand-written note is propped between the glass and the lace curtain. The note, in French, advises readers: "Open 9am. Closed 1pm. In other hours or in emergency please telephone the National Police." Definitely my idea of

177

a laid- back cop shop.

Time to leave. I drove away from Bourg Madame and was searching for a narrow unpaved farm road that according to my map should lead north east above the town from behind the Gendarmarie and would after a few Ks link me with D class back roads on which I intended to travel from here all through France to Italy. I found the unpaved road but after passing a few Ks through fields planted with sunflowers and maize my road forked at the entrance of a thickly grown pine forest. One route through the trees was reduced to a track where a blue painted fingerpost stuck in the ground pointed me toward La Maison Perdue. Intrigued, I followed the sign through the forest and came to a rock-walled small house and stables set in a clearing in the trees. Four cars stood in front of the stables.

The buildings were covered with climbing dog roses and out front had a sign reading "Restaurant La Maison Perdue" swinging from an old gibbet type post. Having taken only coffee so far this day I decided I would splash the cash and stop for lunch. In my medieval frame of mind and with rampant imagination I became inadvertently embroiled in a Comédie Française/Anglaise replay of the historic French/ English wars.

The dining room had six polished long wooden tables with high backed dining chairs under a beamed and plaster ceiling and with some framed artwork on the walls. There were four leather armchairs and a beaten brass-topped table in front of a fireplace containing an iron coalscuttle filled with wild flowers. A TV stood on a side table near the fireplace. A sideboard carried glasses, bottles and carafes of wine, more flowers.

The restaurant was empty of clients except for a party of six people eating salad at one of the dining tables. I could see the entrance to a kitchen at the rear of the room. A bell tinkled when I entered, and an extraordinarily pretty chestnut-haired girl dressed in country costume came out of the kitchen, walked toward me and bid me Bon Jour, I made my reply and gestured appreciation for her beauty. She tilted her chin, gave me a saucy smile and waved me to a table. I returned her smile and I sat. The girl next handed me a menu and told me that her father, (the proprietor and chef) would be along in a moment. She smiled again and swayed back to the kitchen. The traditional scene was set: Tavern rake and serving wench.

La Maison Perdue

The TV was on low volume at a news station showing German Chancellor Helmut Kohl making a state visit to France and begging forgiveness from President of France, Jacques Chiraq for Germany having been the cause of WWII. Chancellor Kohl blushingly throws himself into the arms of M Le President and buries his face in Chiraq's chest. (I kid you not). The President smiles benignly for the cameras and pats Kohl on the back. (There, there, now, what is half a million or so dead French citizens between friends? Even for the second time around?) I am thinking that it is amazing what some people will do to, or for each other when determined to sell automobiles and pork, aircraft and wine.

A sniff at my side tells me that the Maitre D is waiting. I look up at this fried egg-eyed florid face on top of several hundred pounds of gastronomized Chef-costumed fat. He smiles through a blast of pre-lunch (and maybe pre-breakfast) liquor fumes, holds up a pencil and note pad and begs my wish. I glance at the menu then order. My choice is as he wishes except for a main course of Blanquette de D'Agneau He remarks my accent "Ah, Messieur is English". He glances at the TV and pointing at the images asks me in English: "What do you sink of zat?" Now this is dodgy, when the question comes I am immersed in watching Jacques Chiraq smothering Helmut Kohl in a smiling bear hug grip while whispering in his ear to remind him of the deal that forgiveness for WWII will cost Germany two of its next years EU votes on agriculture, the acceptance of at least two union raises in the costs of manufacture and delivery of French made avionics parts for the Eurofighter airplane soon to be entering service in the Luftwaffe, purchase of at least 12 Airbus 360s, plus being screwed out of umpteen zillion Euros in unbalanced trade with France over the next fifty or so years. AND—Kohl can "Take it or leave it." The French have learned to blitzkrieg bop. The first thing that comes into my head is to be diplomatic. I turn to the restaurant owner and say: "At least Chiraq is showing some socialistic forgiving spirit and at last in France—World War Two is over." Le Chef blusters, eye popped, his complexion pales, he positively pulses, he reverberates in 3D apoplexy. The girl comes toward me with a wild rose in a glass and cocks a hip as she places it on the table. I wink, she grins. Papa catches the exchange and almost boils over. With a look at me intended to burn my nenes off—and a gesture at the TV which would have dislocated Mussolini's elbow Le Chef departs to the kitchen with muttered words like "Chiraq—Cochon Socialiste, Sale Boche, Idiot Anglais, Mais—Les Pauvre Sabines," trailing behind him. Too late I see over the entrance to the kitchen—a map of Corsica mounted in a frame of embroidered Napoleonic bees and—a printed portrait of the Fabled Short Ass Himself in full color military drag. M Le Chef is an Empire Fanatic. AND- politics, women and food in France are a heady and volatile mixture. I suspect immediately zat I am in ze deep ca-ca and not going to get a second chance. By my pacifist views I have behaved worse than Fou. With my observed wink at his daughter I have committed Sacrilage du Sacre Bleu. War has been declared, this Rabid Royalist and Defender de la Fleur De France is on the rampage. The lowlife guttersnipe English wandering tramp of unknown lineage is NOT going to get HIS daughter. The daughter glances my way then shakes out her hair in preparation for yet another necessary sweetening of a customer on the long list of those sentenced to suffer a political/ romantic demise. Bringing me a hopefully fortifying half carafe of house red to prepare me for the coming ordeal she pours me some wine, lifts a questioning eyebrow as I sip, nods to my nod and goes again to the kitchen. I am left to realize that I personally am going to pay for the French humiliation at Agincourt, where, in a single day of battle we English killed about eight thousand Frenchmen and they only killed two hundred of ours,—(A percentage in soccer goal-scoring terms of their losing by forty to one.) Then there is the conquering and long occupation of Normandy by medieval English armies and the pre-marital puffing up of a French Queen Catherine by an English King Henry to be reckoned for; there is a toasted dyke named Jean D'Arc, plus the battle of Waterloo. Another supposed serious insult to France is the WWI refusal of British army quartermasters to purchase horsemeat from French victuallers during the battle of the Somme. (Our dead horses they stole from the battlefields then butchered and tried to sell back to us). Also there is the WWII allied liberation of Paris then all of France. These things Le Maitre,—M Le Chef,—is not prepared to overlook. I prepare for battle by psyching myself up. Who does he think he is, this upstart aristocrat? This closet kitchen Clausewitz! This pretender to the mixing bowl of Escoffier! This

Clochard from the basement of Le Métro Les Dauphins! Heh? HEH? The Daughter emerges from the kitchen and puts on the dining room sideboard a basket of croutons sprinkled with fresh parsley, then a huge bowl of Escargot a la Catalan swimming in onion gravy with garlic heads and diced bacon. This delight is for the diners at the other occupied table. She and the Escargot glide pass my table. I am almost slavering as I tremblingly admire this artful scouting reconnaissance across my front. The news on the TV changes to Weather which promises to drown me between here and Toulouse. While I remain still hungry yet goggling at images of sliding vehicles and pouring rain, girl and a rabbit pie pass my eyes and nose. Looking like the promise of Paradise this pie has a golden dome at least 15 centimeters high, is garnished with strips of smoked ham and topped with a ring of baked thin apple slices and fresh basil leaves. It looks so light it appears to float above the platter. My fellow diners ooh and aah. I hope against hope for mercy and begin reciting my chant of contrition. M Le Chef knows how to turn the thumbscrews. I get a dispatch from my general command center warning me to expect no quarter when M. Le Chef appears in the dining room and switches the TV to a re-run of "Dr Frankenstein"

Frankenstein's monster is being laid into with electro-shock therapy in the cellar. Perfect timing by Messieur Le Maitre, he is planning serious campaign torture.

Le Chef returns to his lair and sure enough there follows a loud rattle of charcoal, the clashing of fire-irons and rotisserie chains; steam casts writhing shadows in the kitchen doorway. A squeak and pop of a cork followed by loud gurgling informs me that Le Chef is limbering up the war machine. Behind the steam there is a sheet of flame and curses as a bucket of boiling oil is thrown in the wrong direction.

The daughter comes toward me, bringing the advance advisors of battle to my table: A cruet set containing salt, pepper, olive oil, le moutard.

The Chefs first musket shots are fired when the girl places before me a plate with deux Vol et Vent de Poulet Fricassee and a generous slice of Terrine de Perdis. I realize this volley is but a prelude to serious battle and her father is intending to weary me by weighing me down with rations of substance as solid as lead shot. He is testing my resistance in case of prolonged siege. Feeling somewhat adventurous I devour everything except the plate to show him I am a trencherman with palisade well set. Next the girl advances avec Une Salade Verte. Papa watches and suffers a set back as this second testing of my line of defense contains only a weak-wristed sabre cut such as is caused by miscalculated lack of bread and sliced lemon. His mortification at this Faux Pas is relieved by a rapid delivery of thick chunks of pain du pays and half a lemon by his eye flashing daughter. She also delivers a speckled fat mountain trout cooked with a fine touch of dill and butter. The fish is so fresh it must have still been swimming while I was parking outside. I pare the trout and take a bite before tackling the salad. Le Chef growls, but nods grudging approval at my *Elan*.

Le Chef wallows back to the kitchen, then pokes his head round the door again to see if I am Déclasse and will eat first all the fish without sampling the salad. I scorn the attempt he has made on my lines with this scheming low blow of a sly strike with fresh water flattery; I address the salad. Parrying the lemon to the side of my plate, leaving it there for him and all to see I abandon etiquette, muster my courage and daringly chew and swallow an undressed lettuce leaf. My tactic has success. M Le Chef gulps, then swells visibly at the daring of this dégeulas uncouth insult.

I ask myself—Does this upstart Sous Apprentice Plongeur Du Plat not realise that he is facing un homme avec beaucoup d'expérience sur les barricades Dans Les Guerres Pour Defense De Le Sandwich?

The hint of prolonged warfare by the late delivery of bread and lemon has rattled me though and as I dress the salad, finish it and trout I am left in apprehension for the imminent attack of the next course.

Noise of weapon sharpening from the kitchen; a thud followed by a squelch as a battle axe is planted and a poignard is thrust by Le Chef—into a side of beef doubling as me. Some accompanying low volume movie death rattles as Frankenstein's monster strangles a couple of TV people.

My neighbours have devoured the rabbit pie. The girl presents a splendid Soufflé Imperial Au Chocolat to these fortunate civilians at the table on the sidelines. The Soufflé doesn't sink. My courage is diminished by this show of military strength. Obviously, I cannot dismiss M Le Chef as being merely a puffed-up pastry.

La Maison Perdue

My adversary strikes frying pans and colanders, launches the slingshots and light artillery to do battle by firing his daughter at me with a salvo of superb devilled clams. They are delicious, but wait, what are these browny balls also on the plate? These are round shot that I cannot account for. Is this disguised granade shrapnel? Even so, I refuse to retreat, I am no Versailles fop. Regardless, I scoff the lot to let him know that I enjoy the clams —AND the other browny balls that I belatedly recognize as a mix of miniature Champignon Provencal Sauté and Preserved Truffles. The Buffoon! I have shown him that I have foiled his slippery suavity. However, I do realize that his strategy of weighing me down to tire me disguises also a stealthy intent whereby to diabolically weaken me by manoeuvres leading me into a most exorbitant costly defense.

From the kitchen -another bout of cork popping with more gurgling.

The girl attempts my distraction by fluffing the flowers on the sideboard. Le Chef is now sufficiently aroused to descend into slightly dubious military manual field tactics. While I am distracted by the lady with flowers Papa tries to outflank me on the blind side, moving as a sneak sapper carrying satchel charge. Appearing suddenly at my table and almost with thumb in plate, (Quelle Blague!) and flicking a cold-blooded flourish he slides before me a fused canister concoction of a King Asparagus Spear with Chou fleur aux Gratin and the recently invented Engineer Corps weapon of a slit silken black fig with grated walnut and an anchovy on top. Thinking to flabbergast and disarm me with this Nouveau Cuisine farcical frippery of the fig—M Le Chef retreats and watches breathlessly from the kitchen doorway. This Mountain Mule is insulting my manhood, but Tante Pis! Braving everything I show him my mettle by first eating chou fleur, fig, and anchovy. Then I reveal just what I think of him and his strategy by turning the King Asparagus Spearhead toward him as Lance Présente, looking at him, looking at it, looking at him again, pause- before eating it. He understands, oh, he understands. But Merde Alors! His eyes now look like spirit levels. Il et vraiment tres dangereuse! Il et vraiment très pissed!

From the sideboard the daughter is watching the battle with a rather sinful smile; she arrives to take my plate away—and plants another half carafe. I wink again and display sarcastic court mannerism by nonchalantly dabbing my mouth with a serviette. The girl chokes back a chuckle. Le Maitre is knocked off balance and turns puce at his daughter's appreciation of this sly seduction by a Sans culotte; he glares at me, glares at the girl. Still, I know –just one more slip from him—then I can hoist him on his own pétard.

Now from the kitchen I can hear heavy artillery loading up and as the girl serves soothing cream cheese and cherries to my neighbors—Frankenstein monster fizzles, smokes from the ears, raises a club and brains the boss. I feel the blow and wait warily for the main bombardment by the whole Artillery De France. I display bravery but am wilting at the imagined threat of a full divisional onslaught.

Le Commandant Chef Grand Marichal De L'armée Française approaches my position with all guns blazing and all flags flying. He marches from the kitchen to my table and places before me the main course I ordered, Blanquette D'Agneau. He bows, chokes back a snigger, retreats close to the fireplace and leans on the mantelpiece to gloat. The plate displays A Masterpiece, a veritable Oeuvre. I am seriously wounded and almost swooned into unconsciousness by the delicious aromatic bouquet from this overwhelming howitzer delivery. I had expected that his main thrust of attack and revenge for all that France and its women allegedly suffered by the machinations of Les Mauvais Anglais would be to serve me something that would look and taste like the Duke Of Wellington's riding breeches served in a sauce boiled down from Madame Pompadour's Saturday night underskirt. Instead, I got lamb I could cut without a knife, braised baby carrots and celery, a steamed small whole onion and, as a twist of the bayonet deep into my Englishness—an exquisitely roasted potato. This scheming scouring of my national sensibilities by the gift of the Pomme de Terre has dealt me a near death-blow! I am almost brought to tears by his perfidious behavior. This man is an utterly unscrupulous warrior, un soldat formidable, he is killing me with kindness. Then, mortified with humiliation I recognize the genius of his calculated callousness. I have been repelled by a Molière Manque, a Tartuffe of Christian Charity and Chicanery !

The artistry of M Le Chef was overwhelming and as I sat and ate my meat in scalded awe I realized that I had been foiled as to his strength of arms and strategic expertise by the oldest trick in the world, he had

completely misled and outgunned me by ruthless tactical use of La Femme Fatale. His daughter, this Salome of the Sûr had surely compiled "The Houris Guide To Venery". Sad but true, I cannot win. These surroundings and situations are his familiar battleground and he wants to make sure that I am bloated horizontal, dead and buried before the coffee, rather than only undone, still alive—and Upright,—when his daughter takes her siesta. I finished the main course, lay down my knife and fork, patted my stomach in resignation for the benefit of M Le Chef and prepared for my surrender to the French.
Now the girl approaches my table with a knowing grin. I am served my just desserts. She delivered the Coup de Grâce of a Bombe Glace Alsace with fresh raspberries. As a consolation and to ensure the quietus on me she slips me an ancient armagnac—and hidden from her father—makes me a small mou.
Turning away from my table she paused, gave me her best profile and breathed a deep sigh to finish me off. Then, springing a curl, she sashayed away to papa. Je suis désolée! I have been thoroughly trounced. I capitulate. I have been rendered down from Roue to Roux then ruefulness and luckily have not been thrown into La Rue. I am reduced and left to simmer.
Devastated by the superior force of culinary arms and feminine guile I offered to retire from the field sans fromage. My offer was politely accepted. My bill arrived with a strong coffee to help me choke it down. The itemized Addition was longer than the Canal du Midi and was of a size for which Robespierre would have rolled my tormentor to the guillotine on a tumbrel. It reflected every single one of my winks, smiles, overt and covert glances at the girl—and Pouffe!- Take Zat—To Jacques Chiraq, Les Boche and to ze Peasant, Socialiste Labour Party Rosbif!
In recognition of their coordinated military expertise I left a fair tip for the daughter and a handshake of true appreciative salutation for her father. They both came outside to bid me goodbye. The weather had cleared. As I started my engine Le chef raised his right hand in the Churchill victory / hippy peace salute. The girl waved to me and flashed a smile that almost shattered the sun.
Driving away I was tempted to snub the French success at Austerlitz by shouting an Arnold Swartzeneggar. Instead, chivalry won. After all,

M Le Chef had fought a battle to guard against a foggy casual tumble of his daughter as well as defending his ground to maintain political position and economic benefit. To remove his enemy from the field he had chosen to feed me some of the finest food that his Vive La France gallantry had on offer.

© Neil Rock

38.

Rockin' through Poland

A few years ago, while driving out of Germany into Poland at Stettin I'm wondering how much has changed since Communism fell. Hopefully, it would be for the better. I had been in several Eastern European and Balkan countries under communist rule between the 1960s and 1989; drab existence and paranoia would be a good description of them then. Even a repeat visit to Bulgaria in 1992 proved that only a veneer of smarmy hypocrisy covered a repressive system much the same as the '60s.

I am waved through Polish immigration and customs with no more than a fleeting glance at the cover of my British passport. Pulling into a gas station, 50 meters or so inside the Polish side of the frontier I am confronted by a full-size vinyl blow-up of Shakira wearing a grass mini-skirt and offering me a plastic pizza. Capitalism has arrived. Put to the vote in Poland it is obvious that communism could not have stood a chance. While tanking up my van, two service guys wash my windscreen and fill my freshwater bottles for coffee on the road. I tip the guys and pay the girl at the cash desk, saying " Thank you" to her in Polish (one of the few words I know) she looks at me in surprise, beams a smile, then curtsies, CURTSIES! and says "Thank you" in English. I am immediately into a feel-good trip.

Outside the gas station a young student is sitting on a rucksack and waiting for a lift. I stop. The guy rushes up to the van, opens the door and burbles a stream of about fifty-five consonants without a vowel in between them. Brain stunned I say " English". A look of scorn appears on the guy's face and I can see that he now believes the truth of all those jokes he has heard about stupid Englishmen. Without moving his head, or moving his eyes away from mine he sticks his left arm straight out from his side, points his finger back down the road the way I have come and says " English", then sticks his right arm out from his side, and now, looking like a scarecrow, he points up the road the way I'm going and says "Gdansk" meaning the Baltic coastal city of Danzig. OK, so I don't laugh. Having got it straight the direction he is heading I nod, beckon him to jump in and we're off. Silence. No communication, he no speka da Ingliz, I no speka ze Polska. Five excruciating minutes of silence is enough. I turn on the cassette player and stick in one of my own compiled 50s Rock 'n' Roll and Rhythm 'n' Blues tapes. After a few numbers from Elmore James, Jerry Lee Lewis, Howlin' Wolf, Wanda Jackson, Billy Lee Riley et al, my hitch-hiker is jaw dropped, stompin', groovin', planning for a DA haircut and ready to move to Memphis. We couldn't speak together but we rolled through the night—solid rockin'.

Late at night and being hungry we looked out for a restaurant and finally came to a roadside truck stop in a grove of trees and bushes on the side of the road. The truck stop roof had a flashing red neon sign of a shivering arrow pointing at the breasts of a naked girl sitting on a bed and holding a cocktail glass. The place was named "The Girly Bar All Nighty". (No hesitation about advertising the menu.) We go inside and after fending off an exotic African bird in tribal drag and a swarm of slinky blondes, one in a thigh-high sky-blue business suit, one in a black and both carrying briefcases, (an up-market ploy to attract truck drivers) we sat to eat and my guy wrote down a few names he knew, Elvis, Rolling Stones, Beatles, followed by a question mark wanting to know who was who in the rock 'n' roll world. Sadly, there is no doubt that all people East of the Iron Curtain were forced to miss out on a lot of fun; this hitchhiker was up for bringing in a revival. I made him a list on his road map. He pointed out to me on the map that he had been on a summer hitchhiking holiday in France. After food we said goodnight to the girls and got our heads down in the van for the rest of the night.

At dawn we moved further on up the road with more good music: John Lee Hooker and some Sister Rosetta Tharpe to warm up the day. About 7 o'clock we came to a village on the edge of a forest where traffic-catch-ing women and children sat by the roadside selling wild raspberries, blueberries, mushrooms, eggs, homemade yogurts and strings of freshly caught eels. I bought us some eggs and chanterelles for an omelet, a couple of yogurts for which we picked our own sweetener of blueberries from the forest floor and we cooked and ate breakfast camped under giant pine trees. Just as we were packing our gear away to leave, two cars drove in amongst the trees and stopped. Each car had two guys in the front and four women in the back. The women got out, the cars drove to a layby and the guys just sat there. The women spaced themselves at intervals along the roadside. Each woman was carrying a handbag in one hand and a mobile phone in the other. It's for sure that these women were selling overripe fruit and not one of them had had a cherry in her basket for a few decades. My pal and I ignored the beckoning. The pimps looked at us stone-faced as we drove past.

A few minutes after breakfast we passed a farm road with a signpost in front pointed to "Megatiti". Polish roads seemed to me to be full of sex. I wasn't stopping though, even if this was Dolly Parton's birthplace. We passed a town named Matti Podless, (poor Matti), then a bar with a sign outside reading—U MAMA BAR, DRINKI UND SMAK. Is this place a red neck fight bar, a junkie hang out or a sado/masochistic massage parlour?

We do some **BB King**. It started to rain. Windows Up. Air guitar from my fellow traveler.

The contrast between beauty and brutal conditions of rural life in Poland was brought home to me while driving on a country road between two poverty blighted villages. After driving through a village of tumble-down brick houses and barns I was impressed to see that kindly past local inhabitants had planted fruit trees along the connecting public roadside pathway for a few kilometers. Plums, cherries, apples, pears and a variety of nuts: free food for passing travelers. Then, while driving in rain and sludge through the unpaved single street of the second village, a place of old tractors, mangy dogs, a smoking garbage heap, dilapidated pine board buildings and wobbly wooden sidewalks, Anna Kournikova's blonde hair braided 14-year-old kid sister double walked out of a rickety shack doorway and joined a bunch of kids skipping to school along the sidewalk boards. I immediately recognized that her schoolbooks or good looks were her only possible means of escape from a surely screaming mad insane future—as driving past the shack doorway I saw the interior was the village abattoir. Her huge, shapeless and hopeless-eyed mother was in there, working amongst cracked sinks and tan-colored peeling linoleum walls, wearing a blood-spattered apron, standing at a chopping block under a single naked light bulb and smashing a cleaver into the head of a scalded pig.

About mid-day we drove into Gdansk and my hitcher guided me through the city. Inside the city and across the entrance to the old walled town a huge hand-painted bedsheet sign—"Coca Cola Café" straddled the street amidst strung up and winking colored lights. The café below was a cracked window framed hole in the wall surrounded by Marlboro ads. A ten feet tall automatic pistol-toting Bruce Willis had a blonde with torn open dress in his arms on a badly hand-painted cinema marquee poster next door. This country is now in The European Union, The European Free Trade Market, but it seems that The USA health destruction market got here first

This city is just like John Le Carre described it in his book "Smiley's People", dull, gray, with dirty early 1900s tramcars screeching on rusting buckled tracks along greasy cobbled streets. Many buildings have WWII bullet and shell-pocked facades. The crowds are shuffling bundled up pedestrians carrying "perhaps" bags and moving past doorway men in turned-up collared raincoats. You know here that the stink of Kremlin communism still lingers, even though the Poles were the first people to successfully break out of the Iron Curtain Prison. But Yes, its' coming, full-on freedom is just around the corner. We stopped for a coffee in Solidarity Square, the site of the first Polish anti-communist risings. At a secondhand junk stall, I found a metal pin button printed with the design of a swastika and a crossed hammer and sickle. Round the rim of the button was written in English "50 years a prisoner, 1939-1989."

Gdansk has an oil refinery pouring out raw fumes so bad that it must be producing the lowest Octane level of operating engine fuel in the world. Vehicles belch blue-black smoke on every street. Within thirty minutes of being in the city, I had a roaring headache and swore to myself that I would never return to Gdansk again. Not even if I was given a VIP front row free ticket by The Pope himself for the Canonization of Lech Walesa.

So, Gdansk is a downer. Mind you, I see that the young ladies are very pretty. OK, not the breathtaking, heart racing, world-winner young Russian Tartar/ Scandinavian mix beauties one sees everywhere in the city of Tallinn, Estonia, but nevertheless, really pretty. In Eastern Europe the difference in looks and health between the younger generations raised in freedom of now and the elders who were straitjacketed by Communist repression is amazing. The young really are striding fresh-faced, heads up to the future. One of the most pleasing things I find in the Baltic States is that Ladies' fashions in the coastal towns are focused still on the 1940s. Now, still, in summer, the girls walk out in swaying knee-length floral print frocks, high or court heels, purse under the shoulder and with freshly brushed and swinging hair. Smart. Assured. Chic. Not tacky, unsure, slick. There are very few sloppy-dressed young girls or pin-lipped and eyebrow ring horrors of either sex anywhere outside of Warsaw.

So, back on the wheels: I want to get my hitcher home and then reach around the Gulf of Danzig to my next camping stop in the town of Elblag. After driving on the coast a few K's we decide it is time for lunch. A few old men are fishing on the banks of the Vistula River, so we stop and buy a few small fish. I open a couple of beers from the van fridge and fry up to Fats Waller and Louis Prima. To my surprise, my Polish pal is right there with this music also. Out comes the roadmap and pencil as he writes down what's what from the cassette covers. A couple of anglers glance our way to check us out, then get their attention back to serious underwater business.

More sex on the road. The counties in Poland are called Gminas. After lunch I drove into a Baltic county called Gmina Puck. (It's there on the map). Some comic wag has changed the sign at the county line to read Gim ia Fuck. They do have great humor in Poland. After all, the Warner Brothers were born in Poland and it doesn't get much funnier than Bugs Bunny and Daffy Duck. And where else can you find a town with a Groucho Marx name like "Wotzyaseyo"?

A few K's further up the road my hitchhiker signaled me to stop at a turn-off to a village and stepped out of the van. He stuck out his hand, we shook. I gave him a rock n' roll cassette. His face was a picture of

complete glee and his eyes told me that his ride with me would be top of the menu at school tomorrow. He would tell his friends that he had ridden home across Poland with a fully certifiable crazed-out boogying rock' n' roller.
WELLLL,—YEAH!

© Neil Rock

39.

Skirt, Skis and Skates

Driving solo on rough cross-country interior roads through Scandinavia; I am heading for the northern-most point one can drive on the planet, North Cape, at the top of Norway. Right now, I am in Swedish Arctic Lapland. The Long Johns and other winter clothing I bought in Estonia feel already like good company. This wind-blasted land has no trees, only stunted bushes. This means I can see the scenery around me, not like the monotonous thousand kilometers of constant pine forest in the interior of Finland, where driving cross country on dirt top logging roads the only view is the cut through the trees ahead, where there is no traffic whatsoever and at crossings the only directional signs are made by ballpoint scribble on pieces of cardboard nailed to tree trunks and placed there to aid loggers. Here in Lapland the land is mostly marsh and frozen open tundra. The country roads are also not busy, apart from occasional wild Moose or Reindeer you might pass half a dozen vehicles a day, Sami road repairers, the odd traveler or dedicated angler. Heading north toward Finnmark, I am already some hundreds of kilometers up inside the Arctic Circle. The cold air in Lapland and onward is so intense that when you come across any of the four or five towns that are scattered amongst the many thousands of empty square kilometers, up here it will have parking places with free of charge electrical heating points attached for you to plug into your vehicle, for sure outside the school and shops. Every couple of hundred Ks or so there are huts with fireplaces, a stack of free firewood, a dining table and bench/bunks to eat and sleep on. Outside, an earth toilet is attached. Good government service, but nobody here in winter, and in summer it is sometimes difficult to sleep in a land where wrapped in parka and sleeping bag you can read a book by the light of the sun all day round without strain, except during dusk at a half-hour each way of midnight. I was here in June the year before but only traveled as far north as Narvik. This trip, the North Cape is my definite target.

Upper Lapland, somewhere in Finnmark, I entered Norway, joined the national road, (the only National road in Norway), and drove upward through the most northern fishing village on earth, at latitude 70 degrees N and only a few Ks south of North Cape. At mid-day the sky was black, cod and herring boats rocking at anchor in angry swells, spume frozen like ice chips was blowing off the Arctic Ocean onto a rock wall across the road and forming an ice coat there at 71 10' 21 and some 800 kilometers up inside the Arctic Circle, on the same latitude with the northern tip of Alaska. Next stop is the North Pole—if you want to swim there.

So, in July 2005, having just passed my 69th young birthday (You gotta do this stuff while you can really enjoy it, right?), I am running the test of this freezing place in summer weather so bad that my heaters were constantly at full power and not my dog nor myself had stepped out of the van in over 24 hours. We were 20Ks from our goal and struggling up a mountain in a Force 5 raging nighttime blizzard. It was 4 degrees below centigrade zero outside and the buffeting wind was rocking my camper on it's springs. Icicles like stalactites hung down from the roof to the ground on the wind side of my vehicle. Suddenly, close in front of my vehicle, through the flying sleet I saw another vehicle's rear lights. Absolutely jaw-dropping amazing—my headlights caught a girl on roller skates, in snow gear, a pack and skis on her back, being towed upward as she clutched a rope fastened to the rear of a truck. I couldn't believe my eyes for the first moments. I gave a blast on my horn and as she lifted her snow goggles and looked up, I pointed to the seat beside me. She shook her head, gave me a thumb up sign and waved me on. I saluted her as I passed. The next morning, we met again on the cliffs at North Cape. I learned that she had been traveling for over 3 months,—along the roads and cross-country mountain sides—on skis and roller skates,—coming north over 2500 kilometers to here from Oslo—to make the longest Ski/Skate run by anybody, ever.

To get here I had driven alone, 11,000 kilometers, from Spain through

Western and Eastern Europe, The Baltic States and Scandinavia. Oh, adventurous me! Who am I kidding? I had a most wonderful trip, driving as far north on the planet as you can go.
But of myself, and the girl on skates at the edge of the Arctic Ocean that year, it was she who had the real courage, BALLS , Writ Large.

© Neil Rock

40.

The Green March

Ah, patriotism, our land of democracy. Defend and protect the motherland. Volunteers to the front, Go! Frequently it is total nonsense. When Morocco invaded the country of Rio Del Oro, (now known as Western Sahara) by a march of over 350,000 unarmed civilian 'volunteers' into that Spanish-held North African country in 1975, it did so against the resolutions of The International Court Of Justice and the United Nations—those resolutions on Western Sahara being that the country had the right to determine its own future following the announcement by Spain of its' intention to abandon its interests there. Although Mauritania also laid claim to Western Sahara, Mauritania had no clout to back it up and so withdrew its claim after attacks on its country by Saharan rebels. King Hassan 2nd of Morocco felt free to invade even before the Spanish left, knowing that the USA and European governments would back his move in exchange for guarantees of continual supplies of phosphates (and Bauxite, a strategic natural rock resource for aluminum, military weaponry, and other products.) There is so much phosphate and bauxite down there that trains 2 miles long, the longest trains in the world, are hauling it day and night from the desert mines to Atlantic Seaboard ports. Mauritania wanted it, Algeria wanted it—and Morocco wanted it. Claiming that historic 19th-century treaties between Saharan tribal rulers, Spain, and the Sultan of Morocco had de facto incorporated Western Sahara into Morocco- allowed King Hassan 2nd to fend off other claims on the territory, including the claims of the fighting Algerian supported Saharan rebel movement -The Polisario Front. The same day that the UN and International Court of Justice

The Green March

announced the right of Western Sahara to self-determination of rule, King Hassan announced his "Green March" peaceful invasion.

Spain, which had held Western Sahara as a 'province' rather than have no riposte against the international community view of it being a colony, (in reality, it was) had been fighting a guerrilla war against the Algerian backed Sahara Polisario Front for control of Western Sahara since 1973. Fighting a conflict generally unreported in news media and in which losses of Spanish troops were rising, Spain decided to withdraw and initiated secret negotiations with the Saharan Polisario Front guerrillas. Managing to prolong public information on the war in Western Sahara being released in the Spanish news media until 1975, the Spanish government, at that time failed to gain UN recognition as De Jure ruler of Western Sahara. They had no choice then but to abandon Western Sahara rather than risk dissent amongst the Spanish public, who were uncertain of what future awaited them as Franco lay dying. The Spanish Government simply could not assure itself that its troops should fight for a Franco-held colony after the Generalissimo's death. Spain could not afford more world criticism than what was already sure to come regarding Franco's period of dictatorship. A continuance of colonialism in Africa could have been seen as a continuance of Franco's dictatorship and could have caused civil unrest in Spain. Taking advantage of Spanish government weakness, King Hassan 2nd of Morocco publicly announced on Moroccan TV that he was seeking volunteers (whom he personally would lead) to march unarmed in a peaceful "Green March" on Western Sahara and so 'liberate' the country from Spain and return it to the Moroccan homeland.

So, on November $3^{rd,}$ 1975 having lunch in a café with a front center view of Tangier Bay and its railroad station, my wife Barbara, and myself, watched in amazement on TV the political exhortations to recruit Green March volunteers. The King (in smart traditional Moroccan dress) was there before us on The Box, extolling the courageous and patriotic duty of unarmed volunteers to leave behind their ALL in order to help their country. It was an emotional appeal. Meanwhile, in real-time, at that very moment down at the Tangier railroad station, we could see baton-wielding police herding together groups of rounded up men and youths and packing them like sardines into commandeered trucks, and into carriages of the Marrakech Express. As this was happening, people on the city streets were running to get indoors and out of sight as fast as possible. Women, children, and old-agers were left alone by the cops. All fit males were being stopped, their identity cards taken off them, pushed into the train or into waiting trucks heading to the Atlantic coastal highway to Rabat and southwest Morocco. They were being sent to 'liberate' Western Sahara, like it or not. ID cards were to be handed back when the owners returned from the march and asked for them at their district police station. The café that Barbara and I were in became crowded as men entered it, seeking to hide. A man hurrying in told everybody that he had just spoken on the phone with relatives in Tetouan and Rabat, who had informed him that men were being rounded up in cities all over the country.

Much martial music on the TV as the King saluted the flag outside his Royal Palace—. Which Royal Palace? in Rabat? Meknes? Fez? Marrakech? Tangier? No diff,' it's the flag! and the King is using it to wind up the citizens. As far as the café customers and the running people in the street are concerned –The Sahara can get stuffed and there isn't a single real volunteer in sight. But—as to Civil Rights and men wanting to stay home—Zip. It was not for nothing that amongst the Moroccan population the rule of Hassan the 2nd was known as 'The Years of Lead.' He really was heavy and nothing ever moved forward unless he said so. Hence the marchers were volunteers. Barbara and I watch as the train is stuffed full to the gills with captives and puffs off south to Marrakech. Then, about 50 commandeered trucks filled with more 'volunteers' guarded by police take off down the highway. Quiet descends- at least until the unwary citizens are out and about again—when more trucks roar into the bay and are also stuffed full of 'volunteers'. It is announced on TV that the King is in Marrakech, awaiting the arrival of his 'most faithful people'. Shots of him outside Le Tour De Hassan, with bodyguards for sure- but waving at the close-by public—are also shown to prove it. Wow! He really is there to lead! A gutsy King and General! Only—Barbara and I—having decided to see what is happening in Marrakech—leave Tangier that night and are parked and breakfasting in our camper the following morning in a roadside copse on the high plateau near the city of Meknes—when suddenly, here comes King

The Green March

Hassan himself, scuttling away from Marrakech, away from the march and anything to do with it, in a motorcade surrounded by screaming horn motorcycle outriders and headed north as fast as his Limo's ass will take him. What was that said on TV about him being in Marrakech and full of piss and vinegar to lead the marchers south?

Arriving at night in Marrakech, Barbara and I see the King again on TV and supposedly still in the city (pre-taped broadcast), as he continues his spiel on the "patriotic marchers, and their effort to 'free' the Saharaouis from the Spanish oppressors." Sleeping anywhere in the city was completely out of the question; nobody knew how many hundreds of trucks and dozens of police cars were parked on the Jemma El Fna and streets for kilometers around it. Yes, there are canteens set up for food, and medical vehicles to care for ill or injured, but I could no more find a safe place to park and sleep than could any other night-time arrivals. Hotels were full and two hundred thousand sleeping, snoring, dozing, and coughing men covered every inch of street ground space in the city center or roamed back and forth trying to stay awake. The city campsite was my next stop, far enough out of town to be not so crowded. Next morning on the Jemma El Fna with images of the King again on TV extolling the peaceful Green March, dozens of green arm-banded, whistle-blowing supervisors organized the loading of men onto the trucks. Bunches of green Moroccan national flags were handed to people on board and the cavalcade left for the Moroccan Sahara border town of Tarfaya about two days drive to the south. Barbara and I had already agreed that going to the border with the marchers was madness for us. We saw no other foreigners witnessing this venture and had every intention of making ourselves absent before the invasion started. Keeping to the rear of the van of this gigantic column of trucks we could hear the roar of men, shouting, singing, and yelling of patriotic songs. At Paradise Valley just north of Agadir, we pulled off the road to camp in the palm oasis and left the wake of the convoy while the marshals were still keeping the mob whipped up and singing in nationalistic fervor.

The marchers crossed the Morocco/Western Sahara border on November the 6th.

The story of The Green March crossing the border into Western Sahara and the returning home of the marchers belongs to journalists. Ac-

199

Second Marriage ceremony 2000   1990

2015   with Barbara 2013

with Marty 2013

with Brice and Ardha   Santa Eulalia, Ibiza 2017

Morrocco 1990

with Montana,
Marty and Renee's daughter
2000

Two Magic Rupees and a Space Chillum

portrait by Claudia 2000's

with Claudia 2000's

with Michael Mills and Marty Graf at Atenea Santa Eulalia, Ibiza
'the office'

Blue Cardigan 2017

with Brice 2016, 80th birthday celebration

Two Magic Rupees and a Space Chillum

with Susan 2017

with Amanda (friend) and Susan 2018

with (friend) Linda 2017

with (friend) Kay at
Es Vedra, Ibiza, 2015

with (friend) Judith 2017

Two Magic Rupees and a Space Chillum

with (friend) Sharon 2018

with (friend) Heather

2016

cording to foreign newspapers, the marchers were offloaded from their vehicles near Tarfaya and marched across the frontier through lines of troops of the Spanish Foreign Legion, whose commanders ordered them not to open fire. This was most fortunate for the Moroccan marchers as the army of the Spanish Foreign Legion is not only an army of very tough battle troops, but also definitely contains some of the most vicious villains in the world, and this army wanted revenge on Morocco for the mass murder of hundreds of Spanish supporters when the Moroccan army had stormed the fortress in the Spanish held city of Ifni on the Atlantic coast in 1954. King Hassan 2nd had gambled on Spain not allowing the Legion to attack by reason of being frightened of international repercussions. He was correct. So, the 'volunteer' marchers, streamed into the desert, then, immediately the Moroccan Authorities were in charge of the Western Sahara capital city of Laayoune, the marchers were transported back across the border, back to Marrakech, then to their respective hometowns.

Spain evacuated from Western Sahara on November 14th.

The lie of this invasion being held to be a march in which the Moroccan population were told that they were peacefully liberating their Sahara brothers from Spanish oppression, rather than the reality of it being an illegal takeover, can be judged by the fact that when it happened, not only was it not reported in the Moroccan news media as anything else other than liberation, but even now, today, 34 years later, it is still illegal for the event to be discussed or information about it published in Morocco. Journalists there have been fined and jailed for trying to do so, newspapers have been closed down. As to Morocco being a democratic country, there are reputed to be more journalists in jail in Morocco than in any other Arab country in the world.

This feat of taking a country by force of mass unarmed civilian invasion is a unique coup in recorded history. That it could be achieved in 1975 on the eve of the latter quarter of the 20th century without interference by the military forces of other countries is a tribute to the machinating mind of King Hassan 2nd in outwitting the Spanish Government. It also displays the level of dictatorship –and foreign support for it, then, as now—which masquerades as democracy in Morocco. Although Hassan's son, King Mohammed the 6th has lifted some of the weight off

The Green March

Hassan—'Years Of Lead' from his people and allows a parliament, Morocco still remains today a total dictatorship.

The Sahraoui people are held down by Moroccan military presence in their country and have been in a state of armed insurrection since the Green March invasion. To no avail, the bauxite and phosphates still roll out exclusively to the profit of the ONA GROUP, a multi-industrial conglomerate controlled by the Moroccan Royal Family.

In the 1980s the Moroccan military constructed a huge wall across Western Sahara, (The Moroccan Wall) and still surrounds the Saharouis with an army as large as the entire Saharoui population. A permanently Western Sahara-based UN troop contingent enforces a cease-fire made in 1995. The Green March was a massive and successful con job whereby one country was absorbed into another through an operation of manipulative cynical public relations.

It was an invasion in which not a single gunshot was fired, nor any person killed. And keeping cool the marchers? Every one of them received a brand-new ID card bearing the Moroccan Royal Coat of Arms and a tribute stating that they are Heroes of The Green March.

In terms of "How To Steal A Country AND Get Away With It" King Hassan the 2nd of Morocco wrote the book.

© Neil Rock 2008

41.

Ethernet

Some random happenings called coincidence are maybe just that, but on occasion, one has to shake one's head at the implausibility of events. The following incidents have often given me pause to wonder and reflect.

One day in 1963 while in London and crossing Gloucester Road, alongside me pulled up a large motorcycle with two men dressed in clothing of animal skins, strings of beads, headbands, and braided Native American long black hair and skin coloring. The driver was a very large guy and in his mid-thirties or so, his sidekick somewhat smaller, slimmer, and younger.. The driver, speaking in a mid-west accent asks me do I know how they can get to the Dover road. So "Yes" I reply, "You keep going straight, cross the bridge over the Thames river, turn immediately left, and after a couple of miles you will see signs reading , "Dover." " Thanks," says the driver and they roar off into the traffic. A couple of years later in a jazz club in Paris, I met a well-dressed cleancut young Chinese American photographer named Joe. We hit it off over Scotch and Miles Davis and so we hung out together at clubs for a couple of weeks until I left for Morocco. Later that year while I am having a coffee in Tangiers' Socco Chico here comes Joe, so again we hang out together, and coffee in the Socco becomes our thing. The day Joe was leaving for Madrid I asked him if he had ever been in London. He replied "Once" I looked at him, flashed back 2 years on the motorcycle passenger, and asked, "Did you ever find the Dover Road?" He said, "Wow! Was that you?" T- PTRRRRrrm..Enrn. Encarnama

Billy The Bat, former proprietor of San Francisco's Bat Man Art Gallery accidentally shot himself dead at home one Christmas Eve in

Ethernet

Kabul while cleaning an automatic pistol and is buried in that city under a bat-shaped headstone. However, a decade before that Christmas as I was having my usual mid-morning coffee in Tangier I noticed that each day this tall bearded skinny figure wrapped in a hooded desert floor-length back burnoose and wearing Spanish boots would pass in front of the cafe. Over a period of weeks, we took to nodding until one morning I wave him over and invite him to coffee. We talk a bit, The Sahara, Atlas Mountains, Marrakech, The Rif, etc, and Billy tells me his name and asks mine. I tell him I am Neil Rock and he then invites me to dinner with him and his wife at their house in the Medina the next night. Finding the house I knock on the door and with the door still locked Billy's wife calls "Who's there?" "Neil Rock," I reply. Bolts are drawn, the door opens and the lady looks at me and says, "You're not Neil Rock." I assure her that I am. "But you are not," says she. Billy shouts for her to let me in and once I am in the house he laughingly tells me that he had not told his wife that I was coming to visit, as he wanted my arrival to be a surprise. Bill and his wife had gone to high school together in California with a friend named Neil Rock who, one day, when he was seventeen had disappeared and had never been heard of since.

Flying from NY to Amsterdam and due to overbooking, my wife and I were bumped up to fly first-class Pan Am for free. Great. As we are ascending the steps to the plane I see a face I know walking from the transit bus toward the plane at the economy class end. When we are off the ground, and as this friend and I have not seen each other for some years past, I ask a flight attendant if she can get him forward to the first-class cabin so we can have a drink. She asks his name and tells me she will ask the captain to address the passengers. Over the airplane intercom, the captain asks Mr. So-and-So to please come forward. The stewardess appears beside my wife and me with a bottle of champagne and three glasses and says "Compliments of the captain" Wonderful! The cabin door opens, my friend walks in and the stewardess turns to him and says, "Hello Michael". He says "Hello Margaret", The stewardess was my friend's girlfriend.

On my way from Ibiza to NY one year for Christmas I stopped overnight with a friend in London. He told me "John Small is living now in NY, you should look him up". I told him that I did not know the man.

211

"Sure you do," says my host," He stayed with you in your apartment on Ibiza. "Never heard of him," I say. The telephone rings and my host picks it up and says, "Yes, Merry Christmas to you too John. Hey, Neil Rock is here on his way to New York and I told him to look you up." He then hands me the phone and the voice at the other end tells me that my host in London has long misunderstood that he (John Small) and I knew each other. He told me he had stayed in my apartment on Ibiza a few days one winter while I was traveling in India. He suggested that we meet in NY and asked where I would be staying. I told him that I would be in the West Village. He tells me that he also is in the West Village and asks which street I will be on and I say Carmine Street. He tells me that he is on Carmine Street and asks me the building number. I tell him the number and he says he is in that same number and is calling from there right now. He asks me which apartment I will be in and I tell him number six. He says that he is across the hall in number five and will see me when I get there. The next night I knocked on his door and there he was

In Helena, Arkansas, after being on the radio as a guest on The King Biscuit Hour Show with Sunshine Sonny Payne, the world's longest working DJ, I was looking out the window at the Mississippi river Helena levee while browsing through records in Bubba's Blues Corner Record Store. On my asking Bubba if he had a particular record and he replying "Yes," then told me that he had heard me on the radio that lunchtime and then invited me to sign his guest book. The names above mine were those of the sons of a blues musician—a decades-long friend of mine from London. I commented on this to Bubba, then the only other person in the shop turned toward me and said, "Now that's a peculiar accent to hear in this part of the world." I was listening to someone with exactly my own accent who turned out to have been born and was still living eight miles from where I grew up in the city of Leeds, England. That evening I phoned my sister at her home in Springfield Virginia and told her of the coincidence of the guest book and meeting this neighbor in this small US Southern town. "Oh really" replied my sister, "Today, while looking at the site for my new house on the Chesapeake Bay, a car pulled up and a lady got out to ask me for information on land prices in the area. As kids in Leeds, we went to the same high school." Two days

Ethernet

later while driving on a backcountry road I stopped to eat at a roadside diner and discovered I was outside the town of Leeds, Alabama. Sure enough, I drove past a street with the name Darfield Place, the same name as the street where my sister and I grew up in Leeds, England.

© Neil Rock

42.

Hi-Ho for No Silver

On a most beautiful autumn Sunday morning in Tennessee, I have just descended from The Smoky Mountains where the All-Great Whoosis has treated me to the yearly abundance of his forest color box. There is no place on earth where a palate of autumn colors glows like this. To see, double-take, gasp, and wonder is just about enough to do the Great Smokeys justice. The sheer beauty of October Fall is overwhelming. Ending an enjoyable drive around 10 of the southern belle states, I am about to turn into North Carolina and homeward to my sister's house in Virginia.

Needing to stop for a leak, I pulled into a roadside rest area, and there met someone whose exemplary goodness has stayed for years in my memory and whose commitment to the spiritual welfare of mankind I sincerely admire.

After parking my vehicle I walked to the service area and was surprised to see a western-saddled chestnut-colored horse tethered to a bush.

Inside the foyer of the rest building, Ladies to the left, Gentlemen to the right, stood six-foot tall Reverend Robert E Harris of Ashville, North Carolina. In black Stetson hat, gray broadcloth and black reverend suit, white shirt, velvet string tie, and polished Texas riding boots—the Reverend was a very noticeable presence as he handed out religious tracts. He was even more noticeable by looking like somewhere between actors Lee Marvin and Steve McQueen. He did not speak, only politely tipped his hat to those people who accepted his papers.

I looked around to check if I was really in a toilet, I was. I just had to ask.

Reverend Harris is the last living preaching Circuit Rider.

Hi-Ho for No Silver

The Circuit Rider travels alone with his horse, blanket, and bible. He rides the backcountry roads bringing The Word to anybody who asks him to speak and rest awhile. He believes that God told him to tell anybody he meets that God has not forgotten that person.

No bed and the Circuit Rider will sleep outdoors on the ground; no meal and he will do without until he gets one. He asks for no money but accepts with grace if offered.

The first Circuit Rider was an English preacher named Francis Asbury, who came to America in the 1700s, saw that his brethren were reluctant to travel out of the towns, and decided to show them the way. He preached for 50 years, rode 270,000 miles, delivered at least a sermon a day, and had a motto of, "Live or Die I Must Ride." All men, even Indian Tribes called him The Man of The Long Road.

He never owned a house or had a home that belonged to him. He never even rented a room. He preached and slept in cabins, barns, taverns, out in forests and fields.

President George Washington said of him, "He is entitled to rank as one of the builders of our nation." Asbury died in 1816, in a cabin at Spottsylvania, Virginia.

So here I am, faced with the last man in America of the line of Circuit Riders on a Sunday morning as he is standing in a Tennessee restroom just for my education by his choice of enlightenment. Telling me that God remembers me wherever I might be.

It does not matter whether or not I believe in the God of any particular religion, or even all of them. It matters most that The Reverend Harris is willing to spend his time on a Sunday morning, not in a church but offering the news to people that God remembers them—by being in the one place he knows that other people on the road just Have to go. He stands and offers them the news in a public toilet.

I repeat that The Reverend Harris is the last Circuit Rider in America. He is without doubt a good person. I think it would be neat should any man in America step forward and prepare to take his place.

© Neil Rock

43.

Christmas in Balafia

Balafia was the name of a dark ages country in what is now Rumania and was ruled over by Vlad Dracula (Vlad the Impaler). Even older is the still existing small settlement also named Balafia that is on Ibiza. The present group of houses here were originally built by the Arabs in the 11th century and although one layer of houses has been built over others the original stone fire towers are intact, having been kept in good condition through the centuries.

Our host told me that Balafia, Ibiza, was the first settlement built on the island. The original inhabitants were Phoenicians who lived in it around 1500 BC; from then to the 19th century it was a defensive fortress against Mediterranean Pirates or other invaders. When marauders were sighted off the coast then the fires would be lit on the roofs of the towers and the island population would pack food and portable valuables and go to the walled enclave of Balafia for protection. Still, today, underground tunnels exist beneath the houses and Phoenician graves over 3000 years old can be found in the walls of pathways and fields. My Christmas was spent at the house of English friends who live in one of the seven house in Balafia. We opened festivities with wine in the afternoon sun while sitting round a fire in the garden and next to one of the towers. Being a bit too warm in the sun to sit close to the fire most of us sat in the shade of a Gazebo. Guests were Spanish, Argentinean, French, German, Irish, American and English. We toasted absent friends who are scattered across the world. Stories were told about life in many different countries and the people we know in remote places. Some stories were of traveling in India and Afghanistan, these countries being where many of us have lived at some time or another, also stories of the roads of Europe and The Balkans, Turkey, Iran, to and from Asia, an overland trip which several of us have driven more than once. Our English/Dutch hostess related having driven her car round the entire Mediterranean coastline countries when she was 22 years old. One friend had hitchhiked from Patagonia to New York and still—now in his 60s—drives tens of thousands of miles round India each winter on a 1940s Enfield Bullet motorcycle. We spoke of a friend who had sailed the South China Seas for three years in a Junk, and of two Canadian brothers who lived 12 years in Indonesia's Ring of Fire and who had sailed with Ambon pirates in the Sulu Sea. I related being one of the three people who were the only people ever to drive a motor vehicle through the Kakrak Pass in the Hindu Kush Mountains of Afghanistan and of driving from Spain to Cap Nord, 800 kilometers above the arctic circle, and on the edge of the Arctic Ocean, as far north as it is possible to drive on the planet, above the final inhabited village on Earth and at the same latitude as the northernmost tip of Alaska.

We toasted a passed on blind American friend who roamed the earth for several decades and who's achievements included hitchhiking and walking overland to the Lapis Lazuli mines in Badakshan on the border of Afghanistan and China, writing a book, having four wives and a large tribe of kids and building three houses in San Miguel Allende in Mexico. We toasted Foxie, the WWII and 1950's Bohemian Queen of Soho, London, who is buried on Ibiza under a headstone with no name, no date of birth or death and which simply reads "To Foxie from all her friends". We spoke of meeting pagans still living in rural areas of Lithuania and Latvia; pagan festivals, carved wooden rune poles and rune stones by sacred trees hidden in forests, pagan altars at country crossroads. We talked about never visited Indian tribes in the Nicobar and Andoman Islands and a friend who has visited the secretive Kogi Indians in the jungles of Colombia and aboriginal tribes in Vanuatu, and of a friend who has worshipped at the effigy of a saint who rules an obscure religion in Colombia. All this and much more. At eating time we sat down to a turkey dinner with all the trimmings and then some. We celebrated the words of Jesus "Do unto others as you would be done by." then Tucked In and noshed our way down to the table cloth through a few bottles and more stories. All in all I must say that this was the best Christmas party I ever attended. Wonderful- and I hope that your Christmas was as exciting.

love, Neil

44.

A Formentera Visit

The stones are hot under my feet, but my pleasure is worth the small discomfort. Shoes tied round my neck I am walking barefoot down the rock-walled lane, past Casas Patatas and Damien's house to Migjorn Beach.
Now I am passing Maria's house, she long gone to join her husband in the island graveyard, but who, during the first week of the first summer I came to Formentera almost fifty years ago invited Dutch Steef and myself to raid her mulberry tree one hot June day. Steef and I were walking down this lane to the beach and eyeing the mulberries when Maria saw us passing by and beckoned us into her yard, pointing to the tree and its fruit she urged us upward. We stripped to swimming shorts and climbed the tree, under the shade of which Maria, in her yellow straw sun hat, her ancient black-clad body shaking with toothless laughing cackles sat on a rope-seated chair knitting a winter wool sweater amongst her flock of goats and sheep. Maria cheered and waved us on as Steef and I filled a shopping bag and our bellies and stained ourselves purple from head to foot with sticky juice. Maria proclaimed it all hilarious and asked us to come back and make a repeat performance any time. That day, scrubbing off the juice with handfuls of sand while standing in the shallows at the beach I threw my finger ring far out in the water as a gift to the Sea Gods and knew at that moment that the Pitiuses Islands were to be my home.
In front and to my left, its roof above the trees, I can see the fire tower that Ellson lived in, a favorite visited place of our island clan and the friendly spirits who lived amongst the pine and juniper brush at the edge of the sea. The spirits, who played in peace and welcomed others have

since abandoned Formentera, disturbed by the increased pace and noise of modern life which began with the first asphalt road laid down from the port of La Savina, to the lighthouse on La Mola, in 1966. They have moved to other Mediterranean Sea bound refuges. All gone. On which of the islands the Mediterranean spirits now live is a story for someone else's life and time.

Passing through the bosque on the dirt path to Brice's house I see that unfortunately the pomegranate trees and the orange orchard have been removed. The red tile roofed fieldstone house, once host to freakdom painters and musicians and a shelter to people of many nations is now the office of a tourism resort of small cottages built over the orchard. The water well that Brice sweated to clean out, lowering himself inside and raising himself up and down the bucket rope by hand is still there. Stopping for a drink from the bucket I notice that the water tastes now salty; over development of tourism accommodations has caused most of the water in the island wells to fall below sea level. Of course, fresh water for the tourist hotels is now delivered by truck. Some few hotels have their own desalination plant.

Along the shoreline past Brice's house, beach towels are spread amongst the pine trees at the waters edge where hidden and noisy Cicadas still reign. Oiled and deeply suntanned summer girls lay like sinuous eels on the sand, island sirens, constantly replenished. A tanga clad male struts by, a chest puffed poseur, striving for attention by flicking his fingers supposedly unconsciously in front of his crotch. But he gets no takers.

Constantino, owner of the Chiringuito on the beach has long passed over, and Pepe, who was his six-year-old cute son helping serve lunch-time and nightfall tables, is now a gray-haired middle-aged married family man running the hotel/restaurant which grew by work of him, his father and mother from being friendly with the few of us foreigners who lived on the island in the mid sixties. Scrabbling in the hard rock soil with arthritic hands to grow a few potatoes, tomatoes and onions is a life of the past; the family look sleek, they own houses, they have a car and a four-wheel drive jeep I see in the carport next to the restaurant parking lot.

Looking Westward toward Cap Barbaria I see new built houses scattered over the countryside. Looking along Migjorn Beach toward La

A Formentera Visit

Mola there are colored parasols and family-filled plastic beach recliners stretching away into the distance. I can see more new houses, several bars and hotels. High up on La Mola itself is a huge residential tourism club, Club La Mola, next to it there is an Iberia Airlines hotel. I decide to ride my rented motorcycle up there to the island end lighthouse.

In 1965 La Mola was still an isolated place, some residents had never left Formentera and one ancient crone was reputed to never have come down off the hill even to visit the other villages. Even in 1969, one autobus a day to the port and back was the limit of public transport. In those days my friends and I owned a mixture of our own transport that was quirky to say the least. Eddy, well, Eddy had a rattling and rapidly wrecked Porsche 911 sports car. What could you expect on an island where gasoline came in rusting cans- on the boat with chickens pigs and passengers from Ibiza- and where there were only rock roads and no asphalt? Our pal Mola George built himself a hallucination of a motorcycle from abandoned bits and pieces of ancient wrecks he found scattered on Ibiza and Formentera. What I remember of this machine is that the motor worked, it had a seat, not a single instrument or light wire was connected to anything, but George was a mechanic wizzard and the bike ran. And, The Raja, he would leave his windmill home on La Mola and drive down to town in Damien's left behind old black and battered wreck of a Bedford van. This van, infamously known to the island locals as El Coche Negro, had no insurance, no ownership papers and we dared not drive it in daylight, so it was our groaning and bone-shaking, sleep- disturbing nighttime marauder. It provided a hair-raising ride of second, top and reverse gears only, even then maybe—if you were lucky. Brice made many wild rides as loadmaster in El Coche Negro while sitting on the floor in the back of the van, cradling the gas tank in his arms to stop it sliding round the van floor while Raja navigated the dust-flying bends. The van would break down and Raj would ride back up la Mola on the second hand Velo-Solex that Gene of the Witches laugh had bought in Paris and ridden down to Barcelona, and which four years later with great care and attention was still working. Often though, if the Velo Solex motor was stopped it would refuse to start again, and sure enough—here came The Raja heading back down La Mola to fix the van and this time pedaling a rattler of a bicycle. The Formentera people didn't think him quite mad but often muttered that Senor Raja was "Un poco particular."

On a visit to La Mola, the certainty of getting there was only if you walked. It was an all day and overnight adventure to walk the rutted rock road from San Fernando and up La Mola. No traffic to hitch on. The timing was planned to reach Es Calo in the afternoon to climb the cliff edge Roman Path to arrive at dusk and cut fresh pine branches to sleep on overnight in the cliff edge cave. Continuing through the forest in the early morning would get you to the Tienda de Correos for mid-morning coffee and to the homes of friends by noon.

There is now a craft market on La Mola, tourists by the busload arriving every summer day, cafes and a restaurant are busy. Like every other place they have come to Hippies have brought business and income to the locals. Quality products are for sale on this market, some of Spain's master craftsmen maintain ateliers in the village.

Late at night La Mola seems still remote and remains intensely quiet. I drink bottled water and eat a sandwich in a copse near Raja's windmill home, salute the stars before bedding down in my sleeping bag—and waiting for sleep I listen for George and The Raja warming up their drums by the fire for a midnight full moon ritual feast. Tribal blood runs river deep in me here even now, I can almost feel stroking the girls I knew, taste the raw red Formentera Wine and smell a honey-basted roasting pig.

In Es Calo this morning for breakfast I see that the lobster trap cave of the restaurant behind the Pension is still there, stocked with fish and crustaceans. Two boatmen still fish out of Es Calo, though the lobsters are not wild anymore but are grown in tanks inside a nearby building. More product to meet the larger summer demand. The Pension is bigger, more up-market.

At Don's Tortuga Bar the original bar price list of cognacs at ten pesetas each and San Miguel beers at eight is framed and hanging on the restaurant wall. Very posh now is La Tortuga, long owned by a crooked former Mayor, a Formentera boy who became a property speculator and tax dodger made good.

July 4[th,] 1966 was a memorable evening at The Tortuga Bar, Don ar-

A Formentera Visit

ranged the first fireworks display ever seen on the island.

"It will be allowed" said the Chief of Police, "but a pyro-technician will be needed. You will only find one in Barcelona or Palma de Mallorca."

"Lo and behold", says Don, "Longini has a license"

"What!?" asks the Chief.

"Where?" asks the Sergeant.

"Welllll," says Don—"I mean, he says so,—it is somewhere,—maybe in a cupboard in Taos, New Mexico, but he has one."

"Well, alright" says the Chief of Police.

Like everything else about Jack Longini- this story about the license is believed. Why not? He is rich beyond Formenteran comprehension. He owns a real motorcycle and the only private World War II army surplus Land Rover between Barcelona and Tunisia—AND his wife is educated, she plays madcap classical music at home on a pump bellows organ. What's more, Longini, is just like anybody else, he always pays his monthly grocery bill on time. The coming firework display was talk for a week. The island bus transported Formentera locals to the nighttime event. The bar garden filled up. There were gabbling gnarled Biddies in straw hats, canvas shoes, black dresses, seven petticoats and be-ribboned pigtails,—and black-suited, grey-shirted farming and fishing spouses everywhere. Come midnight, with lanterns in the fig trees and where the display was mounted along the rear wall of the garden, Longini lit the fuse. OH Jack! Dozens of locals and foreigners froze in stunned amazement as everything boomed in a most spectacular multi-colored, up, down, horizontal, every direction cart-wheeling skyrocket crackling, fountain cascade, whistle screamer whiz-bang of simultaneous gunpowder blast. In ten seconds of overpowering shock—La Tortuga garden exploded. When the noise grew to awed silence and the smoke cleared it was understood by all locals that America had great power and clearly also good luck in that miraculously nobody had been hit. Longini, even if a tad deaf now but only slightly singed was immediately and unanimously declared to be insane. Most of the Formentera people were homeward bound in the bus within sixty second's flat. Now, La Tortuga is staid, by the steak and bratwurst menu it could be in Blackpool or Berlin.

In San Fernando, La Fonda Pepe international meeting wall is gone, built over now. The traveling world once spent their evenings here.
Do you remember the fisherman who sat and rolled a flower round in his mouth while reading the Spanish dictionary little by little, through cover to cover? Remember? Propped in his chair in the cool of the evenings outside La Fonda Pepe door? Inside the bar—where Pepe's son, Julian, now holds sway—the walls still have Jack Longini cracking his whip on his motorcycle while chasing admiring cooing and running ladies. And Gings' Pepe still dances on his fountain of water wealth while holding on to his hat. Apart from a new bottle rack over the bar—if a chair, table or anything but a lick of paint has changed in this room in five decades it really isn't noticeable.
The old tienda of Maria still stands at the San Fernando roadside and is now very spruced up to meet these tourism times. Once, in a cave of a hanging everything from sausages, smoked fish, hand woven rope, feather dusters, boots, Sparta grass brooms, and hand knit wool sweaters—to shelves of wines, canned fruits, paella pans and toilet rolls, Maria served the customers. Her husband, yet another ubiquitous Pepe, seated amongst bags of grains, beans and firewood while being permanently and totally stoned and with eyes like road maps, supervised the cash drawer. Both have long ago departed from this life on his cloud of Pota smoke and cognac fumes.
In 1965, one black and stormy rain pouring winter night near to this shop I saw the most remarkable occurrence of good fortune. A flash of lightning struck a rock in a nearby field and a speed ripping horizontal traveling sizzling lightning bolt flashed across the road between the bicycle frame and legs of my friend Brice as he peddled on unaware toward the town. He didn't see it happen.
Sam, vacationing with me once at Freddie's house close to the Tortuga Bar was also foreign to recognition that certain things in nature might impede his progress. When confronted with the fact that the Pozo Negro of the house we were staying in was a limited slow soak-away of a mere crack in volcanic rock and only twenty centimeters deep, fifteen centimeters wide and half a meter long, which did not allow the inhabitants of the house to use both the toilet and the shower in the bathroom on the same day, Sam announced that he would dig a Pozo of the like he

had seen on a dude ranch in Texas. Filled with giant and small pebbles hauled from the beach and topped with earth and grass seeds for osmosis filtering, Sam, working with only a pick and shovel dug this soak away Pozo Negro two meters deep and three meters square in only two days, and in a cactus patch—without finding even a single stone in the dirt. Hit no rock! On Formentera?

In Es Pujols, riding through streets of high-rise tourist apartment blocks, supermarkets, bars and hamburger/waffle joints, riding along the beach front road, passing souvenir stores, more Bars and discotheques it is not possible for me to admire what has been exchanged for what was once a quiet cove containing four shacks built by an appreciative Englishman for the rowing boats of local fishermen. Gone is the pine branched roofed restaurant where Mola George traded for dinner his spear diving daily caught fish. On the far point headland had stood the island's then only tourist hotel, the Hostal Roca Plana. In front of me now, a middle aged northern European woman, totally naked except for sandals and a handbag she carries, steps off the beach and crosses the road while dodging traffic. She walks past racks of inflatable toys, T shirts and Snickery postcards and goes into a supermarket to do some shopping. Not a policeman or anybody else seems to care that she is starkers in town. A Euro is a Euro and the locals sold their souls to the tourist season long ago. And, well, what is one naked woman in town compared with the day trip boatloads of flouncing camp young men disembarking and stripping to nude on Es Palmador Island every summer day. They, my dearies,—soft-soaped every night in Ibiza by boat ticket touts trolling the leather and feather bars of the La Peña drag strip now known as The Street of The Virgins—are laid out all summer long for sale or for rent in front of the trendy beach bars at the Es Palmador meat market. And Illietas is so crowded that where once you rode or walked your bicycle across the salt pan paths there is now a concrete car park and you must stop and pay to park everything on wheels except a baby carriage.

In San Francisco, now spruce with its new bars and boutiques, the old long closed Republican hang out, the Bar Fonda Plate re-opened once the Generalissimo Dictator was dead and is now the shopping gossip stop of many of the old foreign Formentera hands. Briefcase Hans, the white suited Austrian property thief is long gone from the island. The locals are not likely to forget that he abandoned his Formentera wife after selling her father's café—twice—and pocketing the cash both times. And Martin, the brilliant yet penniless painter who loved that lady once and was refused her hand, languished in despair then joined the Spanish Foreign Legion. He escaped and is now living and working in Paris to art world acclaim and monetary success.

On the road down to the port the ruin of the old civil war prison has been bulldozed into the ground, carrying deeper into it the bodies of Formentara Republicans murdered there by Franco's, Fascist Guardia. The tourists with their sundowners on the towel and swimsuit draped balconies of nearby Pensions and hotels know nothing of the agony of the island relatives.

Roll on-Roll off sea-going vehicle ferries carrying container trucks, cars and passengers arrive and leave La Savina to and from Ibiza, Valencia and Denia several times every summer day. Even in winter the Ibiza/Formentera high speed ferries keep on running. The car ferry would have cost me 110 Euros ($150) to get here and back from Ibiza with my camper van. 'Struth! Even then I cheated by not staying in a hotel. The local police do not allow any camping or sleeping in vehicles on Formentera, I was lucky while sleeping overnight beside my motorcycle on La Mola not to be arrested.

With mixed feelings as my ship leaves the port for Ibiza. I do raise a final smile as the ghost of Deaf Henry's yacht surfaces on the old jetty. In my memory is a roaring, wild bottle waving, garbage strewing, drunken and rave up birthday party that friends threw for this eccentric old character on board his boat in the spring of 1962—and his wife screaming in his ear, "Stop this, Henry! Stop it! It's a terrible mess!" Henry replied: "It doesn't bother me mate, I'm stone Deaf "

Leaning on the deck rail as the ship leaves, I nod to the memory and laugh. I am taking that laugh home with me to Ibiza.

© Neil Rock 2009

45.

A Tangier Day

Tangier: Just another day. If now, at 72 years old I still could climb the city hills I would again explore and enjoy the alleys and hidden corners in the heart of the Tangier Medina. During the years 1961, '62 and into the spring of '63, Tangier was my home. I lived high at the top of the Medina in a whitewashed rooftop room overlooking the entire city; the view was to Spain across The Straits of Gibraltar, inland toward the Rif Mountains and far up the coast toward Cap Spartel.

Early every morning after being shook out of bed by the cock and his chickens living in a hutch attached to the outside wall of my rooftop home I would descend through the waking streets of Tangier craftsmen, the copper workers, tinsmiths, box makers, basket weavers and toy carvers. My path was down into the area near the port to visit the doughnut maker, who lived, slept and worked encased in a soot-covered and oil-stained djellabah, alongside a pile of charcoal, a can of cooking oil and a large iron skillet on the fire in the blackened smoke-walled doorway of a boarded-up ruined old house in a narrow alley behind a souvenir bazaar. The doughnut maker would be open for business with fire lit, be hand spinning long ropes of dough and have several dough rings frying crisply in the pan by 7AM. Joining the line of street urchins, early housewives and gossiping grandmothers I would voice my order, then, handed my couple of hot doughnuts fresh from the pan and strung on a knotted loop of Sparta grass I would leave with 'Ba' S'lemas' for everybody and climb the hill to enjoy mint tea, my doughnuts and a first sipsi of the day on the lookout balcony of the café of my friend Ab' Kada (Abdel Kadir) the fisherman. Ab' Kada would have the water boiling and often would perk up my waking hours by garnishing my early morning tea with a fresh leaf or bud from the wild Datura plant growing up from a crack in the corner of the balcony. And he would slide me a sugar filled saucer as a doughnut dip.

Ab'Kada's café, on the corner of a shining white sun-dazzled alley and the steep stepped winding hilly street of the Rue Des Cretians had two tables and six chairs on the outdoor balcony, a rug to sit on inside the only room and a pile of old fishing nets along the back wall of the room where the nets doubled as a couch for anybody wishing to snooze some hours away. The café balcony was relaxation area and open-air office space for those few of us with lives most slow and easy and whose living at that time it was to search the bazaars for anything we could sell on the occasional trip across the sea to Torremolinos, Marbella and in my case—a yearly trip to my home country. Early mornings at Ab'Kada's were most treasured peaceful preparation to our hopefully fruitful day.

The personal working domain of Ab'Kada was a six by three foot kitchen corner in an alcove behind the café doorway. Summer, winter, with customers or not, Ab'Kada hummed to himself, fired up his sipsi every half hour or so and regularly fanned the coals in the charcoal burner. A powerful singing bird lived in the café, between an encroaching beam of early morning sunlight and an evening dash of sunset glow—on a perch close to the ceiling, up high beside the kitchen doorway and near to the café entrance. The bird kept its voice in beautiful trim from the aromas of kif, the hanging bunches of bruised fresh mint—and the cooling rising steam of the teakettle. Everyday it sang for us, performing like a Diva. Feeding the bird pine nuts and raisins, Ab'Kada encouraged it to worship with the Muezzins in the minarets of the mosques from near to many miles away. That bird knew in every waking hour of every living day—that God Is Great. A door at the end of the lookout balcony led to Ab'Kada's storeroom of fishing gear, half of which room was rented out to One Eyed Moses and converted by Mose into a sculptor's workshop/studio apartment. Moses was a most favorite 'son' of Ab'Kada and—in his striped djellabah, with his one-eyed roaming glare, shoulder-length wild hair and Benzedrine powered excitable wood bashing eccentricity. Moses was as much a figure from the realm of fantasy as was our raggedy sweater and baggy pants-clad host –Ab'Kada, the shiny domed, kif puffing, crimped walnut brown and cheek-wizened smiling alchemist of the magic teas.

Looking down over the edge of the balcony into the Rue Des Cretians I sometimes spied the early morning performance of the servants working alongside the outer courtyard wall of the palace of Barbara Hutton, the Woolworth multi-millionaire heiress. The household staff would be busy brushing mats, beating carpets, sunning and watering the patio plants. With the Major Domo supervising them the servant girls worked diligently, but occasionally were to be frowned on by him if caught shooting an upward swift-eyed glance to the café balcony from behind the fronds of potted palms These girls were knowingly ensured of getting a quick grin and a wink from me, maybe a finger wiggle, any of which shook them with giggles. Sloe and shy eyed maidens most, but some—rumptious Berber women—rolling tongues in laughing cheeks while audaciously shaking plump middles. At times of the year Ms. Hutton would be in residence and I would occasionally see the lady with opium wobbled Cambodian Prince fourth or fifth husband walking on the steep cobbled lane outside the crenellated front wall of the palace. The frozen-faced Prince, in bespoke tailored beige colored stylish cut tropical suit, with ebony walking stick and shiny brogue Lobb shoes, he,—being somewhat often more stoned than I—was usually being held up for walking to and from the Hutton stately motor car by a couple of young stalwarts from the household entourage. His stilted wooden soldier-like demeanor drew glances from the locals, but then his South Asia-type fez, common red, but more a flattened pork pie variety than the higher sand pie style of the Moroccan Gentleman caught the eye and drew the attention of any aware person anyway.

From the café balcony it was also possible for me to look straight down directly onto the heads of people moving up and down the cobbled stairway of the Rue des Cretians as they went to and from the depths of the Medina. Children, leaping downwards would be yelling and calling to each other while racing down the hill, while adults would be treading carefully and elderly folk leaning backwards for balance against gravity on the steps. Those persons puffing their way to the top would have their djelabahs hitched to shanks while climbing upward. My house was that way, uphill, past Ms. Hutton's palace and further, past shops with bright green doors hung with gleaming hand-dyed reed mats and interiors filled with rolls of even gaudier furnishing materials. As the street opened onto the lookout point across the sea to Spain and onto the palm treed square where I lived, a purple-flowered Bougainvillea shaded a broad stoop which housed a haughty well groomed and horns polished tethered white goat who guarded a small boy hand spinning colored silk braids at his place of work outside his father's caftan-making workshop.

After breakfast at Ab'Kada's, first—a scouring of the Medina markets and a few tourist souvenir emporiums—then a visit to the Zoco Grande (The Great Market) was order of the day. No doubt good fortune from Allah had brought me to walk to work through curbside mountains of fruit and vegetables, through air redolent of the heaped full sacks in the spice market, the hanging bundles of medicinal and culinary herbs and the scented mystique in the Ladies street of perfumeries. On the Square of the Zoco Grande, rummaging through piles of goods both junk and useful, off-loaded onto the ground from buses, carts, the backs of Berber tribeswomen and donkeys, or while rifling through the musty interiors of many dusky shops I would some days find some objects to trade elsewhere, things for me to sell on the occasional trip to Spain or to the UK, maybe a piece of silver jewelry, an antique caftan, an embroidered tent hanging, ceramics or brassware. There might be an expensive carpet or piece of furniture to which I could steer a cruise ship visitor or a tourist from the Mamounia Hotel. Some merchants would seek out and hold for me anything they thought that I could earn a sales commission from. My rivals searched the markets too of course. There were a few other foreign hawk-eyed scavengers haggling the street markets even in those years, a couple of us even furnished our own houses and bought our own wardrobes there. Occasionally I would drive my beat-up Renault car as far as to the markets in Tetuan for hand made and painted wooden tables and wall mirrors. Sometimes I made a trip to the foothill Rif Mountain town of Ouezzane to buy pieces of embroidered stripe patterned cotton, or lengths of hand-woven pure white wool. The soft warm materials were much loved as blankets or cushion covers by the few British Ex-Pat wives of house and yacht owners along the towns of the Spanish Costa Del Sol. Tassel hooded

A Tangier Day

burnouse cloaks provided the young ladies of the Kings Road and the Knightsbridge Sloane Rangers with enjoyment of a pre-Flower Power period in trendy Moorish winter fashion.

After a morning of working the markets, the time to sundown passed lazily. Each Friday, for friends and acquaintances a Cous Cous lunch was served in the restaurant of Achmed, a local folk music entrepreneur. Achmed's eatery lay close to the seaward side of the city wall, near the old guardroom from the bygone days of the Cherifian Sultans. Serious local debates as well as some discussion amongst my friends during transatlantic telephone calls have deliberated on Achmed serving the best tasting Cous Cous in the world. Well now—I can truly say that since those days I have enjoyed a seven-vegetable chicken Cous Cous by the master chef in the finest hotel in Marrakech—and dined on a super sized rack of lamb and whole chicken whopper at the invitation of King Hassan the 2nd at the Casablanca racetrack. Even so, in my early Tangier days Achmed won the taste test. Most days, though, a lunch at home of lamb kebabs and a salad usually saw me off to bed for a siesta until late afternoon, when once again Ab'Kada's lookout balcony was the meeting place, this time for sundown coffees with our sipsis.

In the evenings after eating out, maybe a dinner of vegetable soup and a fried fresh fish with hot newly baked bread and a melon I would meet up with Moses or some other of the four or five foreigners living in the Medina and go to The Dancing Boy Café. Inside a ramshackle building, approached by a raised and narrow walkway for archers along the inner side of the old city wall and through a tall dark doorway, there was a short passage leading into a huge teahouse built atop the south-east corner of the ramparts and with a long row of glass windows overlooking the string of night lamps and rows of date palms along the beach of the Tangier Bay. Smoke browned raw plaster walls, beamed ceiling, and a wooden floor strewn with sawdust contained the tearoom with its' rough wooden tables and chairs. There was a clay brick hearth with brazier for tea making and next to it, musical instruments hung from nails in the wall above a raised stage.

The teahouse had the finest nighttime entertainment in North Africa. A group of Bedouin Musicians and a gyrating young teenage Dancing Boy would raise the souls of the customers for hours with stirring desert and mountain songs. Dressed in an ankle length pale green satin dress, sequin bordered white head scarf, flower embroidered white veil, bright red thick felt hip belt, with henna'd bare feet and hands, his body shimmering to drums, tambour and oud, there was not a woman on the planet who could out dance Adni, the Saharaoui dancing boy from the desert town of Tantan. From 8pm to midnight, six nights a week for several young teenage years Adni shook up and mesmerized desert and mountain men in town for the night—like few female dancers ever could. We, the audience in attendance, clapped to the hypnotic pulsing rhythms of the night, tapped our feet to the beat, swayed to and fro in a thick haze of kif smoke, snacked on salted sunflower seeds, on custard rolls sprinkled with rosewater and were refreshed with mint tea. Never to be forgotten. Sometimes Paul Bowles, Achmed Yacoubi, Batman Billy, George and Tatiana Andrews or some other aficionado of the music would bring visitor friends, sometimes maybe two or three other foreign tourists each month would follow the sound of the music along the alleys and were welcomed at the Dancing Boy Café. So it was that Adni himself was finally captured one winter night at seventeen years old, by a dark-haired French girl dancer from Marseilles. They lived together as lovers, deep in the Medina and—once having had a woman—Adni could never dance for men again. He was subject then to a wise desert law enforced to avoid jealous fights and killings. But while Adni did dance, those of us privileged to watch knew we were seeing a master entertainer and sorcerer beguiler of men. Acknowledged as maestros, Adni and the musicians never worked a night other than it ended with them smiling and nodding their thanks to the crowd as they picked up the many coins and a few banknotes strewn around their feet. There is now no place with entertainment like this other than in the tents of the Bedu camel caravans in the deep Sahara Desert. South of the Atlas Mountains the tradition of houri dancers in desert tents is one of boys, not one of girls, there are no women in the long-distance trade caravans crossing the vast and harsh Sahara. When, The Dancing Boy Café closed for the night, a climb up the Rue Des Cretians to my house ended my day.

During the uncountable trips that I have since made to Tangier and

A Tangier Day

many other of Morocco's Medinas and bazaars it seems that the day is incomplete without the final hours of listening to live Berber and Bedouin music. The Dancing Boy Café has long ago ceased to be open and a tourism variety is probably operating its fakery in some uptown hotel. Now, if I returned to Tangier again, I could sip mint tea with Ab'Kada's grandson while warming my bones with a sipsi in the café balcony sun, watch for the ghosts of friends and the girls of the Hutton household. I could again search the bazaars for profit and listen more frequently in the night for the beat of mountain and desert music that continues living in my heart and soul. If now at 72 years old, I still could climb the city hills.

© Neil Rock

APPENDIX

PROBLEM

United Nations Presentation on Environment & Tourism

Abstract: My paper to The United Nations World
Conference
On Sustainable Tourism.
Lanzarote, Spain, April 22nd to 25th, 1995

ENVIRONMENTAL STANDARDS AS A MAJOR FACTOR
DETERMINING ECONOMIC PERFORMANCE OF
TRADITIONAL AND EMERGING TOURISM DESTINATIONS

Neil Rock
Friends Of The Earth International

With the proliferation of tourism offers in the constantly expanding holiday market, the tendency has been created to evaluate offers in a black and white structure. The traditional seasonal beach and winter sport destinations are being qualified as declining and worn out, the so-called, "green, soft, tourism" offers and destinations are being marketed as being "responsible," and, "new". Are the traditional destinations to be abandoned and relegated to dereliction by being regarded as only yet another consumer used up and thrown away product? Are not many of the newly fashionable, "alternative" destinations themselves to follow suit as they too fall victims to excessive use?
As in the manufacture of the majority of products where producers fail to install necessary environmental safeguards, so the developers of tour-

APPENDIX

ism ignore the installation of an adequate environmentally supportive infrastructure that will be the major contributor to long term economic and social stability. In the life cycle of a tourism destinations the degradation of the product can become early apparent, as is the case in many destinations where the establishment of carrying capacity during the planning stage has generally not been considered.

In response to increasing awareness and mounting criticism of the comportment of tourism developers, some regulatory instruments by governments and voluntary measures by some elements of the tourism industry are now in place. However the failure by most governments to implement regulations and the reluctance of the tourism industry to have standards imposed upon it, plus the exclusion of the public from the decision making process at both ends of the tourism channels, has resulted in

the current measures not sufficiently embracing the range of problems to be necessarily treated to bring stability of environmental and economic performance for the benefit of all stakeholders in tourism.

This paper presents some recent initiatives undertaken as environmental protection exercises in the reach to sustainable tourism and seeks to stimulate cross sector alliances to identify achievable solutions to extend the service life of all tourism destinations.

Two results of my paper.

1
THE UN CHARTER ON SUSTAINABLE TOURISM
* Article 15

The travel industry, together with government bodies and NGOs whose activities are related to tourism, shall draw up specific frameworks for positive and preventive actions to secure sustainable tourism development and establish programs to support the implementation of such practices. They shall monitor achievements, report on results and exchange their experiences.

2
THE INTERNATIONAL TOURISM PARTNERS COMMITTEE
1996 , 1997–1998

Mr Peter Shackleton, Secretary, UN World Tourism Organization.
Mme Helene Genot, Manager, Industry/Environment Office, UN Environmental Programme.
Dr Rebecca Wood, Secretary, World Travel And Tourism Council
Ms Karen Fletcher, Director, International Hoteliers Environmental Initiative Group.
Ms Janet Jackson, Secretary, British Airways Holidays.
Dr Michael Iwand, Director, TUI Environmental Programme.
Mr Paul Thornton, Director, Horizon Holidays.
Mr Neil Rock, Project Coordinator, Friends Of The Earth Mediterranean Network.

APPENDIX

Two Magic Rupees and a Space Chillum

www.ingramcontent.com/pod-product-compliance
Lightning Source LLC
Chambersburg PA
CBHW072049110526
44590CB00018B/3095